ABOUT THIS PUBLICATION

FOR SERVICE ASSISTANCE

Customer Service
1.704.898.0770

North Carolina General Statues is published by The Muliti-Media Group of Greater Charlotte in Charlotte, North Carolina. Copyright 2015 by the Multi-Media Group of Greater Charlotte. This book or parts thereof may not be reproduced in any form, stored in a retrieval system, or transmitted in any form by any means—electronic, mechanical, photocopy, recording or otherwise—without prior written permission of the publisher, except as provided by United States of America copyright law.

The records required by U.S. Code 2257(a) through (c) and the pertinent regulations 28 C.F.R. Cli. 1, Part 75 with respect to this publication and all materials associated with such records are maintained by The Multi-Media Group of Greater Charlotte, Publisher and available for review by Attorney General.

www.visionbooks.org

Copyright © 2015 by MMGGC
All rights reserved!

TID: 5108139
ISBN (10) digit: 1503246353
ISBN (13) digit: 978-1503246355

123-4-56789-01239-Paperback
123-4-56789-01239-Hardback

First Edition

090520140547

Printed in the United States of America

2015 EDITION

North Carolina Criminal Law And Procedure-Pamphlet # 86

Printed In conjunction with the Administration of the Courts

North Carolina Criminal Law and Procedure
Pamphlet Reference Guide

Chapters	Pamphlet
Chapter 1 Civil Procedure	1
Chapter 1 Civil Procedure (Continue)	2
Chapter 1A Rules of Civil Procedure	2
Chapter 1B Contribution.	2
Chapter 1C Enforcement of Judgments.	2
Chapter 1D Punitive Damages.	2
Chapter 1E Eastern Band of Cherokee Indians.	2
Chapter 1F North Carolina Uniform Interstate Depositions and Discovery Act.	2
Chapter 2 - Clerk of Superior Court [Repealed and Transferred.]	3
Chapter 3 - Commissioners of Affidavits and Deeds [Repealed.]	3
Chapter 4 - Common Law	3
Chapter 5 - Contempt [Repealed.]	3
Chapter 5A - Contempt	3
Chapter 6 - Liability for Court Costs	3
Chapter 7 - Courts [Repealed and Transferred.]	3
Chapter 7A – Judicial Department	3
Chapter 7A – Continuation (Judicial Department)	4
Chapter 7A – Continuation (Judicial Department)	5
Chapter 7B - Juvenile Code	5
Chapter 8 - Evidence	6
Chapter 8A - Interpreters for Deaf Persons [Recodified.]	6
Chapter 8B - Interpreters for Deaf Persons	6
Chapter 8C - Evidence Code	6
Chapter 9 - Jurors	6
Chapter 10 - Notaries [Repealed.]	6
Chapter 10A - Notaries [Recodified.]	6
Chapter 10B - Notaries	6
Chapter 11 - Oaths	6
Chapter 12 - Statutory Construction	6
Chapter 13 - Citizenship Restored	6
Chapter 14 - Criminal Law	7
Chapter 14 –Criminal Law (Continuation)	8
Chapter 15 - Criminal Procedure	9
Chapter 15A - Criminal Procedure Act (Continuation)	10
Chapter 15A - Criminal Procedure Act (Continuation)	11
Chapter 15B - Victims Compensation	11
Chapter 15C - Address Confidentiality Program	11
Chapter 16 - Gaming Contracts and Futures	11
Chapter 17 - Habeas Corpus	11

Chapter 17A - Law-Enforcement Officers [Recodified.]	11
Chapter 17B - North Carolina Criminal Justice Education and Training System [Recodified.]	11
Chapter 17C - North Carolina Criminal Justice Education and Training Standards Commission	11
Chapter 17D - North Carolina Justice Academy	11
Chapter 17E - North Carolina Sheriffs' Education and Training Standards Commission	11
Chapter 18 - Regulation of Intoxicating Liquors [Repealed.]	12
Chapter 18A - Regulation of Intoxicating Liquors [Repealed.]	12
Chapter 18B - Regulation of Alcoholic Beverages	12
Chapter 18C - North Carolina State Lottery	12
Chapter 19 - Offenses against Public Morals	12
Chapter 19A - Protection of Animals	12
Chapter 20 - Motor Vehicles	13
Chapter 20 - Motor Vehicles (Continuation)	14
Chapter 20 - Motor Vehicles (Continuation)	15
Chapter 20 - Motor Vehicles (Continuation)	16
Chapter 21 - Bills of Lading	17
Chapter 22 - Contracts Requiring Writing	17
Chapter 22A - Signatures	17
Chapter 22B - Contracts Against Public Policy	17
Chapter 22C - Payments to Subcontractors	17
Chapter 23 - Debtor and Creditor	17
Chapter 24 – Interest	17
Chapter 25 – Uniform Commercial Code	18
Chapter 25 – Uniform Commercial Code (Continuation)	19
Chapter 25A – Retail Installment Sales Act	20
Chapter 25B - Credit	20
Chapter 25C - Sales of Artwork	20
Chapter 26 - Suretyship	20
Chapter 27 - Warehouse Receipts [Repealed.]	20
Chapter 28 - Administration [Repealed.]	20
Chapter 28A - Administration of Decedents' Estates	20
Chapter 28B - Estates of Absentees in Military Service	20
Chapter 28C - Estates of Missing Persons	20
Chapter 29 - Intestate Succession	21
Chapter 30 - Surviving Spouses	21
Chapter 31 - Wills	21
Chapter 31A - Acts Barring Property Rights	21
Chapter 31B - Renunciation of Property and Renunciation of Fiduciary Powers Act	21
Chapter 31C - Uniform Disposition of Community Property Rights at Death Act	21
Chapter 32 - Fiduciaries	21
Chapter 32A - Powers of Attorney	21
Chapter 33 - Guardian and Ward [Repealed and Recodified.]	21

Chapter 33A - North Carolina Uniform Transfers to Minors Act	21
Chapter 33B - North Carolina Uniform Custodial Trust Act	21
Chapter 34 - Veterans' Guardianship Act	22
Chapter 35 - Sterilization Procedures	22
Chapter 35A - Incompetency and Guardianship	22
Chapter 36 - Trusts and Trustees [Repealed.]	22
Chapter 36A - Trusts and Trustees	22
Chapter 36B - Uniform Management of Institutional Funds Act [Repealed.]	22
Chapter 36C - North Carolina Uniform Trust Code	22
Chapter 36D - North Carolina Community Third Party Trusts, Pooled Trusts	23
Chapter 36E - Uniform Prudent Management of Institutional Funds Act	23
Chapter 37 - Allocation of Principal and Income [Repealed.]	23
Chapter 37A - Uniform Principal and Income Act	23
Chapter 38 - Boundaries	23
Chapter 38A - Landowner Liability	23
Chapter 39 - Conveyances	23
Chapter 39A - Transfer Fee Covenants Prohibited	23
Chapter 40 - Eminent Domain [Repealed.]	23
Chapter 40A - Eminent Domain	23
Chapter 41 - Estates	23
Chapter 41A - State Fair Housing Act	23
Chapter 42 - Landlord and Tenant	23
Chapter 42A - Vacation Rental Act	23
Chapter 43 - Land Registration	23
Chapter 44 - Liens	24
Chapter 44A - Statutory Liens and Charges	24
Chapter 45 - Mortgages and Deeds of Trust	24
Chapter 45A - Good Funds Settlement Act	24
Chapter 46 - Partition	24
Chapter 47 - Probate and Registration	25
Chapter 47A - Unit Ownership	25
Chapter 47B - Real Property Marketable Title Act	25
Chapter 47C - North Carolina Condominium Act	25
Chapter 47D - Notice of Settlement Act [Expired.]	25
Chapter 47E - Residential Property Disclosure Act	25
Chapter 47F - North Carolina Planned Community Act	25
Chapter 47G - Option to Purchase Contracts	25
Chapter 47H - Contracts for Deed	25
Chapter 48 - Adoptions	26
Chapter 48A - Minors	26
Chapter 49 - Bastardy	26
Chapter 49A - Rights of Children	26
Chapter 50 - Divorce and Alimony	26
Chapter 50A - Uniform Child-Custody Jurisdiction and	

Enforcement Act	26
Chapter 50B - Domestic Violence	26
Chapter 50C - Civil No-Contact Orders	26
Chapter 51 - Marriage	26
Chapter 52 - Powers and Liabilities of Married Persons	27
Chapter 52A - Uniform Reciprocal Enforcement of Support Act [Repealed.]	27
Chapter 52B - Uniform Premarital Agreement Act	27
Chapter 52C - Uniform Interstate Family Support Act	27
Chapter 53 - Banks	27
Chapter 53A - Business Development Corporations and North Carolina Capital Resource Corporations	28
Chapter 53B - Financial Privacy Act	28
Chapter 54 - Cooperative Organizations	28
Chapter 54A - Capital Stock Savings and Loan Associations [Repealed.]	28
Chapter 54B - Savings and Loan Associations	29
Chapter 54C - Savings Banks	29
Chapter 55 - North Carolina Business Corporation Act	30
Chapter 55A - North Carolina Nonprofit Corporation Act	31
Chapter 55B - Professional Corporation Act	31
Chapter 55C - Foreign Trade Zones	31
Chapter 55D - Filings, Names, and Registered Agents for Corporations, Nonprofit Corporations, and Partnerships	31
Chapter 56 - Electric, Telegraph and Power Companies [Repealed.]	31
Chapter 57 - Hospital, Medical and Dental Service Corporations [Recodified.]	31
Chapter 57A - Health Maintenance Organization Act [Recodified.]	31
Chapter 57B - Health Maintenance Organization Act [Recodified.]	31
Chapter 57C - North Carolina Limited Liability Company Act.	31
Chapter 58 - Insurance.	32
Chapter 58 - Insurance (Continuation)	33
Chapter 58 - Insurance (Continuation)	34
Chapter 58 - Insurance (Continuation)	35
Chapter 58 - Insurance (Continuation)	36
Chapter 58 - Insurance (Continuation)	37
Chapter 58 - Insurance (Continuation)	38
Chapter 58A - North Carolina Health Insurance Trust Commission [Recodified.]	38
Chapter 59 - Partnership.	39
Chapter 59B - Uniform Unincorporated Nonprofit Association Act.	39
Chapter 60 - Railroads and Other Carriers [Repealed and Transferred.]	39
Chapter 61 - Religious Societies	39
Chapter 62 - Public Utilities	39

Chapter 62 - Public Utilities (Continuation)	40
Chapter 62A - Public Safety Telephone Service And Wireless Telephone Service	40
Chapter 63 - Aeronautics	40
Chapter 63A - North Carolina Global TransPark Authority	40
Chapter 64 - Aliens	40
Chapter 65 – Cemeteries	40
Chapter 66 - Commerce and Business	41
Chapter 67 - Dogs	41
Chapter 68 - Fences and Stock Law	41
Chapter 69 - Fire Protection	41
Chapter 70 - Indian Antiquities, Archaeological Resources and Unmarked Human Skeletal Remains Protection	42
Chapter 71 - Indians [Repealed.]	42
Chapter 71A - Indians	42
Chapter 72 - Inns, Hotels and Restaurants	42
Chapter 73 - Mills	42
Chapter 74 - Mines and Quarries	42
Chapter 74A - Company Police [Repealed.]	42
Chapter 74B - Private Protective Services Act [Repealed.]	42
Chapter 74C - Private Protective Services	42
Chapter 74D - Alarm Systems	42
Chapter 74E - Company Police Act	42
Chapter 74F - Locksmith Licensing Act	42
Chapter 74G - Campus Police Act	42
Chapter 75 - Monopolies, Trusts and Consumer Protection	42
Chapter 75A - Boating and Water Safety	43
Chapter 75B - Discrimination in Business	43
Chapter 75C - Motion Picture Fair Competition Act	43
Chapter 75D - Racketeer Influenced and Corrupt Organizations	43
Chapter 75E - Unlawful Activities in Connection With Certain Corporate Transactions	43
Chapter 76 - Navigation	43
Chapter 76A - Navigation and Pilotage Commissions	43
Chapter 77 - Rivers, Creeks, and Coastal Waters	43
Chapter 78 - Securities Law [Repealed.]	43
Chapter 78A - North Carolina Securities Act	43
Chapter 78B - Tender Offer Disclosure Act [Repealed.]	43
Chapter 78C - Investment Advisers	43
Chapter 78D - Commodities Act	43
Chapter 79 - Strays [Repealed.]	43
Chapter 80 - Trademarks, Brands, etc.	44
Chapter 81 - Weights and Measures [Recodified.]	44
Chapter 81A - Weights and Measures Act of 1975.	44
Chapter 82 - Wrecks [Repealed.]	44
Chapter 83 - Architects [Recodified.]	44

Chapter 83A - Architects	44
Chapter 84 - Attorneys-at-Law	44
Chapter 84A - Foreign Legal Consultants	44
Chapter 85 - Auctions and Auctioneers [Repealed.]	44
Chapter 85A - Bail Bondsmen and Runners [Recodified.]	44
Chapter 85B - Auctions and Auctioneers	44
Chapter 85C - Bail Bondsmen and Runners [Recodified.]	44
Chapter 86 - Barbers [Recodified.]	44
Chapter 86A - Barbers	44
Chapter 87 - Contractors	44
Chapter 88 - Cosmetic Art [Repealed.]	44
Chapter 88A - Electrolysis Practice Act	44
Chapter 88B - Cosmetic Art	45
Chapter 89 - Engineering and Land Surveying [Recodified.]	45
Chapter 89A - Landscape Architects	45
Chapter 89B - Foresters	45
Chapter 89C - Engineering and Land Surveying	45
Chapter 89D - Landscape Contractors	45
Chapter 89E - Geologists Licensing Act	45
Chapter 89F - North Carolina Soil Scientist Licensing Act	45
Chapter 89G - Irrigation Contractors	45
Chapter 90 - Medicine and Allied Occupations	45
Chapter 90 - Medicine and Allied Occupations (Continuation)	46
Chapter 90 - Medicine and Allied Occupations (Continuation)	47
Chapter 90 - Medicine and Allied Occupations (Continuation)	48
Chapter 90A - Sanitarians and Water and Wastewater Treatment Facility Operators	48
Chapter 90B - Social Worker Certification and Licensure Act	48
Chapter 90C - North Carolina Recreational Therapy Licensure Act	48
Chapter 90D - Interpreters and Transliterators	48
Chapter 91 - Pawnbrokers [Repealed.]	48
Chapter 91A - Pawnbrokers Modernization Act of 1989	48
Chapter 92 - Photographers [Deleted.]	48
Chapter 93 - Certified Public Accountants	48
Chapter 93A - Real Estate License Law	49
Chapter 93B - Occupational Licensing Boards	49
Chapter 93C - Watchmakers [Repealed.]	49
Chapter 93D - North Carolina State Hearing Aid Dealers and Fitters Board.	49
Chapter 93E - North Carolina Appraisers Act	49
Chapter 94 - Apprenticeship	49
Chapter 95 - Department of Labor and Labor Regulations	49
Chapter 95 - Department of Labor and Labor Regulations (Continuation)	50
Chapter 96 - Employment Security	50
Chapter 97 - Workers' Compensation Act	50
Chapter 97 - Workers' Compensation Act (Continuation)	51

Chapter 98 - Burnt and Lost Records	51
Chapter 99 - Libel and Slander	51
Chapter 99A - Civil Remedies for Criminal Actions	51
Chapter 99B - Products Liability	51
Chapter 99C - Actions Relating to Winter Sports Safety and Accidents	51
Chapter 99D - Civil Rights	51
Chapter 99E - Special Liability Provisions	51
Chapter 100 - Monuments, Memorials and Parks	51
Chapter 101 - Names of Persons	51
Chapter 102 - Official Survey Base	51
Chapter 103 - Sundays, Holidays and Special Days	51
Chapter 104 - United States Lands	51
Chapter 104A - Degrees of Kinship	51
Chapter 104B - Hurricanes or Other Acts of Nature	51
Chapter 104C - Atomic Energy, Radioactivity and Ionizing Radiation [Repealed and Recodified.]	51
Chapter 104D - Southern States Energy Compact	51
Chapter 104E - North Carolina Radiation Protection Act	51
Chapter 104F - Southeast Interstate Low-Level Radioactive Waste Management Compact [Repealed]	51
Chapter 104G - North Carolina Low-Level Radioactive Waste Management Authority Act of 1987 [Repealed]	51
Chapter 105 - Taxation	51
Chapter 105 - Taxation (Continuation)	52
Chapter 105 - Taxation (Continuation)	53
Chapter 105 - Taxation (Continuation)	54
Chapter 105A - Setoff Debt Collection Act	55
Chapter 105B - Defaulted Student Loan Recovery Act	55
Chapter 106 - Agriculture	55
Chapter 106 - Agriculture (Continue)	56
Chapter 106 - Agriculture (Continue)	57
Chapter 107 - Agricultural Development Districts [Repealed.]	57
Chapter 108 - Social Services [Repealed and Recodified.]	57
Chapter 108A - Social Services	57
Chapter 108B - Community Action Programs	58
Chapter 108C Medicaid and Health Choice Provider Requirements.	58
Chapter 108D Medicaid Managed Care for Behavioral Health Services.	58
Chapter 109 - Bonds [Recodified.]	58
Chapter 110 - Child Welfare	58
Chapter 111 - Aid to the Blind	58
Chapter 112 - Confederate Homes and Pensions [Repealed.]	58
Chapter 113 - Conservation and Development	58
Chapter 113 - Conservation and Development (Continuation)	59

Chapter 113A - Pollution Control and Environment	59
Chapter 113A - Pollution Control and Environment (Continuation)	60
Chapter 113B - North Carolina Energy Policy Act of 1975	60
Chapter 114 - Department of Justice	60
Chapter 115 - Elementary and Secondary Education [Repealed.]	60
Chapter 115A - Community Colleges, Technical Institutes, and Industrial Education Centers [Repealed.]	60
Chapter 115B - Tuition and Fee Waivers	60
Chapter 115C - Elementary and Secondary Education	60
Chapter 115C - Elementary and Secondary Education (Continuation)	61
Chapter 115C - Elementary and Secondary Education (Continuation)	62
Chapter 115C - Elementary and Secondary Education (Continuation)	63
Chapter 115D - Community Colleges	63
Chapter 115E - Private Educational Facilities Finance Act [Recodified]	63
Chapter 116 - Higher Education	63
Chapter 116 - Higher Education (Continuation)	63
Chapter 116A - Escheats and Abandoned Property [Repealed.]	64
Chapter 116B - Escheats and Abandoned Property	64
Chapter 116C - Continuum of Education Programs	64
Chapter 116D - Higher Education Bonds	64
Chapter 116E -Education Longitudinal Data System	64
Chapter 117 - Electrification	64
Chapter 118 - Firemen's and Rescue Squad Workers' Relief and Pension Funds [Recodified.]	64
Chapter 118A - Firemen's Death Benefit Act [Repealed.]	64
Chapter 118B - Members of a Rescue Squad Death Benefit Act [Repealed.]	64
Chapter 119 - Gasoline and Oil Inspection and Regulation	64
Chapter 120 - General Assembly	65
Chapter 120 - General Assembly (Continuation)	66
Chapter 120 - General Assembly (Continuation)	67
Chapter 120C - Lobbying	67
Chapter 121 - Archives and History	67
Chapter 122 - Hospitals for the Mentally Disordered [Repealed.]	67
Chapter 122A - North Carolina Housing Finance Agency	67
Chapter 122B - North Carolina Agricultural Facilities Finance Act [Repealed.]	67
Chapter 122C - Mental Health, Developmental Disabilities, and Substance Abuse Act of 1985	67
Chapter 122C - Mental Health, Developmental Disabilities, and Substance Abuse Act of 1985 (Continuation)	68

Chapter 122D - North Carolina Agricultural Finance Act	68
Chapter 122E - North Carolina Housing Trust and Oil Overcharge Act	68
Chapter 123 - Impeachment	69
Chapter 123A - Industrial Development [Repealed.]	69
Chapter 124 - Internal Improvements	69
Chapter 125 - Libraries	69
Chapter 126 - State Personnel System	69
Chapter 127 - Militia [Repealed.]	69
Chapter 127A - Militia	69
Chapter 127B - Military Affairs	69
Chapter 127C - Advisory Commission on Military Affairs	69
Chapter 128 - Offices and Public Officers	69
Chapter 128 - Offices and Public Officers (Continuation)	70
Chapter 129 - Public Buildings and Grounds	70
Chapter 130 - Public Health [Repealed.]	70
Chapter 130A - Public Health	70
Chapter 130A - Public Health (Continuation)	71
Chapter 130A - Public Health (Continuation)	72
Chapter 130B - Hazardous Waste Management Commission [Repealed.]	72
Chapter 131 - Public Hospitals [Repealed.]	72
Chapter 131A - Health Care Facilities Finance Act	72
Chapter 131B - Licensing of Ambulatory Surgical Facilities [Repealed.]	72
Chapter 131C - Charitable Solicitation Licensure Act [Repealed.]	72
Chapter 131D - Inspection and Licensing of Facilities	72
Chapter 131E - Health Care Facilities and Services	72
Chapter 131E - Health Care Facilities and Services (Continuation)	73
Chapter 131F - Solicitation of Contributions	73
Chapter 132 - Public Records	73
Chapter 133 - Public Works	74
Chapter 134 - Youth Development [Recodified.]	74
Chapter 134A - Youth Services [Repealed.]	74
Chapter 135 - Retirement System for Teachers and State Employees; Social Security; Health Insurance Program for Children	74
Chapter 135 - Retirement System for Teachers and State Employees; Social Security; Health Insurance Program for Children	75
Chapter 136 - Transportation	75
Chapter 136 - Transportation (Continuation)	76
Chapter 137 - Rural Rehabilitation [Repealed.]	76
Chapter 138 - Salaries, Fees and Allowances	76
Chapter 138A - State Government Ethics Act	76

Chapter 139 - Soil and Water Conservation Districts	76
Chapter 140 - State Art Museum; Symphony and Art Societies	76
Chapter 140A - State Awards System	76
Chapter 141 - State Boundaries	76
Chapter 142 - State Debt	76
Chapter 143 - State Departments, Institutions, and Commissions	77
Chapter 143 - State Departments, Institutions, and Commissions (Continuation)	78
Chapter 143 - State Departments, Institutions, and Commissions (Continuation)	79
Chapter 143 - State Departments, Institutions, and Commissions (Continuation)	80
Chapter 143A - State Government Reorganization	80
Chapter 143B - Executive Organization Act of 1973	80
Chapter 143B - Executive Organization Act of 1973 (Continuation)	81
Chapter 143B - Executive Organization Act of 1973 (Continuation)	82
Chapter 143C - State Budget Act	83
Chapter 143D - The State Governmental Accountability and Internal Control Act	83
Chapter 144 - State Flag, Official Governmental Flags, Motto, and Colors	83
Chapter 145 - State Symbols and Other Official Adoptions.	83
Chapter 146 - State Lands	83
Chapter 147 - State Officers	83
Chapter 148 - State Prison System	84
Chapter 149 - State Song and Toast	84
Chapter 150 - Uniform Revocation of Licenses [Repealed.]	84
Chapter 150A - Administrative Procedure Act [Recodified.]	84
Chapter 150B - Administrative Procedure Act	84
Chapter 151 - Constables [Repealed.]	84
Chapter 152 - Coroners	84
Chapter 152A - County Medical Examiner [Repealed.]	84
Chapter 153 - Counties and County Commissioners [Repealed.]	84
Chapter 153A - Counties	84
Chapter 153A - Counties (Continuation)	85
Chapter 153B - Mountain Resources Planning Act	85
Chapter 153C - Uwharrie Regional Resources Act	85
Chapter 154 - County Surveyor [Repealed.]	85
Chapter 155 - County Treasurer [Repealed.]	85
Chapter 156 - Drainage	85

Chapter 156 – Drainage (Continuation)	86
Chapter 157 - Housing Authorities and Projects	86
Chapter 157A - Historic Properties Commissions [Transferred.]	86
Chapter 158 - Local Development	86
Chapter 159 - Local Government Finance	86
Chapter 159 - Local Government Finance (Continuation)	87
Chapter 159A - Pollution Abatement and Industrial Facilities Financing Act [Unconstitutional.]	87
Chapter 159B - Joint Municipal Electric Power and Energy Act	87
Chapter 159C - Industrial and Pollution Control Facilities Financing Act	87
Chapter 159D - The North Carolina Capital Facilities Financing Act	87
Chapter 159E - Registered Public Obligations Act	87
Chapter 159F - North Carolina Energy Development Authority [Repealed.]	87
Chapter 159G - Water Infrastructure	87
Chapter 159H - [Reserved.]	87
Chapter 159I - Solid Waste Management Loan Program and Local Government Special Obligation Bonds	87
Chapter 160 - Municipal Corporations [Repealed And Transferred.]	87
Chapter 160A - Cities and Towns	88
Chapter 160A - Cities and Towns (Continuation)	89
Chapter 160B - Consolidated City-County Act	89
Chapter 160C - Baseball Park Districts [Repealed.]	90
Chapter 161 - Register of Deeds	90
Chapter 162 - Sheriff	90
Chapter 162A - Water and Sewer Systems	90
Chapter 162B Continuity of Local Government in Emergency.	90
Chapter 163 Elections and Election Laws.	90
Chapter 163 Elections and Election Laws. (Continuation)	91
Chapter 164 Concerning the General Statutes of North Carolina.	92
Chapter 165 Veterans.	92
Chapter 166 Civil Preparedness Agencies [Repealed.]	92
Chapter 166A North Carolina Emergency Management Act.	92
Chapter 167 State Civil Air Patrol [Repealed.]	92
Chapter 168 Persons with Disabilities.	92
Chapter 168A Persons With Disabilities Protection Act.	92

§ 156-91. Manner of construction across railroad.

(a) Duty of Railroad. - After the contract is let and the actual construction is commenced, if the work is being done with a floating dredge, the superintendent in charge of construction shall notify the railroad company of the probable time at which the contractor will be ready to enter upon the right-of-way of such railroad and construct the work thereon. It shall be the duty of the railroad to send a representative to view the ground with the superintendent of construction and arrange the exact time at which such work can be most conveniently done. At the time agreed upon the railroad company shall remove its rails, ties, stringers, and such other obstructions as may be necessary to permit the dredge to excavate the channel across its right-of-way. The work shall be so planned and conducted as to interfere in the least possible manner with the business of the railroad.

(b) Utilities Commission to Settle. - If the superintendent of construction and the railroad company shall not be able to agree as to the exact time at which such work can be done, including the time of beginning and the time to be consumed in such work, either party may give written notice thereof to the chairman of the Utilities Commission of the State, and thereupon the Utilities Commission shall cause an investigation to be made, and, after hearing both parties, shall fix the time of beginning such work and the time to be consumed in the work of construction, and the final determination of the Utilities Commission thereon shall be binding upon the superintendent of construction representing the district and the railroad company, and the work shall be done in such time as may be fixed by the Utilities Commission.

(c) Penalty for Delay. - In case the railroad company refuses and fails to remove its track and allow the dredge to construct the work on its right-of-way, it shall be held as delaying the construction of the improvement, and such company shall be liable to a penalty of twenty-five dollars ($25.00) per day for each day of delay, to be collected by the board of drainage commissioners for the benefit of the drainage district as in the case of other penalties. Such a penalty may be collected in any court having jurisdiction, and shall inure to the benefit of the drainage district.

(d) Payment of Expense. - Within 30 days after the work is completed an itemized bill for actual expenses incurred by the railroad company for opening its tracks shall be made and presented to the superintendent of construction of the drainage improvement. Such bill, however, shall not include the cost of putting in a new bridge or strengthening or enlarging an old one. The superintendent of construction shall audit this bill and, if found correct, approve the same and file it with the secretary of the board of drainage commissioners. The commissioners shall deduct from this bill the cost of the excavation done by the dredge on the right-of-way of the railroad company at the contract price, and pay the difference, if any, to the railroad company. (1909, c. 442, s. 28; 1911, c. 67, s. 7; C.S., s. 5348; 1933, c. 134, s. 8; 1941, c. 97, s. 1.)

§ 156-92. Control and repairs by drainage commissioners.

Whenever any improvement constructed under this Subchapter is completed it shall be under the control and supervision of the board of drainage commissioners. It shall be the duty of the board to keep the levee, ditch, drain, or watercourse in good repair, and for this purpose they may levy an assessment on the lands benefited by the maintenance or repair of such improvement in the same manner and in the same proportion as the original assessments were made, and the fund that is collected shall be used for repairing and maintaining the ditch, drain, or watercourse in perfect order: Provided, however, that if any repairs are made necessary by the act or negligence of the owner of any land through which such improvement is constructed or by the act or negligence of his agent or employee, or if the same is caused by the cattle, hogs, or other stock of such owner, employee, or agent, then the cost thereof shall be assessed and levied against the lands of the owner alone, to be collected by proper suit instituted by the drainage commissioners. It shall be unlawful for any person to injure or damage or obstruct or build any bridge, fence, or floodgate in such a way as to injure or damage any levee, ditch, drain, or watercourse constructed or improved under the provisions of this Subchapter, and any person causing such injury shall be guilty of a Class 3 misdemeanor, and upon conviction thereof may only be fined in any sum not exceeding twice the damage or injury done or caused. (1909, c. 442, s. 29; C.S., s. 5349; 1947, c. 982, s. 1; 1993, c. 539, s. 1075; 1994, Ex. Sess., c. 24, s. 14(c).)

§ 156-93. Construction of lateral drains.

The owner of any land that has been assessed for the cost of the construction of any ditch, drain, or watercourse, as herein provided, shall have the right to use the ditch, drain, or watercourse as an outlet for lateral drains from such land;

and if the land be of such elevation that the owner cannot secure proper drainage through and over his own land, or if the land is separated from the ditch, drain, or watercourse by the land of another or others, and the owner thereof shall be unable to agree with such others as to the terms and conditions on which he may enter their lands and construct the drain or ditch, he may file his ancillary petition in such pending proceeding to the court, and the procedure shall be as now provided by law. (1909, c. 442, s. 30; 1915, c. 43, s. 1; 1917, c. 152, s. 3; C.S., s. 5350.)

Article 7A.

Maintenance.

§ 156-93.1. Maintenance assessments and contracts; engineering assistance, construction equipment, etc.; joint or consolidated maintenance operations; water-retardant structures; borrowing in anticipation of revenue.

(a) The board of drainage commissioners may annually levy maintenance assessments in the same ratio as the existing classification of the lands within the district. The amount of these assessments shall be determined by the board of drainage commissioners of the district. The proceeds of these assessments shall be used for the purpose of maintaining canals of the drainage district in an efficient operating condition and for the necessary operating expenses of the district. Notice of the meeting at which the board of drainage commissioners determines the amount of the annual levy shall be mailed to the owners, as shown on the county tax records, of all property subject to assessment, or shall be published once a week for two successive calendar weeks in a newspaper having general circulation in the area. The notice shall be sent or published not more than 30 days nor less than 10 days prior to the meeting, and shall state the time, place, and purposes of the meeting. Any interested person has the right to be heard at the meeting prior to the drainage commissioners taking any action on the proposed assessment. In the event that any interested and aggrieved party disagrees with the said assessment, he may, within 20 days of the mailing of the notice of the assessment, file with the clerk for the county wherein the proceeding is pending, a notice specifically setting forth his objection. The Secretary of the District shall file in the records of the proceeding a certification setting forth the date of the mailing of the notice of the annual maintenance assessments. The clerk shall thereupon notify the senior resident superior court judge of such district who shall set the objection down for hearing at the earliest possible time. The court shall hear the matter upon the objections duly set forth in the notice of objection.

The board of drainage commissioners shall have the authority to employ engineering assistance, construction equipment, superintendents and operators for the equipment necessary for the efficient maintenance of the canals, or the maintenance may be done by private contract made after due advertisement as required for the original construction work.

(b) The board of drainage commissioners of a drainage district may join with the commissioners of one or more districts for the purpose of employing engineering assistance, equipment, superintendents and equipment operators for the maintenance of the canals in the several districts desiring to coordinate their maintenance operations and the drainage districts desiring to coordinate a common maintenance force may have a common office with the necessary employees for the furtherance of the joint operations for maintenance. The districts may coordinate their work without regard to county lines.

(c) The board of commissioners of a drainage district may, individually or jointly with the commissioners of other drainage districts, purchase, lease, rent, sell, or otherwise dispose of at public or private sale, equipment for the original construction or maintenance of the canals in the individual or joint districts or the said drainage districts may make contracts with private construction firms for the maintenance and construction of their canals. Contracts made with private construction companies are to be advertised as provided for the contract for the original construction of the canals.

The drainage districts may use the equipment owned by them for the purpose of maintenance of the canals and the construction of extensions to the system of canals in the individual or several drainage districts.

(d) The drainage districts desiring to consolidate their maintenance services and equipment may set up a board composed of one member from each district for the purpose of control and use of the personnel and equipment employed on a joint basis, and in all matters coming before the joint board, the representative of each district shall have a voting strength equal to the proportionate acreage of his drainage district as compared with the total acreage of the combined districts.

(e) The collection of the annual maintenance assessments shall be made by the county tax collector. The board of county commissioners of the county in which a drainage district is located shall upon the request of the board of drainage commissioners of the said district cause to be shown on the tax statement or notice issued by the county to its taxpayers the amount due the drainage district by the landowners in the same manner as other special assessments are shown thereon. This amount shall be collected by the county tax collector in the same manner as county taxes and deposited to the credit of the district in which the land is located.

(f) The provisions for maintenance as set forth in this Article and elsewhere in this Subchapter III shall include water-retardant structures and the operation of such.

(g) The board of commissioners may borrow money in anticipation of revenue from maintenance assessments, as hereinbefore provided for, from which assessments the loan shall be repaid. The amount which the commissioners may borrow shall not be limited to the revenues anticipated for any one year. The terms and provisions of such loan shall be approved by the clerk of the superior court which approval shall be requested in the form of a petition and order in the proceeding by virtue of which the district was organized. The proceeds of said loan shall be used only for purposes set forth in Article 7A of Chapter 156. (1949, c. 1216; 1959, c. 597, s. 4; 1961, c. 614, s. 8; 1989 (Reg. Sess., 1990), c. 959, s. 4; 1991, c. 634.)

Article 7B.

Improvement, Renovation, Enlargement and Extension of Canals, Structures and Boundaries.

§ 156-93.2. Proceedings for improvement, renovation and extension of canals, structures and equipment.

The board of commissioners may construct, renovate, improve, enlarge and extend the drainage systems and water-retardant structures and any equipment of the district, by complying with the following provisions:

(1) The commissioners shall file with the clerk of the superior court in the county in which the district was organized, a petition which sets forth the need for the improvements requested and a general description of the proposed improvements.

(2) Upon the filing of the petition, the clerk shall then appoint a board of viewers with the same composition and qualifications as is required by G.S. 156-59. He shall direct the board of viewers to consider the proposals of the board of commissioners and report to him (i) whether or not the improvement proposed will benefit the lands sought to be benefited and (ii) whether or not the proposed improvement is practicable.

The board of viewers shall make their report to the clerk within 30 days after their appointment unless the time shall be extended by the court upon the showing of a meritorious cause for the extension.

(3) a. If the board of viewers shall report (i) that none of the improvement proposed will benefit the lands sought to be benefited, or (ii) that it is not practicable, the petition of the board of commissioners shall be dismissed and shall not be submitted again within six months thereafter.

b. If the board of viewers shall report (i) that part or all the improvement proposed will benefit the lands sought to be benefited and (ii) the proposed improvement is practicable, then the clerk shall fix a time and place for a hearing upon said report. The said hearing shall be no less than 20, nor more than 30, days after the filing of said report.

(4) Notice of said hearing shall be given as follows:

a. Posting and publication:

1. Posting at the courthouse door of the county in which the proceeding is pending;

2. Posting at five conspicuous places within the district;

3. The notice shall be posted at least 20 days prior to said hearing;

4. Publication in a newspaper with general circulation within the area once a week for three successive weeks.

b. Contents:

1. The notice shall state the time and place for the hearing;

2. Describe in general terms the improvements proposed;

3. That the court will consider and adjudicate the report of the board of viewers.

(5) At the date appointed for the hearing the clerk shall hear and determine any objections that may be offered to the said report. The clerk may make such modifications and changes which tend to increase the benefits of the proposed work or improvement.

(6) a. If the clerk shall adjudicate that (i) none of the improvements proposed will benefit any of the lands sought to be benefited or (ii) that none of the improvements are practicable, he shall dismiss the proceedings and the petition shall not be submitted again within six months thereafter.

b. If the clerk shall approve the said report, he shall then direct the board of viewers to prepare a further and detailed report which shall include the following:

1. Specific plans and profiles together with estimates of the cost of the work recommended by the said board of viewers and an estimate of all other costs including those incurred by the board of viewers;

2. If directed by the clerk, a new property map of the district which shall show thereon the general location of each tract of land which will be benefited by the proposed work;

3. A statement showing the classification of benefits to be received by the several tracts of lands. This classification shall be determined and shown in the same manner as is provided for in G.S. 156-71. The board of viewers may adopt the original classification. Only those lands to be benefited by the proposed work shall be classified for assessment.

The board of viewers shall have, insofar as applicable, the same powers and duties as relate to the final report as are required and provided in Article 5 by G.S. 156-69, 156-70, 156-70.1 and 156-71.

The board of viewers shall make their report to the clerk within 60 days after their appointment. The clerk may extend this time upon the showing of meritorious cause for the extension.

The expense of the board of viewers, their assistants, and all costs incurred by them shall be paid from any surplus funds of the district, as defined in this Subchapter, or if such are not sufficient, by the same means of financing as are available for such purposes when the district is originally organized. The estimate of the expenditures shall be shown in its report and all amounts of money expended shall be reimbursed when funds are available.

(7)   Upon the filing of the said report, the clerk shall fix a time and a place for a hearing thereupon.

(8)   The notice of the hearing upon said report shall be given in the same manner as required for the notice of the proposed work as required by the preceding subdivision (4) which relates to the preliminary hearing.

Also, a notice of said hearing shall be mailed at least 10 days prior to the hearing, to those landowners as their names appear upon the statement of classification of benefits filed with the report of the board of viewers and whose names and addresses are shown on the tax scrolls of the county wherein their land is situated. The attorneys for, or commissioners of, the district shall use due diligence to determine the said names and addresses from the tax scrolls.

The filing with the clerk of the superior court of a certificate by the attorney for, or the commissioners of, the district, that due diligence has been used to obtain the names and addresses from the tax scrolls and that notice has been mailed to those persons at the address shown, shall be sufficient showing that this provision has been complied with. The certificate shall state the names, addresses and dates to whom such notice was mailed.

(9)   At the date set for the hearing any landowner may appear in person, or by counsel, and file his objections in writing to the report of the board of viewers. It shall be the duty of the clerk to carefully review the report of the board of viewers and the objections filed thereto and make such changes as are necessary to render substantial and equal justice to all landowners in the district.

If the clerk shall adjudicate that the benefits which will accrue to the lands affected are greater than the cost of the improvements, the report of the board of viewers shall be confirmed. The clerk shall then direct the commissioners of the district to proceed with the improvements as approved.

If, however, the clerk finds that the cost of the improvements is greater than the resulting benefits that will accrue to the lands affected, the clerk shall dismiss the proceedings.

(10) Any landowner, party petitioner, or the drainage district may, within 10 days after the entry of the order or judgment by the clerk upon the report of the board of viewers, appeal to the superior court in session time or in chambers. The procedures for taking appeal under Article 27A of Chapter 1 of the General Statutes apply, except as provided otherwise by this Subchapter. All of the terms and provisions of G.S. 156-75 apply to the appeal. (1961, c. 614, s. 1; 1969, c. 192, s. 2; 1999-216, s. 21.)

§ 156-93.3. Extension of boundaries.

The boundaries of a drainage district may be extended upon compliance with the requirements and procedures as follows:

(1) The request for extension shall be made by the board of commissioners of the district, in the form of a petition in the name of the drainage district, to the clerk of the superior court of the county wherein the district was originally organized. The proceeding may be ex parte or adversary.

(2) The area proposed to be included within the boundaries of the district must be either:

a. Located upstream and adjacent to the existing boundary of the district and must have as its only source of drainage either:

1. The canals of the district; or

2. Natural or artificial drain ways which empty into or are benefited by the canals of the district; and

3. Must be within the watershed of the existing district; or

b. Adjacent to the existing boundary of the district and have a common outfall with the existing district.

(3) a. In the event the area meets the requirements of (2)a, it shall only be necessary for the petition to be filed by the board of commissioners of the district.

b.	In the event the area meets the requirement of (2)b of this section, the owners of fifty percent (50%) or more of the land area which it is proposed to include or forty percent (40%) or more of the resident landowners who will be benefited within such area, must join with and be petitioners with the commissioners of the existing district, asking for the extension of boundaries and inclusion of land within the existing district.

Should the area proposed to be included within the boundary of the enlarged district embrace one or more existing drainage districts, the commissioners of any such district or districts may join in a petition to the court asking for the extension of boundaries of the existing district.

The joinder in the petition by the commissioners of such drainage district in the name of the district shall have the effect of including in the petition all of the land within said existing drainage district to the same extent as if the petition had been signed individually by each landowner of the district. The total acreage in such district or districts shall be included as land in the petition in determining whether or not the requirements under this section have been complied with.

(4)	Upon filing of the petition for extension of the boundaries, the clerk of the superior court shall appoint a board of viewers with the same composition and qualifications as is required by G.S. 156-59. The board of viewers shall examine the area proposed to be included within the boundaries of the district to determine whether or not, in their opinion, it is feasible and equitable to include said area within the boundaries of the district, and report their finding to the court. The report must be made within 30 days after the appointment of said board of viewers. The time for filing said report may be extended by the clerk upon a showing of a meritorious cause for the extension.

(5)	If the board of viewers shall report that the proposed extension of boundary is not feasible or equitable, the petition shall be dismissed and shall not be submitted again until after six months from date of dismissal.

(6)	a.	If the board of viewers shall report that the proposed extension of boundary is feasible and equitable, then the clerk of the superior court shall order the board of viewers to make a further and detailed report which shall include a map of the area that is proposed to be annexed which shall show:

1.	Boundaries of the existing district;

2. Boundaries of the proposed extension;

3. A general location of each individual tract of land which will be benefited.

b. In the event no additional work is proposed, the board of viewers shall report the following:

1. The allocation of benefits derived from the existing canals, structures or other improvements, between the existing district and the area to be included within the boundaries of the existing district, which shall be a percentage figure and shall be the major factor for the determination of the requirements set forth in the succeeding paragraphs 2 and 3;

2. The amount of money, if any, which the owners of the land to be included within the district should pay for the use of the canals, structures or other improvements of the district;

3. The percent of the cost of maintenance and operating expenses which the owners of the land to be included, should pay;

4. Classification of the additional lands as to benefits derived from the existing canals, structures or other improvements of the district which shall be in accordance with the provisions of G.S. 156-71. The area of the existing district shall not be classified, unless directed by the clerk of the superior court;

5. The names and addresses of the landowners within the areas proposed to be included insofar as may be determined from the tax records of the county;

6. Such other information as may be appropriate or as may be directed by the clerk of the superior court.

c. In the event additional work is proposed, the report of the board of viewers shall also contain the information required in G.S. 156-93.2, as it applies to the final report of the board of viewers.

(7) The board of viewers shall file their detailed or final report within 60 days after their appointment. The time for filing of said report may be extended by the clerk upon a showing of meritorious cause for the extension.

(8) Upon the filing of said report those landowners in the area to be included who are not parties to the proceedings and who do not desire to sign

the petition, shall be made parties defendant. Summons shall be served upon the defendants in the manner required for special proceedings. There shall be attached to and served with the summons, in lieu of a copy of the petition or final report, a statement which shall set forth (i) the purpose of the proceedings and (ii) that the report of the board of viewers is on file in the office of the clerk of the superior court and may be examined by persons interested.

(9) The attorney for, or the commissioners of, the district shall use due diligence to give notice to every landowner within the area proposed to be included, who has not signed the petition asking for such extension of boundaries and/or the proposed improvements.

The filing of a certificate by the attorney for, or the commissioners of, the district that due diligence has been used to notify each of said defendant landowners shown by the report of the board of viewers, either by personal service or by publication, shall be sufficient showing of compliance with this provision. The certificate shall contain the names of such landowners served personally, the date of service and the names of those served by publication and the date of service by publication.

(10) Upon filing of said certificate the clerk shall fix a time and place for a hearing upon said report, which date shall be no less than 20 days after filing of said certificate.

(11) Notice of said hearing shall be given as follows:

a. Posting and publication:

1. Posting at the courthouse door of the county in which the proceeding is pending;

2. Posting at five conspicuous places in the district and in the area to be included;

3. The notice shall be posted at least 20 days prior to the said hearing;

4. Publication in a newspaper with general circulation within the area once a week for three successive weeks;

5. Mailing a copy of the notice to those persons for whom an address is shown in the certificate filed by the attorney for, or commissioners of, the district.

b.   Contents:

1.   The notice shall state the time and place for the hearing;

2.   Describe in general terms the area proposed to be included and work proposed, if any;

3.   That the court will consider and adjudicate the report of the board of viewers.

(12)   At the date set for hearing any landowner may appear in person or by counsel and file his objection in writing to the report of the board of viewers. It shall be the duty of the clerk to carefully review the report of the board of viewers and the objection filed thereto and make such changes as are necessary to render substantial and equal justice to all of the landowners and the existing district.

(13)   The clerk shall, after making adjustments in the report of the board of viewers, if any, determine:

a.   If the area(s) of land sought to be included, or any part thereof, is, or will be, benefited by the canals, structures or other improvements of the district.

b.   If such area(s) should equitably be included within the boundary of the district because of the benefits received or to be received from the district.

c.   If the requirements of the preceding subdivision (3)b, if applicable, are met.

If the clerk shall determine that all of the three preceding requirements are met, he shall direct that the area(s) of land to be included within the boundaries of the district, in accordance with the provisions of the report of the board of viewers, as approved.

(14)   If the clerk shall determine either:

a.   That no part of the area proposed to be included is or will be benefited by the canals, structures or other improvements of the district and equitably should not be included within the boundaries of the district; or

b. That the requirements of the preceding subdivision (3)a or b, whichever is applicable, have not been complied with; he shall dismiss the proceeding.

(15) Any landowner, party petitioner, or the drainage district may, within 10 days after the entry of an order or judgment by the clerk upon the report of the board of viewers, appeal to the superior court in session time or in chambers. The procedures for taking appeal under Article 27A of Chapter 1 of the General Statutes apply, except as provided otherwise by this Subchapter. All of the terms and provisions of G.S. 156-75 apply to the appeal.

(16) The duties and powers of the board of commissioners as to those lands included within the district by the current proceedings shall be the same as to those in the original proceeding. (1961, c. 614, s. 1; 1965, c. 1143, s. 4; 1969, c. 192, s. 3; cc. 440, 1002; 1999-216, s. 22.)

§ 156-93.4. Coordination of proceedings under §§ 156-93.2 and 156-93.3.

In the event a proceeding shall be instituted as provided for in G.S. 156-93.2 and shall also include the extension of boundaries, as provided for in G.S. 156-93.3, the provisions of G.S. 156-93.2 and 156-93.3 shall be coordinated and if there shall be any conflict as to procedure, that provided for in G.S. 156-93.3 shall be followed. (1961, c. 614, s. 1.)

§ 156-93.5. Assessments and bonds for improvement, renovation, enlargement and extension.

The board of drainage commissioners shall, for the purposes set forth in this Article, levy the necessary assessments and may issue bonds or other debentures for the purpose of providing funds for the construction or acquisition of any of the improvements or works authorized by this Article. The time and manner of levying assessments and the issuance of bonds or other debentures and the terms thereof shall be the same as provided for in Article 8 of Subchapter III. (1961, c. 614, s. 1.)

§ 156-93.6. Rights-of-way and easements for existing districts.

All drainage districts heretofore created shall be deemed to own an easement or right-of-way in and to those lands upon which there are existing canals and spoil banks.

Whenever the proposed repairs, maintenance or other improvements make it necessary for the drainage district to acquire additional land for easements or right-of-way, the procedure to secure the same shall be in accordance with G.S. 156-70.1. (1961, c. 614, s. 1.)

§ 156-93.7. Existing districts may act together to extend boundaries within watershed.

If there shall be more than one drainage district in a drainage basin, or watershed, the board of drainage commissioners of any of the districts may initiate or join separately or collectively with the commissioners of one or more of other drainage districts, in the drainage basin or watershed, and/or with the owners of land within the drainage basin, whose lands are not included within an existing drainage district in a petition to the court, asking for the creation of a larger drainage district, or the extension of boundaries of one of the existing districts.

The joinder in the petition by the commissioners of an existing drainage district, acting in the name of the district, shall have the effect of including all of the land assessed within the drainage district, in the petition asking for the creation of the larger drainage district or the extension of boundaries of an existing district. The total area of assessed land, within the existing drainage district shall be included, as land in the petition, in determining whether or not the requirement of G.S. 156-93.3 (3) b have been fulfilled.

The provisions of this section shall apply in proceedings provided for in G.S. 156-93.2 and 156-93.3. (1961, c. 614, s. 1; 1965, c. 1143, s. 5.)

Article 8.

Assessments and Bond Issue.

§ 156-94. Total cost for three years ascertained.

After the classification of lands and the ratio of assessments of the different classes to be made thereon has been confirmed by the court, the board of drainage commissioners shall ascertain the total cost of the improvement, including damages awarded to be paid to owners of land, all costs and incidental expenses, and also including an amount sufficient to pay the necessary expenses of maintaining the improvement for a period of three years after the completion of the work of construction, not exceeding ten per centum (10%) of the estimated actual cost of constructing the drainage works or the contract price thereof if such contract has not been awarded, and after deducting therefrom any special assessments made against any railroad or highway, and, thereupon, the board of drainage commissioners, under the hand of the chairman and secretary of the board, shall certify to the clerk of the superior court the total cost, ascertained as aforesaid; and the certificate shall be forthwith recorded in the drainage record and open to inspection of any landowner in the district. (1909, c. 442, s. 31; 1911, c. 67, s. 8; C.S., s. 5351; 1923, c. 217, s. 4.)

§ 156-95. Assessment and payment; notice of bond issue.

If the total cost of the improvement is less than an average of twenty-five cents (25¢) per acre on all the land in the district, the board of drainage commissioners shall forthwith assess the lands in the district therefor, in accordance with their classification, and said assessment shall be collected in one installment, by the same officer and in the same manner as State and county taxes are collected, and payable at the same time. In case the total cost exceeds an average of twenty-five cents (25¢) per acre on all lands in the district, the board of drainage commissioners shall give notice for three weeks by publication in some newspaper published in a county in which the district, or some part thereof, is situated, if there be any such newspaper, and also by posting a written or printed notice at the door of the courthouse and at five conspicuous places in the district, reciting that they propose to issue bonds for the payment of the total cost of the improvement, giving the amount of bonds to be issued, the rate of interest that they are to bear, and the time when payable. Any landowner in the district not wanting to pay interest on the bonds may, within 15 days after the publication of such notice, pay to the county treasurer the full amount for which his land is liable, to be ascertained from the classification sheet and the certificate of the board showing the total cost of the improvement, and have his lands released from liability to be assessed for the improvement; but such land shall continue liable for any future assessment for maintenance or for any increased assessment authorized under the law. (1909, c. 442, s. 32; 1911, c. 67, s. 9; C.S., s. 5352.)

§ 156-96. Failure to pay deemed consent to bond issue.

Every person owning land in the district who shall fail to pay to the treasurer the full amount for which his land is liable, as aforesaid, within the time above specified, shall be deemed as consenting to the issuance of drainage bonds, and in consideration of the right to pay his proportion in installments, he hereby waives his rights of defense to the payment of any assessments which may be levied for the payment of bonds, because of any irregularity, illegality, or defect in the proceedings prior to this time, except in case of an appeal, as hereinbefore provided, which is not affected by this waiver. The term "person" as used in this Subchapter includes any firm, company, or corporation. (1909, c. 442, s. 33; 1911, c. 67, s. 10; C.S., s. 5353; 1963, c. 767, s. 4.)

§ 156-97. Bonds issued.

At the expiration of 15 days after publication of notice of bond issue the board of drainage commissioners may issue bonds of the drainage district for an amount equal to the total cost of the improvement, less such amounts as shall have been paid in in cash to the treasurer. Bonds issued by the board of drainage commissioners shall comply with the following provisions:

(1)   The bonds shall be serial bonds;

(2)   The denomination of the bonds shall be not less than one hundred dollars ($100.00) nor more than one thousand dollars ($1,000);

(3)   The interest upon said bonds shall not be more than fourteen percent (14%) per annum, from the date of issue and payable semiannually;

(4)   The first annual installment of principal shall fall due not less than three years nor more than six years after the date of the bonds;

(5)   Each annual installment of principal shall be not less than two percent (2%) nor more than ten percent (10%) of the total bonds authorized;

(6) If the total amount of bonds to be issued does not exceed ten percent (10%) of the total amount of the assessment, the board of commissioners may, in their discretion, not issue any bonds and in lieu thereof issue assessment anticipation bonds which shall mature over a period of not less than four nor more than 10 years and shall be payable in equal annual installments. The interest rate on said assessment anticipation bonds shall not be more than fourteen percent (14%) per annum;

(7) The board of commissioners may issue bond anticipation note or notes to be redeemed and paid upon the sale and delivery of bonds herein provided for. If such bond anticipation note or notes are issued, at the discretion of the commissioners, such may be done after the bonds have been sold and prior to the printing and delivery of said bonds and must be paid from the proceeds of said bonds when delivered. (1909, c. 442, s. 34; 1911, c. 67, s. 11; 1917, c. 152, s. 12; C.S., s. 5354; 1923, c. 217, s. 5; 1955, c. 1340; 1957, c. 1410, s. 1; 1961, c. 601, s. 1; 1963, c. 767, s. 4; 1969, c. 878; 1985, c. 136, ss. 1, 2.)

§ 156-97.1. Issuance of assessment anticipation notes.

In lieu of the bonds provided for in G.S. 156-97, the board of drainage commissioners may issue assessment anticipation notes of the district for an amount not to exceed the assessment levied by the commissioners and approved by the clerk of the superior court, less such amounts as shall have been paid in in cash to the treasurer. It shall be optional with the board of drainage commissioners in issuing assessment anticipation notes to issue serial notes in any denominations bearing not more than fourteen percent (14%) interest from the date of issue, payable semiannually. The first annual installment of principal shall be due not less than one year nor more than two years after date thereof, and each annual installment of principal shall not be less than two percent (2%) nor more than twenty-five percent (25%) of the total amount of notes authorized and issued.

Such assessment anticipation notes, when issued, shall have the same force and effect of bonds issued under the provisions of this Article and shall be collectible in the same manner.

The commissioners may issue either serial notes or an amortized note. (1957, c. 912, s. 2; 1961, c. 601, s. 3; 1963, c. 767, ss. 4, 7; 1985, c. 136, s. 3.)

§ 156-98. Form of bonds and notes; excess assessment.

All bonds and notes authorized and issued shall be signed by the chairman and secretary of the board of drainage commissioners and the corporate seal of the district affixed thereto, and the interest coupons shall be authenticated by the facsimile signature of the secretary, and both the principal and interest coupons shall be payable at some bank or trust company to be designated by the board of drainage commissioners and incorporated in the body of the bond. The form of the bond shall be authorized by the board of drainage commissioners or by the board and the purchaser of the bonds jointly, at the option of the board.

All bonds of reclamation districts shall have that fact noted upon the face of the bond, either by stamping or printing the same thereon. All bonds of improvement districts shall also have that fact noted upon their face.

For the purpose of meeting any possible deficit in the collection of annual drainage assessments or any deficit arising out of unforeseen contingencies there shall be levied, assessed and collected during each year when either the interest or principal or both interest and principal on the outstanding bonds shall be due, an assessment as will yield ten percent (10%) more than the total of interest and principal due in such years; that is to say, for every one hundred dollars ($100.00) of principal and interest, or either, due in any one year, there shall be levied, assessed and collected a sufficient drainage assessment to yield one hundred and ten dollars ($110.00) for such year. When this excess of drainage tax so levied, assessed and collected shall accumulate so that the aggregate surplus in the hands of the treasurer of the district shall amount to more than fifteen percent (15%) of the total principal of the bonds of the district outstanding and unpaid, then such surplus above fifteen percent (15%) thereof may be available for expenditure by the board of drainage commissioners in the maintenance and upkeep of the drainage work in such district in the manner provided by law: After all the drainage assessments have been collected except the last assessment, if the surplus which has accumulated amounts to more than five percent (5%) of the total issue of bonds of the district, then and in such event the board of drainage commissioners may in their discretion apply such excess above five percent (5%) toward the reduction of the total amount embraced in the last assessment, reducing the same pro rata as to each tract of land embraced in the district, and having regard to the classification, to the end that such reduction shall be fairly and justly made. As to such surplus as shall accumulate in the hands of the treasurer of the district over and above all obligations of the district which may be due, the treasurer is hereby directed to deposit same in some solvent bank or banks at the highest rate of interest obtainable therefor, and the said treasurer shall be authorized, if he deems it necessary, to demand satisfactory security for such deposits; but the said treasurer shall reserve the right to demand a repayment at any time upon giving not exceeding 30 days' notice thereof. Whereas the proceeds of the first drainage assessment may not be collected and in the hands of the treasurer of the district prior to the maturity of the first and second semiannual installments of interest upon the issue of bonds, the treasurer of the district is hereby directed to pay the interest coupons first maturing and also the interest coupons next maturing, if necessary, out of funds in his hands for the purpose of maintaining the improvement for the period of three years after the completion of the work or construction. As a surplus fund with the treasurer arising out of the annual additional assessment of ten per centum (10%) shall accumulate in any one year in excess of fifteen per centum (15%) of the total principal of the bonds of the district outstanding and unpaid, as herein provided, the treasurer shall transfer in each of such years such surplus fund to the fund for maintaining the improvement after completion, as a reimbursement of the fund formerly withdrawn therefrom for the payment of the first and second installments of interest coupons until such reimbursement shall be fully made. The treasurer shall thereafter keep separate accounts of the proceeds of such additional ten percent (10%) assessment remaining each year after the payment of all maturing obligations, and also a separate account of the funds provided for maintaining the improvement for the period of three years after completion of improvement and all payments therefrom and reimbursements thereto. (1917, c. 152, s. 13; C.S., s. 5355; 1923, c. 217, s. 6; 1927, c. 98, s. 5; 1961, c. 601, s. 2.)

§ 156-99. Application of funds; holder's remedy.

The commissioners of the district may sell the bonds or notes of the district for not less than par and devote the proceeds to the payment of the work as it progresses and to the payment of the other expenses of the district provided for in this Subchapter. The proceeds from the sale of the said bonds or notes shall be for the exclusive use of the levee or drainage district specified therein. A copy of said bonds or notes shall be recorded in the drainage record. If serial bonds or notes are issued it shall only be necessary to record the first numbered bond or note, with a statement showing the serial numbers, the amount and the due dates of principal and interest.

There shall be set out specifically in the drainage record of said proceeding, a description of the lands embraced in the district for which the tax or assessment has not been paid in full, and which is subject to the lien of the said obligations. A reference to the tract number on the map of the district as recorded in the drainage proceedings or in the office of the register of deeds is sufficient description.

If any installment of principal or interest represented by the bonds and notes shall not be paid at the time and in the manner when the same shall become due and payable, and such default shall continue for a period of six months, the holders of such bonds or notes upon which default has been made may have a right of action against the drainage district or the board of drainage commissioners of the district, its officers, including the tax collector and treasurer, directing the levying of a tax or special assessment as herein provided, and the collection of same, in such sum as may be necessary to meet any unpaid installments of principal and interest and costs of action; and such other remedies are hereby vested in the holders of such bonds or notes in default, as may be authorized by law and the right of action is hereby vested in the holders of such bonds or notes upon which default has been made, authorizing them to institute suit against any officer on his official bond for failure to perform any duty imposed by the provisions of this Subchapter.

The official bond for the tax collector and treasurer shall be liable for the faithful performance of the duties herein assigned them. Such bond may be increased by the board of county commissioners. (1909, c. 442, s. 34; 1911, c. 67, s. 11; c. 205; C.S., s. 5356; 1923, c. 217, s. 7; 1963, c. 767, s. 8.)

§ 156-100. Sale of bonds.

In making the sale of drainage bonds the board of drainage commissioners shall prepare a notice of such sale containing the usual and appropriate information regarding the terms and provisions of the bonds, and shall publish the same for at least a period of two weeks in at least one paper of general circulation published within the State and in at least one other newspaper of large circulation among the buyers of bonds, in which they shall invite sealed bids from prospective purchasers to be opened on a certain day, and may require a cash deposit to accompany all bids, and shall reserve the right to reject any and all bids. In such notice the commissioners may hold in reserve information as to the date when the first installment of principal shall fall due, the annual installments of principal to be paid, the number of years within which the serial bonds are to be paid, the form of the bonds, and the name of the bank or trust company at which the interest coupons and the installments of principal are to be made payable, and shall state that the information and data so withheld may subsequently be agreed upon between the drainage commissioners and the purchaser of the bonds; or the board of drainage commissioners in their advertisement asking bids may make optional propositions in the respects above recited, inviting bids as to each kind of bond so proposed. The board of drainage commissioners shall accept the highest bona fide bid for such bonds and issue and sell the same accordingly, provided the highest bid shall equal or exceed the par value of the bonds with any accrued interest thereon. If no satisfactory bid shall be received, the board of drainage commissioners may readvertise the bonds for sale in the manner above provided, or they may accept any private bid for the bonds at not less than their par value, with any accrued interest thereon. The board of drainage commissioners shall in good faith make diligent effort to sell the bonds at a price not less than their par value, with accrued interest. Bonds of any drainage district heretofore sold or contracted to be sold by the Local Government Commission in the manner provided by the Local Government Act, either alone or in conjunction with the board of drainage commissioners, shall be deemed to have been lawfully sold or contracted to be sold. (1909, c. 442, s. 34; 1911, c. 67, s. 11; 1917, c. 152, s. 15; C.S., s. 5357; 1941, c. 142.)

§ 156-100.1. Sale of assessment anticipation notes.

Should assessment anticipation notes be issued by a drainage district under the provisions of G.S. 156-97.1, the board of drainage commissioners may accept any private bid for said assessment anticipation notes at not less than their par value, with accrued interest thereon without the necessity of advertising the sale hereof as is provided for in the sale of bonds under the provisions of G.S. 156-100. (1957, c. 912, s. 3.)

§ 156-100.2. Payment of assessments which become liens after original bond issue.

Payment of assessments not included in the original bond or note issue shall be financed in the following manner:

(1) In the event of appeal from the order of the clerk of superior court approving the final report of the board of viewers, the assessment approved by the appellate court shall be due and payable 30 days from the entry of the final order in said appeal.

(2) In the event land should be included within the district for any other reason, the assessment thereon shall be due and payable 30 days after the date of the agreement or court order by which said land is included.

(3) In the event the assessments referred to in the preceding subdivisions (1) and (2) are not paid at the expiration of the said 30-day period, then the commissioners may provide for installment payments of said assessment upon such terms as may be approved by the clerk of the superior court who has jurisdiction of the said drainage proceeding.

The commissioners of the district may issue bonds or notes for an amount equal to the total of the installment payments, upon terms as approved by the clerk of the superior court. The lien of the assessment, the rights of the bond or note holder, and all other liabilities and rights shall be the same as prescribed in this Subchapter III for other bonds and notes of the district. (1963, c. 767, s. 9.)

§ 156-100.3. Sinking fund.

The commissioners of the drainage district may establish a sinking fund to be used to pay bonds and notes issued by the district. The terms and conditions by which the said sinking fund is established shall be approved by the clerk of the superior court who has jurisdiction of said district. (1963, c. 767, s. 10.)

§ 156-101. Refunding bonds issued.

In any case where the board of drainage commissioners of any drainage district have issued or may issue bonds for the purpose of constructing or completing the drainage works in such district, the payment of which at maturity would in the judgment of the board of drainage commissioners be an unreasonable burden on the owners of the lands in such district assessed for the payment of such bonds and interest, or if it shall appear for other good and substantial reasons that the welfare of the district and the owners of lands therein would be promoted thereby, the board of drainage commissioners shall have the power to refund such bonds, or any part thereof, and issue new bonds equal to the amount of bonds outstanding and unpaid, or any part thereof. The new or refunding bonds shall bear a rate of interest not exceeding six percent (6%) payable semiannually, and shall be divided into such annual installments not exceeding ten percent (10%) and not less than five percent (5%) of the outstanding bonds so refunded. The new assessments shall be levied and collected with which to pay the principal and interest on the bonds in the manner provided by law. The first installment of principal on the bonds so refunded may be made payable at a certain date in the future not exceeding six years from the date of the refunding bonds, and in the meantime annual assessments shall be levied and collected for the payment of the interest. (1917, c. 152, s. 14; C.S., s. 5358.)

§ 156-102. Drainage bonds received as deposits.

The State Treasurer is authorized to receive drainage bonds issued by drainage districts in North Carolina as deposits from banks, insurance companies, and other corporations required by law to make deposits with the State Treasurer: Provided, that the Attorney General shall have approved the form of such bonds. (1917, c. 152, s. 7; C.S., s. 5359.)

§ 156-103. Assessment rolls prepared.

The board of drainage commissioners shall immediately prepare the assessment rolls or drainage tax lists, giving thereon the names of the owners of land in the district and a brief description of the several tracts of land assessed and the amount of assessment against each tract of land. The first of these assessment rolls shall be due and payable on the first Monday in September following the date of such bonds, and shall provide funds sufficient for the payment of interest on such bonds for one year. The second assessment roll shall make like provision for the payment of the interest for one year. Annual assessment rolls shall thereafter provide funds sufficient to meet the interest for one year on the issue of bonds outstanding. During the year previous to maturity of any annual installment due upon the principal of said bonds there shall be an assessment roll sufficient to provide funds for the payment of both the interest for one year and for the payment of the annual installment due upon the principal of the bonds. Such annual assessments shall be made from year to year to provide funds to meet the interest for one year and the annual installment of the principal due upon the bonds outstanding, until the whole principal due upon the outstanding bonds and the interest thereon shall be fully paid. In making up such assessment rolls there shall be included ten percent (10%) additional as provided in G.S. 156-98. Each of the assessment rolls shall specify the time when collectible and be numbered in their order, and the amounts assessed against the several tracts of land shall be in accordance with the benefits received, as shown by the classification and ratio of assessments made by the viewers. These assessment rolls shall be signed by the chairman of the board of drainage commissioners and by the secretary of the board. There shall be four copies of each of the assessment rolls, one of which shall be filed with the drainage record, one shall be filed with the chairman of the board of drainage commissioners, who shall carefully preserve the same, one shall be preserved by the clerk of the court, without change or mutilation, for the purposes of reference or comparison, and one shall be delivered to the sheriff, or other county tax collector, after the clerk of the superior court has appended thereto an order directing the collection of such assessments, and the assessments, shall thereupon have the force and effect of a judgment as in the case of State and county taxes. If the drainage commission which has assessed the lands of a drainage district prior to March 11, 1919, shall file the aforesaid four copies of assessment rolls within six months from April 1, 1919, the filing of such assessment rolls shall have the same legal effect as if filed strictly in accordance with this section immediately after the preparation of such assessment rolls. The State having authorized the creation of drainage districts and having delegated thereto the power to levy a valid tax in furtherance of the public purposes thereof, it is hereby declared that drainage districts heretofore or hereafter organized under existing law or any subsequent amendments thereto are created for a public use and are political subdivisions of the State. (1911, c. 67, s. 12; 1917, c. 152, s. 9; 1919, c. 282, s. 1; C.S., s. 5360; 1921, c. 7; 1923, c. 217, s. 8.)

§ 156-104. Application of amendatory provisions of certain sections; amendment or reformation of proceedings.

All the provisions of Chapter 217 of the Public Laws of 1923 amendatory of G.S. 156-71, 156-75, 156-83, 156-94, 156-97, 156-98, 156-99 and 156-103 shall apply to all drainage districts which shall hereafter be organized, and also to all districts where proceedings for the organization thereof have been instituted and are now pending and where the bonds have not been actually issued, sold, and delivered to the purchaser thereof. If it shall be necessary to amend or reform any of the pleadings or orders made by the court or any action taken by the board of drainage commissioners in any drainage proceedings instituted and pending before March 6, 1923, full authority is granted to make any such amendments, to the end that the said drainage proceedings shall conform with the provisions hereof. (1923, c. 217, s. 9; C.S., s. 5360(a).)

§ 156-105. Assessment lien; collection; sale of land.

The assessments shall constitute a first and paramount lien, second only to State and county taxes, upon the lands assessed for the payment of the bonds and interest thereon as they become due, and shall be collected in the same manner and by the same officers as the State and county taxes are collected. The assessments shall be due and payable on the first Monday in September each year, and if the same shall not be paid in full by the thirty-first day of December following, it shall be the duty of the sheriff or tax collector to sell the lands so delinquent. The sale of lands for failure to pay such assessments shall be made at the courthouse door of the county in which the lands are situated, between the hours of 10 o'clock in the forenoon and four o'clock in the afternoon of any date except Sunday or another legal holiday when the courthouse is closed for transactions, which may be designated by the board of drainage commissioners. After any such sale date has been designated by the board of drainage commissioners, if for any necessary cause the sale cannot be made on that date, the sale may be continued from day to day for not exceeding four days, or the lands may be readvertised and sold on any day which the board of drainage commissioners may or shall designate during the same hours and without any order being obtained therefor during the same calendar year. Nothing in this section shall be construed to require any order from any court for any sale or resale held hereunder. The existing general tax law in force when sales are made for delinquent assessments shall have application in redeeming lands so sold; and in all other respects, except as herein or otherwise modified or amended, the existing law as to the collection of State and county taxes shall apply to the collection of such drainage assessments. No bid at any sale shall be received unless sufficient in amount to discharge all the drainage assessments and other charges due by the delinquent lands or owner thereof, together with all costs and expenses of sale. If no sufficient bid be received, the board of drainage commissioners of the district shall be deemed the purchaser in its corporate capacity at a sum sufficient to pay all assessments which are due and costs as above stated, and shall be entitled to receive a certificate of purchase and deed in the manner provided by law for purchasers at tax sales. The board of drainage commissioners shall only be required to pay to the sheriff the costs and expenses of sale before receiving a certificate of purchase. The board of drainage commissioners of the district in their corporate capacity shall be in like position and have the same rights and be subject to the same duties as the purchaser of lands at any tax sale under the general law. If the board of drainage commissioners shall have been the purchaser of lands so sold, the amount paid in redemption by the owner, or any person having an estate therein or lien thereon, shall include the sum bid therefor plus the penalty. The board of drainage commissioners shall pay to the sheriff or tax collector the amount representing their bid at the sale of said lands before they shall be entitled to receive a deed therefor, which the sheriff shall pay to the treasurer of the drainage district in the same manner as other funds received by him. The board of drainage commissioners, after acquiring a deed for said lands, may hold the same as an asset of the district, and shall be liable for the payment of all drainage assessments and State and county taxes accruing after the sale at which the district was a bidder, and in all respects be deemed the owner of said lands and subject to the same privileges and liabilities as any other landowner, including the right to convey the said lands for a consideration and pay the proceeds of said sale to the treasurer of the district, which may be distributed by the drainage commissioners for the benefit of the district in the same manner as other district funds.

If any sheriff or tax collector failed for any reason to collect drainage assessments upon lands in any drainage districts due in 1917, or any subsequent years, and further failed to make valid sales of the lands so delinquent in the payment of such assessments, then and in such event the existing sheriff or tax collector is hereby authorized and directed to proceed to collect such unpaid drainage assessments, with interest thereon from the dates when such assessments respectively became due, and in default of payment being made he is further authorized to make sales of such lands as may be in default at any time hereafter, at the times and in the manner authorized by law as amended herein; and the purchaser at said sales shall acquire title to such lands in the manner provided by law. If the sheriff or tax collector in office at the time such assessments were in default has since died or gone out of office, the powers herein given shall be exercised by the existing sheriff or tax collector.

The 1931 amendment to this section shall have the same force and effect from and after April 13, 1931, as if it had been ratified and enacted prior to the first day of January, 1929, and no sale of drainage lands held under the provisions of section 5361 shall be deemed or declared void by reason of the fact that they may not have been held on the day specified in section 5361 of the Consolidated Statutes prior to this amendment. (1911, c. 67, s. 12; 1917, c. 152, s. 9; C.S., s. 5361; Pub. Loc. 1923, c. 88, ss. 3, 4, 5; 1931, c. 273; 2003-337, s. 12.)

§ 156-106. Assessment not collectible out of other property of delinquent.

Only the land assessed in the drainage proceeding shall be liable for the drainage tax or assessment, and no other property of the landowner shall or may be sold for said drainage tax or assessment: Provided, that this section shall not apply to any drainage bond sold and delivered prior to March 7, 1927, or to any litigation pending at that time. (1919, c. 282, s. 2; C.S., s. 5362; 1927, c. 139.)

§ 156-107. Sheriff in good faith selling property for assessment not liable for irregularity.

The sheriff who executes upon property for the collection of drainage assessments under the provisions of this Article shall not be liable either civilly or criminally if he shall sell such property in good faith, even though such sale is irregular or for any cause illegal. (1919, c. 282, s. 4; C.S., s. 5363.)

§ 156-108. Receipt books prepared.

The clerk of the superior court in each county where one or more drainage districts have been established shall be required to have prepared annually during the month of August a form of receipt, with appropriate stubs attached and properly bound, for the drainage assessments due on each tract of land as recited in the assessment rolls. This bound book of tax receipts or bills shall be indorsed "Drainage assessments of the (here give the name of the district) for the county of____, delivered to the sheriff or tax collector as of the first Monday in September, 19____, for collection as required by law," and the same indorsement shall be printed at the top of each tax bill or blank receipt. Each tax bill or blank receipt shall contain a blank space for the name of the owner of the property, the amount of the annual drainage tax, the amount of maintenance tax, if any, and a receipt at the bottom of the same, followed by a blank line for the signature of the tax collector. This bound book of tax bills or receipts, with the blanks duly filled in, shall be delivered to the sheriff or tax collector on the first Monday of September of each year. The necessary cost of printing and binding such book of tax bills or receipts and the filling in of the same shall be a proper charge against such drainage district and shall be paid by the board of drainage commissioners. (1917, c. 152, s. 9; 1919, c. 208, s. 2; C.S., s. 5364.)

§ 156-109. Receipt books where lands in two or more counties.

Where any drainage district which has been established contains lands located in a county or counties other than the county in which the district was established, the clerk of the superior court of the county in which the district was established shall have prepared annually during the month of August a form of tax bills or receipts, with appropriate stubs attached, covering all the lands in the drainage district located in such other county or counties, and in the form herein provided for the county in which the district has been established, and have the same substantially bound in book form. He shall also fill in the blanks of such tax receipts ready for the signature of the collector. On a page in such bound book after the tax bills or receipts there shall be appended an order directed to the sheriff or tax collector in the county in which such lands are located, which shall be in substantially the following form: State of North Carolina - County of _____The Sheriff or Tax Collector of _____ County: This is to certify that the foregoing tax bills or blank receipts embrace the drainage assessments made on certain lands in the county of_____, which are located in and are a part of (here insert the name of the drainage district), which district was established in the county of _____ . These assessments are due on the first Monday of September, 19____, and must be paid and collected within the time required by law. You will make monthly settlements of your collections with the treasurer of _____County, being the county in which the district was established, and in all other respects you will discharge your duties as sheriff or tax collector as required by law. In witness whereof, I have hereunto set my hand and official seal, this _____day of_____, 19____

_____,

Clerk Superior Court _____County.

Thereupon such drainage assessments in such county shall have the force and effect of a judgment upon the lands so assessed, as in the case of State and county taxes, and shall in all other respects be as valid assessments as those levied upon lands in the county in which the district was established. The auditor for drainage districts herein authorized shall also examine the records and accounts of the sheriff of such county. In the establishment and administration of the drainage districts the clerk of the superior court, the treasurer, and the chairman of the board of drainage commissioners shall have jurisdiction over the lands and the collection of drainage assessments in the county or counties other than the county in which the district was established to the same extent as in the county where such district was established: Provided, that in those counties which do not have a county treasurer, then the auditor provided for in this Subchapter shall perform the duties required by this section for the county treasurer. (1917, c. 152, s. 11; C.S., s. 5365; 1963, c. 767, s. 4.)

§ 156-110. Authority to collect arrears.

If any sheriff or tax collector was authorized to collect drainage assessments in any year prior to 1917, and failed to collect any part of such drainage assessments, and is now out of office, or is still holding the office of sheriff or tax collector, then and in such event such sheriff or tax collector, regardless of the expiration of his term of office, is hereby authorized and directed to proceed to the collection of such unpaid drainage assessments, and in default of payment being made, he is further authorized to make sales of such lands as may be in default at the times and in the manner authorized by law during the year 1917, 1918 or 1919. (1917, c. 152, s. 9; C.S., s. 5366.)

§ 156-111. Sheriff to make monthly settlements; penalty.

The sheriff or tax collector shall be required to make settlements with the treasurer on the first day of each month of all collections of drainage assessments for the preceding month, and to pay over to the treasurer,the money so collected, for which the treasurer shall execute an appropriate receipt, to the end that the treasurer may have funds in hand to meet the payments of the interest and principal due upon the outstanding bonds as they mature. If any sheriff or tax collector shall fail to comply with the law for the collection of drainage assessments, or in making payments thereof to the treasurer as provided by law, he shall be guilty of a Class 1 misdemeanor and he shall likewise be liable in a civil action for all damages which may accrue either to the board of drainage commissioners or to the holder of the bonds, to either or both of whom a right of action is given. (1911, c. 67, s. 12; 1917, c. 152, s. 9; C.S., s. 5367; 1963, c. 767, s. 4; 1993, c. 539, s. 1076; 1994, Ex. Sess., c. 24, s. 14(c).)

§ 156-112. Duty of treasurer to make payment; penalty.

It shall be the duty of the treasurer, and without any previous order from the board of drainage commissioners, to provide and pay the installments of interest at the time and place as evidenced by the coupons attached to the bonds, and also to pay the annual installments of the principal due on the bonds at the time and place as evidenced by the bonds. The treasurer shall be guilty of a Class 1 misdemeanor if he shall willfully fail to make prompt payments of the interest and principal of the bonds, and he shall likewise be liable in a civil action for all damages which may accrue either to the board of drainage commissioners or to the holder of such bonds, to either or both of whom a right of action is hereby given. (1911, c. 67, s. 12; C.S., s. 5368; 1963, c. 767, s. 4; 1993, c. 539, s. 1077; 1994, Ex. Sess., c. 24, s. 14(c).)

§ 156-113. Fees for collection and disbursement.

The fee allowed the sheriff or tax collector for collecting the drainage tax as hereinbefore prescribed shall be two percent (2%) of the amount collected, and the fee allowed the treasurer for disbursing the revenue obtained from the sale of drainage bonds shall be one percent (1%) of the amount disbursed: Provided, that no fee shall be allowed the sheriff or tax collector or treasurer for collecting or receiving the revenue obtained from the sale of the bonds hereinbefore provided for, nor for disbursing the revenue raised or paying off such bonds; provided, that where the sheriff, tax collector or treasurer is on a salary basis, the fees herein set out shall not be charged. (1911, c. 67, s. 13; C.S., s. 5369; 1925, c. 271, s. 1; 1957, c. 562; 1963, c. 767, s. 4.)

§ 156-114. Conveyance of land; change in assessment roll; procedure.

(a) Status of Land Fixed. - The boundaries of lands as surveyed and mapped, the ownership thereof, and the classification and assessment thereof as appears in the final report and map and upon the assessment roll, shall be and remain as of the time when the district was established and the final report of the board of viewers was approved by the court. No conveyance or devise of land or devolution by inheritance after the petition has been filed or the owner thereof has been served with the original summons, either by personal service or by publication, shall affect the status or liability of such land as a part of such drainage district, except as herein provided.

(b) Conveyance before Final Report. - If the owner of any lands included in such district shall, after the filing of the petition, and after being served with the original summons and before the approval of the final report, convey the whole or any part of such lands, or the title thereto shall be otherwise changed, then and in such event the grantor and grantee or new owner, or either, may file a petition in an ancillary proceeding before the clerk of the superior court setting forth the facts, with a description of the lands conveyed either in part or the entire body of land, together with a description of the land excepted and not conveyed. If the grantor or grantee or new owner, in whole or in part, file such petition, the other not so joining shall be served with notice of same. The clerk may require the petitioner to attach to the petition a map showing the boundaries of the entire body of land as it appears in the record of the proceedings, and also showing the part conveyed. If the ownership of such land has been changed by devise or inheritance, or any joint ownership has been changed by partition, such new owner may file a petition as herein provided. Such petition shall conclude with a prayer that the grantee or new owner be made a party to the proceeding. The court after a hearing may make the grantee or new owner a party to the drainage proceeding and shall certify to the engineer and viewers a description of the land so conveyed or held by the new owner, with directions to verify the boundaries and to classify the land to the same extent as if the grantee was the original party. Any part of such lands not so conveyed shall be and remain a part of the district.

(c) Conveyance after District Established. - After the district shall be established, the lands classified, the final report approved, and the assessment roll filed, no conveyance of any land in the district shall affect or change the existing status or liability of such land as to assessment charges or otherwise, except in the manner herein defined. When the title and ownership of any tract of land embraced in the district have been changed or vested in others by grant, devise, or inheritance, or by partition between joint owners, subsequent to the establishment of the district, the assessment roll may be amended in the following manner: The grantor and grantee, or the new owners, may file a petition with the chairman of the board of drainage commissioners alleging that the ownership of the land has changed, and the manner thereof, in whole or in part. If the whole body of land as appears in the final report or on the assessment roll has changed ownership, a general description consistent with such final report and map shall be sufficient. If the ownership of the body of land has changed only as to part thereof, the petition shall contain a description of the part thereof claimed by the new owners, and the number of acres and the classifications, or the several classes if it be in more than one class, and also a description of that part of the land the title to which remains in the original owner, with the number of acres and with the classification and the several classes if it contains more than one class of land. The petition shall so describe the land and the number of acres in each class as to that part of which the ownership has changed as to maintain the number of acres originally assessed, and the class or classes in which the same has been assessed, and the chairman of the board of drainage commissioners may require the petitioners to have the lands surveyed, and submit a map if the same shall be necessary.

(d) Duty of Chairman of Drainage Commissioners and Clerk. - The chairman of the board of drainage commissioners shall present this petition to the clerk of the superior court at any time thereafter, not later than the first Monday in July following. It shall be the duty of the clerk to examine and verify the facts set forth in the petition, and particularly to determine if the number of acres assessed and the classes thereof against the new owners added to the number of acres and the classes assessed against that part of the land, the title to which has not changed, shall equal the total number of acres and the classes so assessed as appear against such entire body of land in the final report and assessment roll. If the clerk shall be so satisfied, he shall enter an order or decree changing the original assessment roll, or the assessment roll as theretofore amended, by adding the name of the new owner with the number of acres assessed in each class, and by amending the number of acres assessed and the classes thereof against the original owner as appears on the original assessment roll or assessment roll as theretofore amended. It shall be the duty of the clerk after such order to make such changes in the assessment roll. It shall be the duty of the clerk of the superior court in making changes in the original assessment roll from time to time to observe and maintain the total number of acres in each class, to the end that the revenue produced from the annual assessment shall not be thereby diminished. The chairman of the board of drainage commissioners, instead of presenting to the clerk of the court each petition of landowners separately, may combine a number of petitions and present the same to the court at one and the same time. The first Monday in

July in each year is hereby set apart as a special day on which petitions for changing the assessment roll may be submitted, at which time the clerk shall hear all petitions not theretofore submitted.

(e) Failure of Chairman of Board to Act. - If the chairman of the board of drainage commissioners shall fail to act when any petition shall be submitted to him as herein provided, or the chairman or any member of the board shall fail to discharge any duty imposed by this section or any other provision of the general drainage law, it is hereby made the duty of the clerk of the superior court, either independently or upon the request of any landowner in the district, to cite such chairman or member to appear before him upon a certain day and show cause why he should not be removed from office, and unless good cause be shown, it shall be the duty of the clerk to remove the chairman or any member of the board of drainage commissioners and to certify his action, to the end that another member may be elected according to law. If the failure of the chairman or any member of the board of drainage commissioners to discharge such duty shall be willful, he shall be guilty of a Class 1 misdemeanor.

(f) When Owner May File Petition with Clerk. - If the grantor and grantee, or all those claiming to have acquired title to any body of land on the assessment roll and whose assessment will be affected, cannot agree upon joinder in a petition to the chairman of the board of drainage commissioners, or if the said chairman fails within a reasonable time to discharge his duty by presenting the petition to the court, then either party interested in the tract of land as it appears on the assessment roll may file a petition with the clerk of the superior court setting forth the facts as to the change in ownership and title of such land, with the description of the entire tract of land and the number of acres in each class, together with a description of that part of the land as to which the ownership has changed, with the number of acres in each class, and pray the court to order that the assessment roll be amended in accordance with the title and interest of the several owners. At the time of filing the petition a summons shall issue to the other parties interested in the tract of land to show cause, on a day certain, why the prayer of the petition should not be granted. Upon the return day the clerk of the court shall hear all the evidence, find the facts, and enter up a judgment directing the appropriate amendment to the assessment roll. It shall be the duty of the clerk to amend the assessment roll in accordance with his judgment.

(g) Effect of Change in Assessment Roll. - No judgment or amendment of the assessment roll shall be valid unless the number of acres and the classes assessed against the original and new owners shall equal the area and classification as contained in the tract of land as it appears on the original assessment roll. This petition may be presented to the court at any time, but the first Monday in July in each year is hereby designated as the day upon which all petitions for amendments to the assessment roll may be submitted. Any amendments to the assessment roll ordered after the last day of August in each year shall not become effective until the first day of September the following year, and the assessment roll as it appears on the first day of September of each year shall constitute the assessment roll to be delivered to the sheriff on the first Monday in September, and he shall collect the drainage assessments as they appear thereon without regard to any changes in title or ownership or any changes in the assessment roll made by the court after the thirty-first day of August. All amendments sought to be made to the assessment roll shall have reference to the assessment roll as it appears at the time the amendment is sought, which shall be either the original assessment roll or as amended; but it shall be the duty of the clerk of the superior court to examine frequently the assessment roll as amended, and before the same shall be further amended, and make certain that the aggregate number of acres in each class as appeared on the original assessment roll shall not be reduced, nor the aggregate annual assessments reduced. Any amendments ordered shall be made on the assessment roll and become due in the following September, and on all subsequent assessment rolls which have not become due or collectible.

(h)   Clerk to Prepare New Assessment Rolls. - It shall be the duty of the chairman and the secretary of the board of drainage commissioners of the district to render to the clerk of the court any clerical assistance involved in changes in the assessment rolls, but the primary duty and responsibility in making such amendments shall remain with the clerk of the superior court, and he shall be held liable for any error or omission which may work a loss to the district or the bondholders. If such amendments to the assessment rolls shall make necessary the preparation of new assessment rolls, the clerk of the superior court shall be required to prepare such new assessment rolls with the clerical assistance of the chairman and secretary of the board of drainage commissioners, and such new assessment rolls shall be signed by the chairman and secretary of the board of drainage commissioners and by the clerk of the superior court before delivery to the sheriff or tax collector as required upon the original assessment rolls. The original assessment rolls shall be preserved by the clerk of the court among his records for future reference.

(i)   Number of Copies. - In the event it shall be necessary to prepare new assessment rolls, the clerk shall prepare four copies, one copy for the drainage record, another for the sheriff or tax collector, another for the chairman of the board of drainage commissioners, and the other for filing and preserving among the records, and which fourth copy shall never be mutilated or interlined, but shall be preserved in its original form for reference. As to all drainage districts heretofore established, the clerk of the court shall prepare an additional copy of all the original assessment rolls for the several years the lands in such districts are assessed and securely preserve the same, at least until all outstanding bonds of the district shall be paid, to the end that they may always be accessible for reference and comparison. It shall not be necessary hereafter to deliver to the sheriff or tax collector a copy of the assessment roll for the current year in which assessments are due and payable, but the copy provided for him may remain among the records of the clerk of the court for safekeeping and reference by him.

(j)   Costs Determined. - As compensation to the clerk of the court for the performance of duties imposed herein, he shall be paid such sum by the board of drainage commissioners of such drainage district as they may deem fair and adequate, and the same is hereby declared a proper charge against said district, but no additional compensation shall be paid to the clerk in those counties where he receives a salary in lieu of fees. Any costs which may accrue in amendments to the assessment rolls shall be adjudged against the parties in interest, in the discretion of the clerk, and such costs shall be paid before the amendment shall become effective. As to all petitions which shall be filed and submitted to the court on the first Monday in July, no costs shall be paid or adjudged against any party in those counties where the clerk and sheriff receive a salary in lieu of fees.

(k)   Chairman Represents Board. - As to all petitions filed with the chairman of the board of drainage commissioners, or as to the discharge of any duty by the chairman required of him under the general drainage law, he shall be presumed to act for the board, and the chairman shall do all things necessary to protect and maintain the interests of the drainage district. If the chairman shall be or become a landowner in the drainage district and may desire an amendment to the assessment rolls, he may file his petition before any other member of the board, or file the same directly with the clerk of the superior court.

(l)   Application of Section. - The provisions of this section shall apply to landowners in districts heretofore established and to drainage proceedings heretofore instituted to the same extent as to drainage proceedings hereafter instituted and established. (1917, c. 152, s. 4; 1919, c. 208, s. 1; C.S., s. 5370; 1993, c. 539, s. 1078; 1994, Ex. Sess., c. 24, s. 14(c).)

§ 156-115. Warranty in deed runs to purchaser who pays assessment.

Where the land assessed by drainage commissioners under the provisions of this Article has been purchased since the making of the assessment by a purchaser for value without notice under a deed of general warranty, and said purchaser pays to the sheriff the amount of said drainage assessment, which is a lien on the land purchased, then such purchaser who pays the said drainage assessment shall have a right of action against the warrantor of his title under the covenant of general warranty contained in his deed for the recovery of the amount paid. (1919, c. 282, s. 3; C.S., s. 5371.)

§ 156-116. Modification of assessments.

(a) Relevy. - Where the court has confirmed an assessment for the construction of any public levee, ditch, or drain, and such assessment has been modified by the court of superior jurisdiction, but for some unforeseen cause it cannot be collected, the board of drainage commissioners shall have power to change or modify the assessment as originally confirmed to conform to the judgment of the superior court and to cover any deficit that may have been caused by the order of court or unforeseen occurrence. The relevy shall be made for the additional sum required, in the same ratio on the lands benefited as the original assessment was made.

(b) Upon Sale of Land for Assessments. - If any person, or any number of persons, claiming to have title to any tract or tracts of land subject to assessment or drainage tax shall fail to pay any annual assessment levied against such lands, and the sheriff or tax collector shall be compelled to sell such lands under the law for the purpose of making such collection, the net proceeds of such sale shall be paid to the treasurer, to be held by him and disbursed for the purpose of paying the current assessment and future annual assessments so far as the proceeds may be sufficient. When the fund in the custody of the treasurer shall be exhausted in the payment of annual assessments against such lands, or there shall not be a sufficient sum to pay the next annual assessment, the treasurer shall immediately give written notice to that effect to the chairman of the board of drainage commissioners of the district, and also to the clerk of the superior court, whereupon the board of drainage commissioners shall institute an investigation of such tract or tracts of land to determine the market value, and if they shall find that the market value is not equal to all the future annual assessments to cover its share of installments of principal and interest on the outstanding bonds, they shall proceed, with the approval of the clerk of the superior court, to make new reassessment rolls on all the remaining lands in the district and increase the sum in sufficient sums to equal the deficit thereby created and such new assessment rolls shall constitute the future assessment rolls until changed according to law, and shall be certified to the tax collector as herein provided in lieu of the former assessment rolls. However, the tract or tracts of land which have been so sold by the tax collector shall continue on the assessment roll in the name of the new owner, but reassessed upon the new basis, and the drainage tax collected at the same time and in the same manner as other lands as long as such lands may have sufficient market value out of which to collect the annual drainage tax, and when such lands shall cease to have such value, or shall be abandoned by the person claiming title thereto, the drainage commissioners may omit the same from the assessment roll with the approval of the clerk of the superior court, but such lands may in the same manner at any time in the future be restored to the assessment rolls.

(c)   Surplus Funds. - If the funds in the hands of the treasurer at any time, arising under this section or in any other manner, shall be greater than is necessary to pay the annual installments of principal and interest, or the annual cost of maintenance of the drainage works, or both, such surplus shall be held by the treasurer for future disbursement for other purposes as herein provided or subject to the order of the board of drainage commissioners.

(d)   Insufficient Funds. - If there shall be any impairment or destruction of the drainage works by any unforeseen cause or occurrence not anticipated, during the period of construction by the contractor, the contractor shall nevertheless repair and complete the works according to the contract and specifications and shall be liable therefor and also his sureties on his bond; but if the contractor shall make default and if there shall be a failure to collect all resulting damages from such contractor and the sureties upon his bond, and it shall thereby be necessary to raise a greater sum of money to complete the drainage works in accordance with the plans, or if for any other unavoidable cause it shall be necessary to raise a greater sum to complete such drainage works, the board of drainage commissioners, having first obtained the approval of the clerk of the superior court, shall prepare new assessment rolls upon all the lands in the district upon the original basis of classification of benefits and increase the same in sufficient sums to equal the deficit thereby created, and the same shall constitute the new assessment rolls until changed according to law, and shall be certified to the tax collector as herein provided.

(e)   Additional Bonds Issued. - If for any of the causes hereinbefore recited in this section, or for any other cause, a sum of money greater than the proceeds of sale of the drainage bonds shall become necessary to complete the drainage system, and the board of drainage commissioners shall determine that the amount to be raised is greater than can be realized from the collection of one annual assessment upon the lands in the district without imposing an undue burden upon the lands, or if it is advisable or necessary to raise the money more expeditiously, then and under such conditions additional bonds may be issued in such aggregate sum as may be necessary.

(f)   Manner of Issue. - The proceedings for the issue of such additional bonds shall be substantially as follows: The board of drainage commissioners shall file their petition with the clerk of the superior court, setting forth all the facts which require the expenditure of more money and the issue of additional bonds to complete the drainage system, which shall be accompanied by the recommendation of the drainage engineer who was one of the original viewers, or some other expert drainage engineer selected by the drainage commissioners; whereupon the court shall issue a notice to all the owners of land within the district reciting the substance of the petition and directing each to appear before the court on a day certain, not less than 20 days after the service upon all the parties, and to show cause, if any they have, why the additional bonds should not be authorized, which notice shall be served personally on each such landowner by reading the same, and by leaving a copy, and if the same cannot be personally served, then it shall be served in the manner authorized by law. Any landowner may file an answer denying any material allegation in the petition or setting forth any valid objection to same before the return day thereof.

Upon the day when the notice is returnable, or on such day as to which the same may have been continued, the court shall proceed to hear the petition and answers. If the court shall find that the allegations of the petition are true, and that the issue of additional bonds is advisable or necessary, the court shall make an appropriate order authorizing and directing the issue of such additional bonds, fixing the amount of such issue, the date of same, the time when the interest and principal shall be payable, and all other matters necessary and appropriate in the premises. Any landowner may appeal from the order of the clerk of the superior court, and on such appeal only the issues raised in the answer shall be considered, and such appeal and the further procedure thereon shall be as prescribed in special proceedings, except as modified by this Subchapter.

After the court shall have ordered the additional issue of bonds, the further procedure as to the assessment rolls, the levying and collecting of the drainage taxes, the disbursement of the revenue therefrom for the payment of such bonds and interest thereon, and all further procedure shall be the same as required for the establishment of drainage districts. The additional bonds issued shall not exceed twenty-five percent (25%) of the total amount originally issued. The additional issue of bonds shall bear six percent (6%) interest per annum and may be made payable in 10 annual installments, or in lesser number of annual installments as nearly equal as may be, as recommended by the board of drainage commissioners and approved by the court. (1909, c. 442, s. 35; 1911, c. 67, s. 15; C.S., s. 5372; 1963, c. 767, s. 4.)

§ 156-117. Subdistricts formed.

Subdistricts may be formed by owners of land in main districts theretofore established in the manner provided for the organization of main districts. Such subdistricts shall have the right to use the ditches or canals of the main districts for outlets. The formation of subdistricts shall not operate to release the lands in any subdistrict from the payment of any assessment or levy made prior to the formation of such subdistricts, nor from any assessment which may thereafter be made for the completion and maintenance of the canals in main districts, or for the payment of the principal and interest on any indebtedness incurred by the main district, nor shall it give the subdistrict any claim on the funds of such main district for its local use. It shall be the duty of the drainage commissioners of the main district to control all matters pertaining to the main district drainage. Drainage commissioners for the subdistricts shall have authority and control over all matters pertaining to drainage within their respective subdistricts, except such work as belongs exclusively to the main district. (1917, c. 152, s. 8; C.S., s. 5373.)

§§ 156-118 through 156-120. Repealed by Session Laws 1961, c. 614, s. 11.

§ 156-121. Redress to dissatisfied landowners.

Anyone owning land which has been reclassified by the board of viewers who is dissatisfied with their classification shall have the same redress as has heretofore been provided where divisions of classification have been made by a petition to the clerk or otherwise. (1923, c. 231, s. 4; C.S., s. 5373(d).)

§ 156-122. Increase to extinguish debt.

If in the opinion of the board of drainage commissioners it would help the sale of the maintenance or improvement bonds, or they would deem it necessary under the provision of G.S. 156-101, they may, with the approval of the clerk of the superior court, add to the amount estimated by the board of viewers a sufficient amount to pay off all outstanding obligations of the district, leaving this their only bond issue. (1923, c. 231, s. 5; C.S., s. 5373(e).)

§ 156-123. Proceedings as for original bond issue.

The compensation of the board of viewers and their assistants, together with all other expenses in connection with this bond issue, shall be paid in the same manner, the duties and power of the clerk, and the duties and power of the board of drainage commissioners, the bonds shall be advertised and sold, divided into such annual installments, bear such a rate of interest, the landowners shall be given the same notices and the same rights to pay cash, the contract shall be let and supervised, and contractor paid the same, as if this was the original bond issue. (1923, c. 231, s. 6; C.S., s. 5373(f).)

§ 156-124. No drainage assessments for original object may be levied on property when once paid in full.

Whenever any assessment has been made or may be made by any drainage district formed under the laws of the State of North Carolina upon any lands in said district, either for construction or maintenance of its system of drainage or for any other purpose, and the particular assessment made against any particular piece of property has been paid or shall be hereafter paid in full, then and in that event no other or further assessment may be made upon said land for the purpose of providing money for the purpose for which the original assessment was made. (1933, c. 504; 1935, c. 469, s. 5.)

§ 156-124.1. Repealed by Session Laws 1961, c. 614, s. 11.

Article 9.

Adjustment of Delinquent Assessments.

§ 156-125. Adjustment by board of commissioners authorized.

The board of commissioners of any drainage district may, in connection with the issuance of bonds for the purpose of refunding outstanding bonds of the district, and in addition to preparing a new assessment roll, for the payment of principal and interest of such refunding bonds, and when the bonds so refunded constitute all of the bonds of the district for which an assessment has been made against property therein, adjust the uncollected delinquent installments of the assessment made upon property in the district, for the payment of principal and interest of the bonds so refunded and for other purposes authorized by law before said bonds were refunded. The adjustment of such delinquent assessments may include reduction of the principal amount of the delinquent installments, not exceeding fifty per centum (50%) thereof, to which reduced installments shall be added interest computed thereon, at a rate not less than the rate of interest of the refunding bonds, from the date of delinquency of said installments to the date of the refunding bonds, and shall include any costs legally incurred for the collection of the same; the date of delinquency shall be deemed to be the first day of December following the date upon which each of said installments became due: Provided, however, all delinquent installments of such assessment shall be adjusted on the same basis and by the same method. (1935, c. 469, s. 1.)

§ 156-126. Extension of adjusted installments.

Upon adjustment of delinquent installments of any assessment as provided herein, the payment of all delinquent installments so adjusted may be extended over a period not exceeding the life of the issue of refunding bonds, but in no event over a period exceeding 20 years. Such extension shall be made by the preparation of assessment rolls, which shall provide for the payment of installments so adjusted in equal annual installments which shall become due annually on September 1, in accordance with the original assessment, and shall bear interest at the rate of four per centum (4%) per annum from December 1 following their due date until paid. Such assessment rolls shall be prepared and filed with the sheriff and the clerk of superior court and receipts shall be prepared and the same shall be collected in the same manner as other assessments of the district. (1935, c. 469, s. 2.)

§ 156-127. Special fund set up; distribution of collections.

The collection of assessments adjusted under this Article and of interest accrued under G.S. 156-126 shall be set aside in a fund and shall be applied as follows: One third of such collections may be used solely for operating and administrative expenses of the district, but the remaining two thirds thereof shall be reserved as additional security for the payment of the refunding bonds, or for the purchase and retirement of such refunding bonds, at prices not exceeding par and accrued interest. (1935, c. 469, s. 3.)

§ 156-128. Approval of adjustments by Local Government Commission.

Any adjustments of delinquent assessments under the provisions of this Article shall be effective only upon approval of the Local Government Commission. (1935, c. 469, s. 4.)

§ 156-129. Amount of assessments limited; reassessments regulated.

The assessments made under this Article shall in no instance, and against no piece of property, be greater in amount than that percent which the percent assessment authorized by this Article bears to the unpaid original assessment upon each piece or tract of property within the district. In no instance, either under this Article or any other law, shall any reassessment be made upon any piece of property for the purpose of providing money for the same purpose for which the original assessment was made, when the original assessment upon said property has been paid, or shall be paid prior to such general reassessment, nor to the extent that the original assessment has been paid. (1935, c. 469, s. 4(b).)

Article 10.

Reports of Officers.

§ 156-130. Drainage commissioners to make statements.

It shall be the duty of the commissioners of all drainage districts in the State of North Carolina organized under the provisions of the laws thereof to file with the clerk of the superior court in the county where such district is organized a monthly statement or account during the course of construction of canals for the district, showing the receipts and expenditures of all funds coming into their hands belonging to such drainage district for the period of one month prior to the day on which the same is filed, and also to post a copy of such statement or account at the courthouse door in the county. After the construction of the canals has been concluded and the drainage commissioners have only to maintain the canals, said drainage commissioners shall only be required to file and post the annual statement required in G.S. 156-131. Such statement or account shall be certified by the chairman of the board of commissioners of each drainage district and shall be attested by the secretary thereof, and a copy thereof shall be filed and kept as a part of the minutes of the district. (1917, c. 72, s. 1; C.S., s. 5374; 1927, c. 98, s. 6.)

§ 156-131. Annual report.

At the end of each fiscal year the board of commissioners of all drainage districts in the State of North Carolina shall file with the clerk of the superior court in the county where the district is organized a verified itemized statement of receipts and expenditures of all funds belonging to the district during the fiscal year just closed. (1917, c. 72, s. 2; C.S., s. 5375; 1957, c. 1410, s. 2.)

§ 156-132. Penalty for failure.

Any board of commissioners of any drainage district in the State, and each of the members thereof, which shall fail or refuse to file the statements or accounts, as provided in G.S. 156-130 and 156-131, shall be deemed guilty of a Class 1 misdemeanor. (1917, c. 72, s. 3; C.S., s. 5376; 1957, c. 1410, s. 3; 1993, c. 539, s. 1079; 1994, Ex. Sess., c. 24, s. 14(c).)

§ 156-133. Auditor appointed; duties; compensation.

The clerk of the superior court for the county where the district was organized, shall annually appoint an intelligent and competent person of sufficient experience, as auditor for each drainage district which levies current assessments or which has accumulated funds. The same person may be auditor of more than one drainage district. The auditor shall annually report to the court as to financial affairs of the drainage district. The auditor may prepare all financial reports required by the drainage law to be made to the court by the commissioners of the drainage district. The compensation of the auditor shall be fixed by the said clerk of the superior court, and shall be paid out of the general, or operating, fund of the district. (1917, c. 152, s. 10; 1919, c. 208, s. 3; C.S., s. 5377; 1959, c. 420; 1963, c. 767, s. 11.)

§ 156-134. Duties of the auditor.

The auditor for the drainage district will be required to examine the assessment roll and the records and accounts of the sheriff or tax collector as to the assessment roll which went into his hands on the previous first Monday in September and for all previous years as to which the records and accounts of the sheriff or tax collector have not been audited.

The auditor shall for each of such years make a report as to each drainage district, showing the total amount of drainage assessments due for each year, the amount collected by the sheriff up to the fifteenth day of May of the following year, the names of the owners of land, and a brief description of the lands on which the drainage assessments have not been paid, and the total amount of unpaid drainage assessments, with any further data or information which the auditor may regard as pertinent.

If the lands in the district lie in other counties, the auditor for the county in which the district was established shall also examine the records of the sheriff or tax collector for such other counties.

The auditor shall also examine the books of the treasurer for similar years, and he shall report the amount of drainage assessments paid to the treasurer by the sheriff or tax collector for each year, and the amounts paid out by the treasurer during such years, and for what purposes paid. It shall be the duty of the sheriff and treasurer to permit the auditor to examine their official books and records and to furnish all necessary information, and to assist the auditor in the discharge of his duties.

The auditor shall make a report to the board of county commissioners on or before the first Monday in July following his appointment, and he shall deliver a duplicate of such report to the chairman of the board of drainage commissioners of each drainage district established in the county.

If the sheriff has not collected all of the drainage assessments, or has not paid over all collections to the treasurer, or if the treasurer has not made disbursements of the drainage funds as required by law, or has not in his hands the funds not so disbursed by him, it shall be the duty of the auditor to so report, and to prepare two certified copies of his report, one of which shall be delivered to the judge holding a session of superior court in the county following the first Monday in July, and a copy to the district attorney of the prosecutorial district as defined in G.S. 7A-60 in which the county is located, and it shall be the duty of such district attorney to examine carefully such report and to institute such action, civil or criminal, against the sheriff or tax collector or the treasurer, as the facts contained in the report may justify, or as may be required by law. (1917, c. 152, s. 10; C.S., s. 5378; 1963, c. 767, s. 4; 1973, c. 47, s. 2; c. 108, s. 97; 1987 (Reg. Sess., 1988), c. 1037, s. 124.)

Article 11.

General Provisions.

§ 156-135. Construction of drainage law.

The provisions of this Subchapter shall be liberally construed to promote the leveeing, ditching, draining, and reclamation of wet and overflowed lands. The collection of the assessment shall not be defeated, where the proper notices have been given, by reason of any defect in the proceedings occurring prior to the order of the court confirming the final report of the viewers; but such order or orders shall be conclusive and final that all prior proceedings were regular and according to law, unless they were appealed from. If on appeal the court shall deem it just and proper to release any person or to modify his assessment or liability, it shall in no manner affect the rights and legality of any person other than the appellant, and the failure to appeal from the order of the court within the time specified shall be a waiver of any illegality in the proceedings, and the remedies provided for in this Subchapter shall exclude all other remedies. (1909, c. 442, s. 37; C.S., s. 5379.)

§ 156-135.1. Investment of surplus funds.

Any drainage district organized under the provisions of Subchapter III of Chapter 156 of the General Statutes and the governing authority of same is hereby authorized and empowered to invest any surplus funds or any funds not needed for the immediate use of the district in United States bonds or any securities or type of investment in which guardians, executors, administrators and others acting in a fiduciary capacity are authorized to make investments by virtue of Article 1 of Chapter 36 of the General Statutes as amended. (1951, c. 1058, s. 1.)

§ 156-136. Removal of officers.

Any engineer, viewer, superintendent of construction or other person appointed under this Chapter may be removed by the court, upon petition, for corruption, negligence of duties, or other good and satisfactory cause shown. (1909, c. 442, s. 38; C.S., s. 5380.)

§ 156-137. Local drainage laws not affected.

This Subchapter shall not repeal or change any local drainage laws already enacted. (1909, c. 442, s. 38 1/2; C.S., s. 5381.)

§ 156-138. Punishment for violating law as to drainage districts.

If any person shall violate any of the provisions of law in reference to drainage districts as provided in this Chapter, or shall leave any log, brush, trash, or other thing where it is liable to wash into an adjacent stream and obstruct the flow of water or cut any tree so as to fall in a stream, or place any other obstruction in a stream in a drainage district, he shall be fined not more than fifty dollars

($50.00) or imprisoned not more than 30 days. (1905, c. 541, ss. 7, 9; Rev., s. 3378; C.S., s. 5382.)

§ 156-138.1. Acquisition and disposition of lands; lease to or from federal or State government or agency thereof.

The district may acquire any lands necessary or convenient to enable it to accomplish the purposes for which the district was established. If the lands cannot be acquired by agreement as to the purchase price, then the power of eminent domain is hereby conferred and the lands may be condemned by the procedure set out in G.S. 156-67 and Chapter 40A of the General Statutes. The land so acquired may be used in a manner and for the purposes the commissioners of the district deem best. If, in the opinion of the drainage commission of the district the lands should be sold, leased or rented, the board may do so, subject to the approval of the clerk of the superior court.

The commissioners of the district may, in their discretion, convey or lease to the State or federal governments, or any of their agencies, with or without consideration, any properties, real or personal, belonging to the district, if in their opinion it is necessary to enable the district to receive State or federal funds available to the district. The terms of a conveyance or lease shall be subject to the approval of the clerk of the superior court of the county in which the district was established.

The commissioners of the district may lease from the State or federal governments any real or personal property needed by the district to enable it to efficiently operate and maintain the district for the purposes for which it was established. The terms of a lease shall be subject to the approval of the clerk of the superior court of the county in which the district was established. (1957, c. 539; 2001-487, s. 38(h).)

§ 156-138.2. Meaning of "majority of resident landowners" and "owners of three fifths of land area."

Wherever in this Subchapter reference is made to a "majority of resident landowners" or "owners of three fifths of the land area," such reference shall be deemed to refer only to lands alleged in a petition or adjudged by the court to be benefited by the proposed construction work. (1959, c. 1312, s. 2.)

§ 156-138.3. Notice.

Unless specifically required by the provisions of this Subchapter, it is not necessary to give notice to any landowner of a motion made to, or order rendered by the clerk of the superior court or the judge of the superior court relating to the affairs of the district, financial or otherwise, except when an assessment is proposed to be made upon his land and then such notice shall be given as is required by the provisions of this Subchapter. This provision for notice of assessment shall not apply to assessments for annual maintenance expenses, which are provided for in this Subchapter, and specifically in Article 7A and G.S. 156-92. (1961, c. 614, s. 3.)

§ 156-138.4. Procedures to be followed in connection with drainage projects that involve channelization.

Every drainage project that involves channelization shall be subject to the procedures set forth in G.S. 139-47. (1971, c. 1138, s. 4.)

SUBCHAPTER IV. DRAINAGE BY COUNTIES.

Article 12.

Protection of Public Health.

§ 156-139. Cleaning and draining of streams, etc., under supervision of governmental agencies.

When the board of commissioners of any county subject to the provisions of this Article shall, by resolution duly adopted, find as facts: (i) that the cleaning out and draining of any portion of any nonnavigable stream, creek or swamp area in such county is necessary and/or desirable to protect and promote the health of the citizens of such county, and (ii) that the agricultural benefits which the lands along such stream or area might receive from such cleaning out and draining would be so negligible as not to justify the levying of any special assessments against such lands on account thereof, it may order, provide for, and accomplish the cleaning out and draining of such portion of such stream, creek or swamp area by, through, and under the supervision and jurisdiction of, the health department, or any sanitary committee, or any drainage commission, or other governmental agency or department of such county. (1943, c. 553, s. 1.)

§ 156-140. Tax levy.

In order to carry out and accomplish the objects and purposes of this Article, the board of commissioners of any such county may annually levy and collect a countywide tax not exceeding two cents (2¢) upon each one hundred dollars ($100.00) in value of the taxable property in such county. (1943, c. 553, s. 2.)

§ 156-141. Article applicable to certain counties only.

This Article shall apply only to those counties which may have a population in excess of 100,000 persons. (1943, c. 553, s. 3.)

Chapter 157.

Housing Authorities and Projects.

Article 1.

Housing Authorities Law.

§ 157-1. Title of Article.

This Article may be referred to as the Housing Authorities Law. (1935, c. 456, s. 1.)

§ 157-2. Finding and declaration of necessity.

(a) It is hereby declared that unsanitary or unsafe dwelling accommodations exist in urban and rural areas throughout the State and that such unsafe or unsanitary conditions arise from overcrowding and concentration of population, the obsolete and poor condition of the buildings, improper planning, excessive land coverage, lack of proper light, air and space, unsanitary design and arrangement, lack of proper sanitary facilities, and the existence of conditions which endanger life or property by fire and other causes; that in such urban and rural areas many persons of low income are forced to reside in unsanitary or unsafe dwelling accommodations; that in such urban and rural areas there is a lack of safe or sanitary dwelling accommodations available to all the inhabitants thereof and that consequently many persons of low income are forced to occupy overcrowded and congested dwelling accommodations; that these conditions cause an increase in and spread of disease and crime and constitute a menace to the health, safety, morals and welfare of the citizens of the State and impair economic values; that these conditions cannot be remedied by the ordinary operation of private enterprise; that the clearance, replanning and reconstruction of such areas and the providing of safe and sanitary dwelling accommodations for persons of low income are public uses and purposes for which public money may be spent and private property acquired; that it is in the public interest that work on such projects be instituted as soon as possible; and that the necessity for the provisions hereinafter enacted is hereby declared as a matter of legislative determination to be in the public interest.

(b) It is hereby further declared that there is a serious shortage of decent, safe and sanitary housing in North Carolina that can be afforded by persons and families of moderate income; that it is in the best interest of the State to encourage programs to provide housing for such persons without imposing on them undue financial hardship; and that in undertaking such programs a housing authority is promoting the health, welfare and prosperity of all citizens of the State and is serving a public purpose for the benefit of the general public. (1935, c. 456, s. 2; 1938, Ex. Sess., c. 2, s. 14; 1941, c. 78, s. 2; 1987, c. 464, s. 1.)

§ 157-3. Definitions.

The following terms, wherever used or referred to in this Article shall have the following respective meanings, unless a different meaning clearly appears from the context:

(1) "Authority" or "housing authority" shall mean a public body and a body corporate and politic organized in accordance with the provisions of this Article for the purposes, with the powers and subject to the restrictions hereinafter set forth.

(2) "Bonds" shall mean any bonds, interim certificates, notes, debentures, obligations, or other evidences of indebtedness issued pursuant to this Article.

(3) "City" shall mean any city or town having a population of more than 500 inhabitants according to the last federal census or any revision or amendment thereto.

(4) "City clerk" and "mayor" shall mean the clerk and mayor, respectively, of the city or the officers thereof charged with the duties customarily imposed on the clerk and mayor respectively.

(5) "Commissioner" shall mean one of the members of an authority appointed in accordance with the provisions of this Article.

(6) "Community facilities" shall include real and personal property, and buildings and equipment for recreational or social assemblies, for educational, health or welfare purposes and necessary utilities, when designed primarily for the benefit and use of the housing authority and/or the occupants of the dwelling accommodation.

(7) "Contract" shall mean any agreement of an authority with or for the benefit of an obligee whether contained in a resolution, trust indenture, mortgage, lease, bond or other instrument.

(8) "Council" shall mean the legislative body, council, board of commissioners, board of trustees, or other body charged with governing the city.

(9) "Farmers of low income" shall mean persons or families who at the time of their admission to occupancy in a dwelling of the authority:

a. Live under unsafe or unsanitary housing conditions;

b. Derive their principal income from operating or working upon a farm; and

c. Had an aggregate average annual net income for the three years preceding their admission that was less than the amount that shall be determined by the authority to be necessary, within its area of operation, to enable them, without financial assistance, to obtain decent, safe and sanitary housing, without overcrowding.

(10) "Federal government" shall include the United States of America, the Federal Emergency Administration of Public Works or any agency, instrumentality, corporate or otherwise, of the United States of America.

(11) "Government" shall include the State and federal governments and any subdivision, agency or instrumentality, corporate or otherwise, of either of them.

(12) "Housing project" shall include all real and personal property, buildings and improvements, stores, offices, lands for farming and gardening, and community facilities acquired or constructed or to be acquired or constructed pursuant to a single plan or undertaking:

a. To demolish, clear, remove, alter or repair unsanitary or unsafe housing; and/or

b. To provide safe and sanitary dwelling accommodations for persons of low income, or moderate income, or low and moderate income; and/or

c. To provide safe and sanitary housing for persons of low income, through payment of rent subsidies from any source; and/or

d. To provide grants, loans, interest supplements and other programs of financial assistance (including rent subsidies in furtherance of a program of home ownership) to persons of low income, or moderate income, or low and moderate income, so that such persons may become owners of their own housing or rehabilitate their own housing; and/or

e. To provide grants, loans, interest supplements and other programs of financial assistance to public or private developers of housing for persons of low income, or moderate income, or low and moderate income.

"Housing project" also includes any project that provides housing for persons of other than low or moderate income, as long as at least twenty percent (20%) of the units in the project are set aside for the exclusive use of persons of low income.

The term "housing project" may also be applied to the planning of the buildings and improvements, the acquisition of property, the demolition of existing structures, the construction, reconstruction, alteration and repair of the improvements and all other work in connection therewith.

(13)   "Mortgage" shall include deeds of trust, mortgages, building and loan contracts or other instruments conveying real or personal property as security for bonds and conferring a right to foreclose and cause a sale thereof.

(14)   "Municipality" shall mean any city, town, incorporated village or other municipality in the State.

(15)   "Obligee of the authority" or "obligee" shall include any bondholder, trustee or trustees for any bondholders, any lessor demising property to the authority used in connection with a housing project or any assignee or assignees of such lessor's interest or any part thereof, and the United States of America, when it is a party to any contract with the authority.

(15a)   "Persons of low income" means persons in households the annual income of which, adjusted for family size, is not more than sixty percent (60%) of the local area median family income as defined by the most recent figures published by the U.S. Department of Housing and Urban Development.

(15b)   "Persons of moderate income" means persons deemed by the authority to require the assistance made available pursuant to this Chapter on account of insufficient personal or family income taking into consideration, without limitation, (i) the amount of the total income of such persons and families available for housing needs, (ii) the size of the person's family, (iii) the cost and condition of housing facilities available, and (iv) the eligibility of such persons and families for federal housing assistance of any type predicated upon a moderate or low and moderate income basis.

(16)   "Real property" shall include lands, lands under water, structures, and any and all easements, franchises and incorporeal hereditaments and every estate and right therein, legal and equitable, including terms for years and liens by way of judgment, mortgage or otherwise.

(17)   "State" shall mean the State of North Carolina.

(18)   "Trust indenture" shall include instruments pledging the revenues of real or personal properties but not conveying such properties or conferring a right to

foreclose and cause a sale thereof. (1935, c. 456, s. 3; 1938, Ex. Sess., c. 2, s. 14; 1941, c. 78, s. 2; 1943, c. 636, s. 1; 1959, cc. 321, 641, 1281; 1961, c. 200, s. 1; 1977, c. 924; 1987, c. 464, ss. 2, 3.)

§ 157-4. Notice, hearing and creation of authority; cancellation of certificate of incorporation.

Any 25 residents of a city and of the area within 10 miles from the territorial boundaries thereof may file a petition with the city clerk setting forth that there is a need for an authority to function in the city and said surrounding area. Upon the filing of such a petition the city clerk shall give notice of the time, place and purposes of a public hearing at which the council will determine the need for an authority in the city and said surrounding area. Such notice shall be given at the city's expense by publishing a notice, at least 10 days preceding the day on which the hearing is to be held, in a newspaper having a general circulation in the city and said surrounding area, or, if there be no such newspaper, by posting such notice in at least three public places within the city, at least 10 days preceding the day on which the hearing is to be held.

Upon the date fixed for said hearing held upon notice as provided herein, an opportunity to be heard shall be granted to all residents and taxpayers of the city and said surrounding area and to all other interested persons. After such a hearing, the council shall determine:

(1) Whether insanitary or unsafe inhabited dwelling accommodations exist in the city and said surrounding area, and/or

(2) Whether there is a lack of safe or sanitary dwelling accommodations in the city and said surrounding area available for all the inhabitants thereof.

In determining whether dwelling accommodations are unsafe or insanitary, the council shall take into consideration the following: the physical condition and age of the buildings; the degree of overcrowding; the percentage of land coverage; the light and air available to the inhabitants of such dwelling accommodations; the size and arrangement of the rooms; the sanitary facilities; and the extent to which conditions exist in such buildings which endanger life or property by fire or other causes.

If it shall determine that either or both of the above enumerated conditions exist, the council shall adopt a resolution so finding (which need not go into any detail other than the mere finding) and shall cause notice of such determination to be given to the mayor who shall thereupon appoint, as hereinafter provided, not less than five nor more than nine commissioners to act as an authority. Said commission shall be a public body and a body corporate and politic upon the completion of the taking of the following proceedings:

The commissioners shall present to the Secretary of State an application signed by them, which shall set forth (without any detail other than the mere recital):

(1)   That a notice has been given and public hearing has been held as aforesaid, that the council made the aforesaid determination after such hearing, and that the mayor has appointed them as commissioners;

(2)   The name and official residence of each of the commissioners, together with a certified copy of the appointment evidencing their right to office, the date and place of induction into and taking oath of office, and that they desire the housing authority to become a public body and a body corporate and politic under this Article;

(3)   The term of office of each of the commissioners;

(4)   The name which is proposed for the corporation; and

(5)   The location of the principal office of the proposed corporation.

The application shall be subscribed and sworn to by each of said commissioners before an officer authorized by the laws of the State to take and certify oaths, who shall certify upon the application that he personally knows the commissioners and knows them to be the officers as asserted in the application, and that each subscribed and swore thereto in the officer's presence. The Secretary of State shall examine the application and if he finds that the name proposed for the corporation is not identical with that of a person or of any other corporation of this State or so nearly similar as to lead to confusion and uncertainty he shall receive and file it and shall record it in an appropriate book of record in his office.

When the application has been made, filed and recorded, as herein provided, the authority shall constitute a public body and a body corporate and politic under the name proposed in the application; the Secretary of State shall make and issue to the said commissioners a certificate of incorporation pursuant to this Article, under the seal of the State, and shall record the same with the application.

If the council, after a hearing as aforesaid, shall determine that neither of the above enumerated conditions exist, it shall adopt a resolution denying the petition. After three months shall have expired from the date of the denial of any such petitions, subsequent petitions may be filed as aforesaid and new hearings and determinations made thereon.

In any suit, action or proceeding involving the validity or enforcement of or relating to any contract of the authority, the authority shall be conclusively deemed to have been established in accordance with the provisions of this Article upon proof of the issuance of the aforesaid certificate by the Secretary of State. A copy of such certificate, duly certified by the Secretary of State, shall be admissible in evidence in any such suit, action or proceeding, and shall be conclusive proof of the filing and contents thereof.

The Secretary of State is authorized and empowered to revoke or to cancel a certificate of incorporation previously issued to an authority or housing authority upon filing in his office a petition and resolution of the council and a petition and resolution of the authority and its members requesting such revocation or cancellation and when the Secretary of State is satisfied that no indebtedness has been incurred or property acquired by said housing authority. (1935, c. 456, s. 4; 1943, c. 636, s. 7; 1961, c. 987; 1971, c. 362, s. 1; c. 599.)

§ 157-4.1. Alternative organization.

(a)   In lieu of creating a housing authority as authorized herein, the council of any city may, if it deems wise, either designate a redevelopment commission created under the provisions of Chapter 160 of the General Statutes to exercise the powers, duties, and responsibilities of a housing authority as prescribed herein, or may itself exercise such powers, duties, and responsibilities. Any such designation shall be by passage of a resolution adopted in accordance with the procedure and pursuant to the finding specified in the first and second paragraphs of G.S. 157-4. In the event the council of any city designates itself to exercise the powers, duties, and responsibilities of a housing authority, then where any act, proceeding, or approval is required to be done, recommended, or approved both by a housing authority and by the council of the city, then the performance, recommendation, or approval thereof once by the council of the city shall be sufficient to make such performance, recommendation, or approval valid and legal. In the event the council of the city designates itself to exercise the powers, duties, and responsibilities of a housing authority, it may assign the administration of the housing programs, projects, and policies to any existing or new department of the city.

(b)   The council of any city which has prior to July 1, 1969, created, or which may hereafter create, a housing authority may, in its discretion, by resolution abolish such housing authority, such abolition to be effective on a day set in such resolution not less than 90 days after its adoption. Upon the adoption of such a resolution, the housing authority of the city is hereby authorized and directed to take such actions and to execute such documents as will carry into effect the provisions and the intent of the resolution, and as will effectively transfer its authority, responsibilities, obligations, personnel, and property, both real and personal, to the city. Any city which abolishes a housing authority pursuant to this subsection may, at any time subsequent to such abolition or concurrently therewith, exercise the authority granted by subsection (a) of this section.

On the day set in the resolution of the council:

(1)   The housing authority shall cease to exist as a body politic and corporate and as a public body;

(2)   All property, real and personal and mixed, belonging to the housing authority shall vest in, belong to, and be the property of the city;

(3)   All judgments, liens, rights of liens, and causes of action of any nature in favor of the housing authority shall remain, vest in, and inure to the benefit of the city;

(4)   All rentals, taxes, assessments, and any other funds, charges or fees, owing to the housing authority shall be owed to and collected by the city;

(5)   Any actions, suits, and proceedings, pending against, or having been instituted by the housing authority shall not be abated by such abolition, but all such actions, suits, and proceedings shall be continued and completed in the same manner as if abolition had not occurred, and the city shall be a party to all such actions, suits, and proceedings in the place and stead if the housing authority and shall pay or cause to be paid any judgments rendered against the

housing authority in any such actions, suits, or proceedings, and no new process need be served in any such action, suit, or proceeding;

(6) All obligations of the housing authority, including outstanding indebtedness, shall be assumed by the city, and all such obligations and outstanding indebtedness shall be constituted obligations and indebtedness of the city;

(7) All ordinances, rules, regulations and policies of the housing authority shall continue in full force and effect until repealed or amended by the council of the city.

(c) Where the governing body of any municipality has in its discretion, by resolution abolished a housing authority, pursuant to subsection (b) above, the governing body of such municipality may, at any time subsequent to the passage of a resolution abolishing a housing authority, or concurrently therewith, by the passage of a resolution adopted in accordance with the procedures and pursuant to the finding specified in G.S. 157-4.1, designate an existing redevelopment commission created pursuant to Article 37 of Chapter 160 of the General Statutes, to exercise the powers, duties, and responsibilities of a housing authority. Where the governing body of any municipality designates, pursuant to this subsection, an existing redevelopment commission created pursuant to Article 37 of Chapter 160 of the General Statutes to exercise the powers, duties, and responsibilities of a housing authority, on the day set in the resolution of the governing body passed pursuant to subsection (b) of this section, or pursuant to subsection (c) of this section:

(1) The housing authority shall cease to exist as a body politic and corporate and as a public body;

(2) All property, real and personal and mixed, belonging to the housing authority or to the municipality as hereinabove provided in subsections (a) or (b), shall vest in, belong to, and be the property of the existing redevelopment commission of the municipality;

(3) All judgments, liens, rights of liens, and causes of action of any nature in favor of the housing authority or in favor of the municipality as hereinabove provided in subsections (a) or (b), shall remain, vest in, and inure to the benefit of the existing redevelopment commission of the municipality;

(4)	All rentals, taxes, assessments, and any other funds, charges, or fees owing to the housing authority or owing to the municipality as hereinabove provided in subsections (a) or (b), shall be owed to and collected by the existing redevelopment commission of the municipality;

(5)	Any actions, suits, and proceedings pending against or having been instituted by the housing authority or the municipality, or to which the municipality has become a party as hereinabove provided in subsections (a) or (b), shall not be abated by such abolition but all such actions, suits, and proceedings shall be continued and completed in the same manner as if abolition had not occurred, and the existing redevelopment commission of the municipality shall be a party to all such actions, suits, and proceedings in the place and stead of the housing authority or the municipality, and shall pay or cause to be paid any judgments rendered in such actions, suits, or proceedings, and no new processes need be served in such action, suit, or proceeding;

(6)	All obligations of the housing authority or the municipality as hereinabove provided in subsections (a) or (b), including outstanding indebtedness, shall be assumed by the existing redevelopment commission of the municipality; and all such obligations and outstanding indebtedness shall be constituted obligations and indebtedness of the existing redevelopment commission of the municipality;

(7)	All ordinances, rules, regulations, and policies of the housing authority or the municipality as hereinabove provided in subsections (a) or (b), shall continue in full force and effect until repealed and amended by the existing redevelopment commission of the municipality.

(d)	A redevelopment commission designated by the governing body of any municipality to exercise the powers, duties and responsibilities of a housing authority shall, when exercising the same, do so in accordance with Chapter 157 of the General Statutes. Otherwise the redevelopment commission shall continue to exercise the powers, duties and responsibilities of a redevelopment commission in accordance with Article 37 of Chapter 160 of the General Statutes. (1969, c. 1217, s. 2; 1971, c. 116, ss. 3, 4.)

§ 157-4.2. Authority budgeting and accounting systems as a part of city or county budgeting and accounting systems.

The council of a city or the board of commissioners of a county may by resolution provide that the budgeting and accounting systems of the city's or county's housing authority (or, if the city's redevelopment commission is exercising the powers, duties, and responsibilities of a housing authority, the budgeting and accounting systems of the redevelopment commission) shall be an integral part of the budgeting and accounting systems of the city or county. If such a resolution is adopted:

(1) For purposes of the Local Government Budget and Fiscal Control Act, the authority (or commission) shall not be considered a "public authority," as that phrase is defined in G.S. 159-7(b), but rather shall be considered a department or agency of the city or county. The operations of the authority (or commission) shall be budgeted and accounted for as if the operations were those of a public enterprise of the city or county.

(2) The budget of the authority (or commission) shall be prepared and submitted in the same manner and according to the same procedures as are the budgets of other departments and agencies of the city or county; and the budget ordinance of the city or county shall provide for the operations of the authority (or commission).

(3) The budget officer and finance officer of the city or county shall administer and control that portion of the city or county budget ordinance relating to the operations of the authority (or commission). (1971, c. 780, s. 37.1; 1973, c. 474, s. 29.)

§ 157-5. Appointment, qualifications and tenure of commissioners.

(a) An authority shall consist of not less than five nor more than eleven commissioners appointed by the mayor and the mayor shall designate the first chair. No commissioner may be a city official. At least one of the commissioners appointed shall be a person who is directly assisted by the public housing authority. However, there shall be no requirement to appoint such a person if the authority: (i) operates less than 300 public housing units, (ii) provides reasonable notice to the resident advisory board of the opportunity for at least one person who is directly assisted by the authority to serve as a commissioner, and (iii) within a reasonable time after receipt of the notice by the resident advisory board, has not been notified of the intention of any such person to serve. The mayor shall appoint the person directly assisted by the authority unless the authority's rules require that the person be elected by other persons who are directly assisted by the authority. If the commissioner directly assisted by the public housing authority ceases to receive such assistance, the commissioner's office shall be abolished and another person who is directly assisted by the public housing authority shall be appointed by the mayor.

(b)   No commissioner who is also a person directly assisted by the public housing authority shall be qualified to vote on matters affecting his or her official conduct or matters affecting his or her own individual tenancy, as distinguished from matters affecting tenants in general. No more than one third of the members of any housing authority commission shall be tenants of the authority or recipients of housing assistance through any program operated by the authority.

(c)   The council may at any time by resolution or ordinance increase or decrease the membership of an authority, within the limitations herein prescribed.

(d)   The mayor shall designate overlapping terms of not less than one nor more than five years for the commissioners first appointed. Thereafter, the term of office shall be five years. A commissioner shall hold office until his or her successor has been appointed and has qualified. Vacancies shall be filled for the unexpired term. A majority of the commissioners shall constitute a quorum. The mayor shall file with the city clerk a certificate of the appointment or reappointment of any commissioner and such certificate shall be conclusive evidence of the due and proper appointment of such commissioner. A commissioner shall receive no compensation for his or her services but he or she shall be entitled to the necessary expenses including traveling expenses incurred in the discharge of his or her duties.

(e)   When the office of the first chair of the authority becomes vacant, the authority shall select a chair from among its members. An authority shall select from among its members a vice-chair, and it may employ a secretary (who shall be executive director), technical experts and such other officers, agents, and employees, permanent and temporary, as it may require, and shall determine their qualifications, duties, and compensation. An authority may call upon the corporation counsel or chief law officer of the city for such legal services as it may require or it may employ its own counsel and legal staff. An authority may delegate to one or more of its agents or employees such powers or duties as it may deem proper. (1935, c. 456, s. 5; 1971, c. 362, ss. 2-5; 1981, c. 864; 1999-146, s. 1.)

§ 157-6. Duty of authority.

The authority shall be under a statutory duty to comply or to cause compliance strictly with all provisions of this Article and the laws of the State and in addition thereto, with each and every term, provision and covenant in any contract of the authority on its part to be kept or performed. (1935, c. 456, s. 6; 1997-455, s. 1.)

§ 157-7. Interested commissioners or employees.

No commissioner or employee of an authority shall acquire any interest direct or indirect in any housing project or in any property included or planned to be included in any project, nor shall he have any interest direct or indirect in any contract or proposed contract for materials or services to be furnished or used in connection with any housing project. If any commissioner or employee of an authority owns or controls an interest direct or indirect in any property included or planned to be included in any housing project, he shall immediately disclose the same in writing to the authority and such disclosure shall be entered upon the minutes of the authority. Failure to so disclose such interest shall constitute misconduct in office. (1935, c. 456, s. 7.)

§ 157-8. Removal of commissioners.

The mayor may remove a commissioner for inefficiency or neglect of duty or misconduct in office, but only after the commissioner shall have been given a copy of the charges against him (which may be made by the mayor) at least 10 days prior to the hearing thereon and had an opportunity to be heard in person or by counsel.

Any obligee of the authority may file with the mayor written charges that the authority is violating willfully any law of the State or any term, provision or covenant in any contract to which the authority is a party. The mayor shall give each of the commissioners a copy of such charges at least 10 days prior to the hearing thereon and an opportunity to be heard in person or by counsel and shall within 15 days after receipt of such charges remove any commissioners of the authority who shall have been found to have acquiesced in any such willful violation.

A commissioner shall be deemed to have acquiesced in a willful violation by the authority of a law of this State or of any term, provision or covenant contained in a contract to which the authority is a party, if, before a hearing is held on the charges against him, he shall not have filed a written statement with the authority of his objections to, or lack of participation in, such violation.

In the event of the removal of any commissioner, the mayor shall file in the office of the city clerk a record of the proceedings together with the charges made against the commissioners and the findings thereon. (1935, c. 456, s. 8.)

§ 157-9. Powers of authority.

(a)   An authority shall constitute a public body and a body corporate and politic, exercising public powers, and having all the powers necessary or convenient to carry out and effectuate the purposes and provisions of this Article, including the following powers in addition to others herein granted:

To investigate into living, dwelling and housing conditions and into the means and methods of improving such conditions; to determine where unsafe, or insanitary dwelling or housing conditions exist; to study and make recommendations concerning the plan of any city or municipality located within its boundaries in relation to the problem of clearing, replanning and reconstruction of areas in which unsafe or insanitary dwelling or housing conditions exist, and the providing of dwelling accommodations for persons of low income, and to cooperate with any city municipal or regional planning agency; to prepare, carry out and operate housing projects; to approve, assist, and cooperate with, as its instrumentality, a nonprofit corporation in providing financing by the issuance by such nonprofit corporation's obligations (which obligations shall not be or be deemed to be indebtedness of a housing authority) for one or more housing projects, pursuant to the United States Housing Act of 1937, as amended, and applicable regulations thereunder, specifically including, but not limited to, programs to make construction and other loans to developers or owners of residential housing, and to acquire, operate or manage such a housing project, and to administer federal housing assistance subsidy payments for such projects; to provide for the construction, reconstruction, improvement, alteration or repair of any housing project or any part thereof; to take over by purchase, lease or otherwise any housing project located within its boundaries undertaken by any government, or by any city or municipality located in whole or in part within its boundaries; to manage as agent of any city or municipality located in whole or in part within its boundaries any housing project constructed or owned by such city; to act as agent for the federal government in connection with the acquisition, construction, operation and/or management of a housing project or any part thereof; to arrange with any city or municipality located in whole or in part within its boundaries or with a government for the furnishing, planning, replanning, installing, opening or closing of streets, roads, roadways, alleys, sidewalks or other places or facilities or for the acquisition by such city, municipality, or government of property, options or property rights or for the furnishing of property or services in connection with a project; to arrange with the State, its subdivisions and agencies, and any county, city or municipality of the State, to the extent that it is within the scope of each of their respective functions, (i) to cause the services customarily provided by each of them to be rendered for the benefit of such housing authority and/or the occupants of any housing projects and (ii) to provide and maintain parks and sewage, water and other facilities adjacent to or in connection with housing projects and (iii) to change the city or municipality map, to plan, replan, zone or rezone any part of the city or municipality; to lease or rent any of the dwelling or other accommodations or any of the lands, buildings, structures or facilities embraced in any housing project and to establish and revise the rents or charges therefor; to enter upon any building or property in order to conduct investigations or to make surveys or soundings; to purchase, lease, obtain options upon, acquire by gift, grant, devise, or otherwise any property real or personal or any interest therein from any person, firm, corporation, city, municipality, or government; to acquire by eminent domain any real property, including improvements and fixtures thereon; to sell, exchange, transfer, assign, or pledge any property real or personal or any interest therein to any person, firm, corporation, municipality, city, or government; to own, hold, clear and improve property; to insure or provide for the insurance of the property or operations of the authority against such risks as the authority may deem advisable; to procure insurance or guarantees from a federal government of the payment of any debts or parts thereof secured by mortgages made or held by the authority on any property included in any housing project; to borrow money upon its bonds, notes, debentures or other evidences of indebtedness and to secure the same by pledges of its revenues, and by mortgages upon property held or to be held by it, or in any other manner; in connection with any loan, to agree to limitations upon its right to dispose of any housing project or part thereof or to undertake additional housing projects; in connection with any loan by a government, to agree to limitations upon the exercise of any powers conferred upon the authority by this Article; to invest any funds held in reserves or sinking funds, or any funds not required for immediate disbursement, in property or securities in which savings banks may legally invest funds subject to their control; to sue and be sued; to have a seal and to alter the same at pleasure; to have perpetual succession; to make and execute contracts and other instruments necessary or convenient to the exercise of the powers of the authority; to make and from time to time amend and repeal bylaws, rules and regulations not inconsistent with this Article, to carry into effect the powers and purposes of the authority; to conduct examinations and investigations and to hear testimony and take proof under oath at public or private hearings on any matter material for its information; to issue subpoenas requiring the attendance of witnesses or the production of books and papers and to issue commissions for the examination of witnesses who are out of the State or unable to attend before the authority, or excused from attendance; and to make available to such agencies, boards or commissions as are charged with the duty of abating or requiring the correction of nuisances or like conditions, or of demolishing unsafe or insanitary structures within its territorial limits, its findings and recommendations with regard to any building or property where conditions exist which are dangerous to the public health, morals, safety or welfare. Any of the investigations or examinations provided for in this Article may be conducted by the authority or by a committee appointed by it, consisting of one or more commissioners, or by counsel, or by an officer or employee specially authorized by the authority to conduct it. Any commissioner, counsel for the authority, or any person designated by it to conduct an investigation or examination shall have power to administer oaths, take affidavits and issue subpoenas or commissions. An authority may exercise any or all of the powers herein conferred upon it, either generally or with respect to any specific housing project or projects, through or by an agent or agents which it may designate, including any corporation or corporations which are or shall be formed under the laws of this State, and for such purposes an authority may cause one or more corporations to be formed under the laws of this State or may acquire the capital stock of any corporation or corporations. Any corporate agent, (i) all of the stock of which shall be owned by the authority or its nominee or nominees or (ii) the board of directors of which shall be elected or appointed by the authority or is composed of the commissioners of the authority or (iii) which is otherwise subject to the control of the authority or the governmental entity which created the authority, may to the extent permitted by law exercise any of the powers conferred upon the authority herein. In addition to all of the other powers herein conferred upon it, an authority may do all things necessary and convenient to carry out the powers expressly given in this Article. No provisions with respect to the acquisition, operation or disposition of property by other public bodies shall be applicable to an authority unless the legislature shall specifically so state.

(b) Notwithstanding anything to the contrary contained in this Article or in any other provision of law an authority may include in any contract let in connection with a project, stipulations requiring that the contractor and any subcontractors comply with requirements as to minimum wages and maximum hours of labor, and comply with any conditions which the federal government may have attached to its financial aid of the project.

(c) To the extent not inconsistent with the Constitution or statutes of this State or the United States, an authority may adopt and enforce rules governing the lawful entry of guests and visitors to its properties, including the visitors and guests of its tenants. Prior to adopting such rules, an authority shall make reasonable efforts to consult with or obtain comments from its tenants or their representatives. Persons who enter or remain on the property of an authority in violation of such rules shall be subject to prosecution as applicable under G.S. 14-159.12 or G.S. 14-159.13.

(d) A housing authority shall not erect or maintain around any lawfully occupied housing units any fence or gate structure that is electrified or that includes spikes or barbed wire. (1935, c. 456, s. 9; 1939, c. 150; 1977, c. 784, s. 1; 1979, c. 690, s. 1; c. 805; 1995, c. 520, s. 2; 2004-199, s. 40; 2011-284, s. 109.)

§ 157-9.1. Moderate income.

(a) Whenever the words "low income" appear in this Chapter, they shall be construed to mean "low and moderate income."

(b) This section applies only to the housing authority of the largest city in a county which has two or more cities with a population of 60,000 or over, according to the most recent decennial federal census.

(c) This section shall apply only to existing, non-federally subsidized structures.

(d) Notwithstanding the provisions of subsections (b) and (c), subsection (a) of this section applies to all counties with an area of 250 square miles or less, and a population of more then [than] 100,000 according to the most recent decennial federal census, and applies to all cities within such counties.

(e) Notwithstanding the provisions of subsections (b), (c), and (d) of this section, subsection (a) of this section applies to the housing authorities of all cities that have a population of less than 20,000 according to the most recent decennial federal census and are the location of a constituent institution of The University of North Carolina that has a student enrollment of more than 10,000 students and applies to the housing authorities of all counties that have a population of less than 80,000 according to the most recent decennial federal census and are the location of a constituent institution of The University of North Carolina that has a student enrollment of more than 10,000 students. (1983, c. 769, s. 1; 1985 (Reg. Sess., 1986), c. 1004, s. 1; 2009-218, s. 1.)

§ 157-9.2. Additional powers.

(a) The findings and purposes set forth in the first three paragraphs of G.S. 122A-2 and in G.S. 122A-5.4(a) are hereby restated and incorporated herein by reference, except that for purposes of incorporating such findings and purposes herein, the phrases "North Carolina Housing Finance Agency" and "Agency" shall read "authority" and the word "Chapter" shall read "Section".

(b) Words and phrases used in this section and not otherwise defined in this Chapter shall be defined as provided in Chapter 122A of the General Statutes, except that for purposes of incorporating such definitions into this section, the phrases "North Carolina Housing Finance Agency" and "Agency" shall read "authority" and the "Chapter" shall read "Section".

(c) An authority shall have all of the powers necessary or convenient to carry out and effectuate the purposes and provisions of this section, including, without limiting the generality of the foregoing, the power:

(1) To make or participate in the making of mortgage loans to sponsors of residential housing; provided, however, that such loans shall be made only upon the determination by the authority that mortgage loans are not otherwise available wholly or in part from public or private lenders upon equivalent terms and conditions;

(2) To make or participate in the making of mortgage loans to persons and families of lower income and persons and families of moderate income for residential housing; provided, however, that such loans shall be made only upon the determination by the authority that mortgage loans are not otherwise

available wholly or in part from public or private lenders upon equivalent terms and conditions;

(3) To make loans to mortgage lenders on terms and conditions requiring the proceeds thereof to be used by such mortgage lenders to originate new mortgage loans to (i) sponsors of residential housing for persons and families of lower income and persons and families of moderate income and (ii) persons and families of lower income and persons and families of moderate income for residential housing. The loans to mortgage lenders and the loans to be made by such mortgage lenders shall be made on such applicable terms and conditions as are set forth in rules and regulations of the authority or otherwise established by the authority; provided, however, that loans shall be made by such mortgage lenders only upon the determination by the authority that such financing is not otherwise available, wholly or in part, from public or private lenders upon equivalent terms and conditions;

(4) To collect and pay reasonable fees and charges in connection with making, purchasing and servicing of its loans, notes, bonds, commitments and other evidences of indebtedness; and

(5) To borrow money to carry out and effectuate its corporate purposes and to issue its obligations as evidence of any such borrowing.

(d) Notwithstanding the provisions of G.S. 157-17.1, the approval of the Local Government Commission shall not be necessary for the issuance of bonds or the incurrence of indebtedness pursuant to this section, and the provisions of the Local Government Finance Act shall not be applicable with respect to bonds issued or indebtedness incurred pursuant to this section. Provided further that notwithstanding any other provision of State law or local ordinance, the approval of the governing body of the county or city in which the housing authority is located shall be necessary for the issuance of bonds or the incurrence of indebtedness pursuant to this section.

(e) This section applies only to housing authorities in any county with an area of 250 square miles or less and a population of more than 100,000 according to the most recent decennial federal census, and applies to all housing authorities of all cities within such counties.

(f) Not later than 30 days prior to making its determination, pursuant to subsections (c)(1), (2) or (3) of this section, that mortgage loans are not otherwise available wholly or in part from public or private lenders upon equivalent terms and conditions, an authority shall give written notice of a proposed financing, including the proposed terms and conditions of the mortgage loans to be made, to the North Carolina Housing Finance Agency. Within 20 days following receipt of such notice, the North Carolina Housing Finance Agency shall respond, in writing, to the authority, and provide the authority with any terms and conditions of mortgage loans which the Agency can make available and which the Agency believes are reasonably relevant to said determination. (1987, c. 423.)

§ 157-9.3. Mixed income projects owned or operated by authorities.

If an authority is the owner or operator of a housing project that includes units for persons of other than low or moderate income, the operating expenses of that project (or of all such projects, together, owned or operated by the authority) shall be met entirely from rents from the project (or projects) together with any rent subsidies provided to low income tenants in the project (or projects). No rent subsidy may be provided to any tenant who is not a person of low income, and no rent subsidy may be paid from bond proceeds. (1987, c. 464, s. 4.)

§ 157-9.4. Multi-family rental housing projects.

(a) If an authority owns, operates, or provides financial assistance to a multi-family rental housing project, at least twenty percent (20%) of the units in the project shall be set aside for the exclusive use of persons of low income. An authority may group projects being developed concurrently in order to meet the requirement of this subsection.

(b) If an authority provides financial assistance to a multi-family rental housing project, the authority shall establish, as a condition of the assistance, requirements and procedures that insure that all units initially set aside for the exclusive use of persons of low income continue to be so used for at least 15 years after the initial date on which at least fifty percent (50%) of the units in the project are occupied. (1987, c. 464, s. 4.1.)

§ 157-10. Cooperation of authorities.

Any two or more authorities may join or cooperate with one another in the exercise, either jointly or otherwise, of any or all of their powers for the purpose of financing (including the issuance of bonds, notes or other obligations and giving security therefor), planning, undertaking, owning, constructing, operating or contracting with respect to a housing project or projects located within the boundaries of any one or more of said authorities. For such purpose an authority may by resolution prescribe and authorize any other housing authority or authorities, so joining or cooperating with it, to act on behalf with respect to any or all of such powers. Any authorities joining or cooperating with one another may by resolutions appoint from among the commissioners of such authorities an executive committee with full power to act on behalf of such authorities with respect to any or all of their powers, as prescribed by resolutions of such authorities. (1935, c. 456, s. 10; 1943, c. 636, s. 2.)

§ 157-11. Eminent domain.

The authority shall have the right to acquire by eminent domain any real property, including fixtures and improvements, which it may deem necessary to carry out the purposes of this Article after the adoption by it of a resolution declaring that the acquisition of the property described therein is in the public interest and necessary for public use. The authority may exercise the power of eminent domain pursuant to the provisions of Chapter 40A.

Property already devoted to a public use may be acquired, provided, that no property belonging to any city or municipality or to any government may be acquired without its consent and that no property belonging to a public utility corporation may be acquired without the approval of the commission or other officer or tribunal, if any there be, having regulatory power over such corporation. (1935, c. 456, s. 11; 1981, c. 919, s. 25.)

§ 157-12. Acquisition of land for government.

The authority may acquire by purchase or by the exercise of its power of eminent domain, as aforesaid, any property real or personal for any housing project being constructed or operated by a government. The authority upon such terms and conditions, with or without consideration, as it shall determine, may convey title or deliver possession of such property so acquired or purchased to such government for use in connection with such housing project. (1935, c. 456, s. 12.)

§ 157-13. Zoning and building laws.

All housing projects of an authority shall be subject to the planning, zoning, sanitary and building laws, ordinances and regulations applicable to the locality in which the housing project is situated. (1935, c. 456, s. 13.)

§ 157-14. Types of bonds authority may issue.

An authority shall have power to issue bonds from time to time in its discretion for any of its corporate purposes. An authority shall also have power to issue or exchange refunding bonds for the purpose of paying, retiring, extending or renewing bonds previously issued by it. An authority may issue such types of bonds as it may determine, including (without limiting the generality of the foregoing) bonds on which the principal and interest are payable from income and revenues of the authority and from grants or contributions from the federal government or other source. Such income and revenues securing the bonds may be:

(1) Exclusively the income and revenues of the housing project financed in whole or in part with the proceeds of such bonds;

(2) Exclusively the income and revenues of certain designated housing projects, whether or not they are financed in whole or in part with the proceeds of such bonds; or

(3) The income and revenues of the authority generally.

Any such bonds may be additionally secured by a pledge of any income or revenues of the authority, or a mortgage of any housing project, projects or other property of the authority.

Neither the commissioners of an authority nor any person executing the bonds shall be liable personally on the bonds by reason of the issuance thereof. The bonds and other obligations of an authority (and such bonds and obligations shall so state in their face) shall not be a debt of any city or municipality and neither the State nor any such city or municipality shall be liable thereon, nor in any event shall such bonds or obligations be payable out of any funds or properties other than those of said authority. The bonds shall not constitute an indebtedness within the meaning of any constitutional or statutory debt limitation of the laws of the State. Bonds may be issued under this Article notwithstanding any debt or other limitation prescribed in any statute.

This Article without reference to other statutes of the State shall constitute full and complete authority for the authorization, issuance, delivery and sale of bonds hereunder and such authorization, issuance, delivery and sale shall not be subject to any conditions, restrictions or limitations imposed by any other law whether general, special or local. (1935, c. 456, s. 14; 1939, c. 150, s. 2.)

§ 157-15. Form and sale of bonds.

The bonds of the authority shall be authorized by its resolution and shall be issued in one or more series and shall bear such date or dates, mature at such time or times, not exceeding 60 years from their respective dates, bear interest at such rate or rates, be in such denominations (which may be made interchangeable), be in such form, either coupon or registered, carry such registration privileges, be executed in such manner, be payable in such medium of payment, at such place or places, and be subject to such terms of redemption (with or without premium) as such resolution or its trust indenture or mortgage may provide.

The bonds may be sold at public or private sale; provided, however, that no public sale shall be held unless notice thereof is published once at least 10 days prior to such sale in a newspaper having a general circulation in the city in which the authority is located and in a financial newspaper published in the City of New York, New York, or in the City of Chicago, Illinois. The bonds may be sold at such price or prices as the authority shall determine.

Pending the authorization, preparation, execution or delivery of definitive bonds, the authority may issue interim certificates, or other temporary obligations, to the purchaser of such bonds. Such interim certificates, or other temporary obligations, shall be in such form, contain such terms, conditions and provisions, bear such date or dates, and evidence such agreements relating to their discharge or payment or the delivery of definitive bonds as the authority may by resolution, trust indenture or mortgage determine.

In case any of the officers whose signatures appear on any bonds or coupons shall cease to be such officers before the delivery of such bonds, such signatures shall, nevertheless, be valid and sufficient for all purposes, the same as if they had remained in office until such delivery.

The authority shall have power out of any funds available therefor to purchase any bonds issued by it at a price not more than the principal amount thereof and the accrued interest; provided, however, that bonds payable exclusively from the revenues of a designated project or projects shall be purchased out of any such revenues available therefor. All funds so purchased shall be cancelled. This paragraph shall not apply to the redemption of bonds.

Any provision of any law to the contrary notwithstanding, any bonds, interim certificates, or other obligations issued pursuant to this Article shall be fully negotiable. (1935, c. 456, s. 15; 1971, c. 87, s. 1; 1977, c. 784, s. 2.)

§ 157-16. Provisions of bonds, trust indentures, and mortgages.

In connection with the issuance of bonds and/or the incurring of any obligation under a lease and in order to secure the payment of such bonds and/or obligations, the authority shall have power:

(1) To pledge by resolution, trust indenture, mortgage, or other contract, all or any part of its rents, fees, or revenues.

(2) To covenant against mortgaging all or any part of its property, real or personal, then owned or thereafter acquired, or against permitting or suffering any lien thereon.

(3) To covenant with respect to limitations on its right to sell, lease or otherwise dispose of any housing project or any part thereof, or with respect to limitations on its right to undertake additional housing projects.

(4) To covenant against pledging all or any part of its rents, fees and revenues to which its right then exists or the right to which may thereafter come into existence or against permitting or suffering any lien thereon.

(5) To provide for the release of property, rents, fees and revenues from any pledge or mortgage, and to reserve rights and powers in, or the right to dispose of, property which is subject to a pledge or mortgage.

(6) To covenant as to the bonds to be issued pursuant to any resolution, trust indenture, mortgage or other instrument and as to the issuance of such bonds in escrow or otherwise, and as to the use and disposition of the proceeds thereof.

(7) To covenant as to what other, or additional debt, may be incurred by it.

(8) To provide for the terms, form, registration, exchange, execution and authentication of bonds.

(9) To provide for the replacement of lost, destroyed or mutilated bonds.

(10) To covenant that the authority warrants the title to the premises.

(11) To covenant as to the rents and fees to be charged, the amount (calculated as may be determined) to be raised each year or other period of time by rents, fees, and other revenues and as to the use and disposition to be made thereof.

(12) To covenant as to the use of any or all of its property, real or personal.

(13) To create or to authorize the creation of special funds in which there shall be segregated

a. The proceeds of any loan and/or grant;

b. All of the rents, fees and revenues of any housing project or projects or parts thereof;

c. Any moneys held for the payment of the costs of operation and maintenance of any such housing projects or as a reserve for the meeting of contingencies in the operation and maintenance thereof;

d. Any moneys held for the payment of the principal and interest on its bonds or the sums due under its leases and/or as a reserve for such payments; and

e. Any moneys held for any other reserves or contingencies; and to covenant as to the use and disposal of the moneys held in such funds.

(14) To redeem the bonds, and to covenant for their redemption and to provide the terms and conditions thereof.

(15) To covenant against extending the time for the payment of its bonds or interest thereon, directly or indirectly, by any means or in any manner.

(16) To prescribe the procedure, if any, by which the terms of any contract with bondholders may be amended or abrogated, the amount of bonds the holders of which must consent thereto and the manner in which such consent may be given.

(17) To covenant as to the maintenance of its property, the replacement thereof, the insurance to be carried thereon and the use and disposition of insurance moneys.

(18) To vest in an obligee of the authority the right, in the event of the failure of the authority to observe or perform any covenant on its part to be kept or performed, to cure any such default and to advance any moneys necessary for such purpose, and the moneys so advanced may be made an additional obligation of the authority with such interest, security and priority as may be provided in any trust indenture, mortgage, lease or contract of the authority with reference thereto.

(19) To covenant and prescribe as to the events of default and terms and conditions upon which any or all of its bonds shall become or may be declared due before maturity and as to the terms and conditions upon which such declaration and its consequences may be waived.

(20) To covenant as to the right, liabilities, powers and duties arising upon the breach by it of any covenant, condition, or obligation.

(21) To covenant to surrender possession of all or any part of any housing project or projects upon the happening of an event of default (as defined in the contract) and to vest in an obligee the right without judicial proceedings to take

possession and to use, operate, manage and control such housing projects or any part thereof, and to collect and receive all rents, fees and revenues arising therefrom in the same manner as the authority itself might do and to dispose of the moneys collected in accordance with the agreement of the authority with such obligee.

(22) To vest in a trustee or trustees the right to enforce any covenant made to secure, to pay, or in relation to the bonds, to provide for the powers and duties of such trustee or trustees, to limit liabilities thereof and to provide the terms and conditions upon which the trustee or trustees or the holders of bonds or any proportion of them may enforce any such covenant.

(23) To make covenants other than in addition to the covenants herein expressly authorized, of like or different character.

(24) To execute all instruments necessary or convenient in the exercise of the powers herein granted or in the performance of its covenants or duties, which may contain such covenants and provisions, in addition to those above specified as the government or any purchaser of the bonds of the authority may reasonably require.

(25) To make such covenants and to do any and all such acts and things as may be necessary or convenient or desirable in order to secure its bonds, or in the absolute discretion of the authority tend to make the bonds more marketable; notwithstanding that such covenants, acts or things may not be enumerated herein; it being the intention hereof to give the authority power to do all things in the issuance of bonds, in the provisions for their security that are not inconsistent with the Constitution of the State and no consent or approval of any judge or court shall be required thereof. (1935, c. 456, s. 16; 1979, c. 690, ss. 2, 3.)

§ 157-17. Power to mortgage when project financed with governmental aid.

In connection with the interim or permanent financing of any project to be permanently financed in whole or in part by a government, or the permanent financing of which is to be secured by a pledge of a government commitment for rental assistance payments, the authority shall also have the power, subject to the consent or approval of any government providing such financing or making such commitment for rental assistance payments, to mortgage all or any part of its property, real or personal, then owned or thereafter acquired, and thereby:

(1) To vest in a government the right, upon the happening of an event of default (as defined in such mortgage), to foreclose such mortgage through judicial proceedings or through the exercise of a power of sale without judicial proceedings, so long as a government shall be the holder of any of the bonds secured by such mortgage.

(2) To vest in a trustee or trustees the right, upon the happening of an event of default (as defined in such mortgage), to foreclose such mortgage through judicial proceedings or through the exercise of a power of sale without judicial proceedings.

(3) To vest in other obligees the right to foreclose such mortgage by judicial proceedings.

(4) To vest in an obligee, including a government, the right in foreclosing any mortgage as aforesaid, to foreclose such mortgage as to all or such part or parts of the property covered thereby as such obligee (in its absolute discretion) shall elect; the institution, prosecution and conclusion of any such foreclosure proceedings and/or the sale of any such parts of the mortgaged property shall not affect in any manner or to any extent the lien of the mortgage on the parts of the mortgaged property not included in such proceedings or not sold as aforesaid. (1935, c. 456, s. 17; 1977, c. 784, s. 3.)

§ 157-17.1. Approval of mortgages by Local Government Commission; considerations; rules and regulations.

(a) With the exception of mortgages under G.S. 157-17, no housing authority may execute any mortgage authorized by this Chapter without the approval of the Local Government Commission.

(b) The Local Government Commission shall consider, in any application by a housing authority for approval of a mortgage, the following issues:

(1) The value of the property, and any other secured indebtedness upon the property;

(2) The ability of the authority to repay the indebtedness secured by the mortgage;

(3) Any other issues it deems necessary to insure the financial soundness of the housing authority.

(c) The Local Government Commission shall adopt rules and regulations to implement this section. (1979, c. 690, s. 5.)

§ 157-18. Remedies of an obligee of authority.

An obligee of the authority shall have the right in addition to all other rights which may be conferred on such obligee subject only to any contractual restrictions binding upon such obligee:

(1) By mandamus, suit, action or proceeding in law or equity (all of which may be joined in one action) to compel the authority, and the commissioners, officers, agents or employees thereof to perform each and every term, provision and covenant contained in any contract of the authority, and to require the carrying out of any or all covenants and agreements of the authority and the fulfillment of all duties imposed upon the authority by this Article.

(2) By suit, action or proceeding in equity to enjoin any acts or things which may be unlawful, or the violation of any of the rights of such obligee of the authority.

(3) By suit, action or proceeding in any court of competent jurisdiction to cause possession of any housing project or any part thereof to be surrendered to any obligee having the right to such possession pursuant to any contract of the authority. (1935, c. 456, s. 18.)

§ 157-19. Additional remedies conferrable by mortgage or trust indenture.

Any authority shall have power by its trust indenture, mortgage, lease or other contract to confer upon any obligee holding or representing a specified amount in bonds, lease or other obligations the right upon the happening of an "event of default" as defined in such instrument:

(1) By suit, action or proceeding in any court of competent jurisdiction to obtain the appointment of a receiver of any housing project of the authority or any part or parts thereof. If such receiver be appointed, he may enter and take possession of such housing project or any part or parts thereof and operate and maintain same, and collect and receive all fees, rents, revenues, or other charges thereafter arising therefrom in the same manner as the authority itself might do and shall keep such moneys in a separate account or accounts and apply the same in accordance with the obligations of the authority as the court shall direct.

(2) By suit, action or proceeding in any court of competent jurisdiction to require the authority and the commissioners thereof to account as if it and they were the trustees of an express trust. (1935, c. 456, s. 19.)

§ 157-20. Remedies cumulative.

All the rights and remedies hereinabove conferred shall be cumulative and in addition to all other rights and remedies that may be conferred upon such obligee of the authority by law or by any contract with the authority. (1935, c. 456, s. 20.)

§ 157-21. Limitations on remedies of obligee.

All property of the authority shall be exempt from levy and sale by virtue of an execution, and no execution shall issue against the same. No judgment against the authority shall be a charge or lien against its property, real or personal. The provisions of this section shall not apply to or limit the right of obligees of any mortgage of the authority provided for in G.S. 157-17, after foreclosure sale thereunder, to obtain a judgment or decree for any deficiency due on the indebtedness secured thereby and to issue execution on the credit of the authority. Such deficiency judgment or decree shall be a lien and charge upon the property of the authority, which may be levied on and sold by virtue of an execution or other judicial process for the purpose of satisfying such deficiency judgment or decree. (1935, c. 456, s. 21; 1979, c. 690, s. 4.)

§ 157-22. Title obtained at foreclosure sale subject to agreement with government.

Notwithstanding anything in this Article to the contrary, any purchaser or purchasers at a sale of real or personal property of the authority whether pursuant to any foreclosure of a mortgage, pursuant to judicial process or otherwise, shall obtain title subject to any contract between the authority and a government relating to the supervision by a government of the operation and maintenance of such property and the construction of improvements thereon. (1935, c. 456, s. 22.)

§ 157-23. Contracts with federal government.

In addition to the powers conferred upon the authority by other provisions of this Article, the authority is empowered to borrow money and/or accept grants from the federal government for or in aid of the construction of any housing project which such authority is authorized by this Article to undertake, to take over any land acquired by the federal government for the construction of a housing project, to take over or lease or manage any housing project constructed or owned by the federal government, and to these ends, to enter into such contracts, mortgages, trust indentures, leases or other agreements as the federal government may require including agreements that the federal government shall have the right to supervise and approve the construction, maintenance and operation of such housing project. It is the purpose and intent of this Article to authorize every authority to do any and all things necessary to secure the financial aid and the cooperation of the federal government in the construction, maintenance and operation of any housing project which the authority is empowered by this Article to undertake. (1935, c. 456, s. 23.)

§ 157-24. Security for funds deposited by authorities.

The authority may by resolution provide that

(1)   All moneys deposited by it shall be secured by obligations of the United States or of the State of a market value equal at all times to the amount of such deposits or

(2) By any securities in which savings banks may legally invest funds within their control or

(3) By an undertaking with such sureties as shall be approved by the authority faithfully to keep and pay over upon the order of the authority any such deposits and agreed interest thereon, and all banks and trust companies are authorized to give any such security for such deposits. (1935, c. 456, s. 24.)

§ 157-25. Housing bonds, legal investments and security.

The State and all public officers, municipal corporations, political subdivisions, and public bodies, all banks, bankers, trust companies, savings banks and institutions, building and loan associations, savings and loan associations, investment companies and other persons carrying on a banking business, all insurance companies, insurance associations, and other persons carrying on an insurance business, and all executors, administrators, guardians, trustees and other fiduciaries may legally invest any sinking funds, moneys or other funds belonging to them or within their control in any bonds issued by a housing authority established (or hereafter established) pursuant to this Article or issued by any public housing authority or agency in the United States, when such bonds are secured by a pledge of annual contributions to be paid by the United States government or any agency thereof, or bonds which may be issued notwithstanding any other limitations of this Chapter, by a not-for-profit corporate agency of a housing authority secured by rentals payable pursuant to section 23 of the United States Housing Act of 1937, as amended, or by rental assistance payments under any other section of said act, as amended, and any such bonds shall be authorized security for all public deposits and shall be fully negotiable in this State; it being the purpose of this Article to authorize any persons, firms, corporations, associations, political subdivisions, bodies and officers, public or private, to use any funds owned or controlled by them, including (but not limited to) sinking, insurance, investment, retirement, compensation, pension and trust funds, and funds held on deposit, for the purchase of any such bonds and that any such bonds shall be authorized security for all public deposits and shall be fully negotiable in this State: Provided, however, that nothing contained in this Article shall be construed as relieving any person, firm or corporation from any duty of exercising reasonable care in selecting securities. (1935, c. 456, s. 25; 1941, c. 78, s. 3; 1971, c. 1161; 1977, c. 784, s. 4.)

§ 157-26. Tax exemptions.

An authority is a local government agency and is exempt from taxation to the same extent as a unit of local government. Property owned by an authority is exempt from taxation in accordance with Article V, § 2 of the North Carolina Constitution. Bonds and other obligations issued by an authority or its corporate agent authorized by this Article to exercise its powers are declared to be issued for a public purpose and to be public instrumentalities. These obligations are exempt from all State, county, and municipal taxation or assessment, direct or indirect, general or special, whether imposed for the purpose of general revenue or otherwise, excluding inheritance and gift taxes, income taxes on the gain from the transfer of the obligations, and franchise taxes. The interest on the obligations is not subject to taxation as income. (1935, c. 456, s. 26; 1953, c. 907; 1973, c. 695, s. 7; 1977, c. 784, s. 5; 1995, c. 46, s. 17.)

§ 157-26.1. Exemption from real estate licensure requirements.

The authority and the regular salaried employees of the authority shall be exempt from the requirements of Chapter 93A of the General Statutes as provided in G.S. 93A-2(c)(8). (1999-409, s. 2.)

§ 157-27. Reports.

The authority shall at least once a year file with the mayor of the city a report of its activities for the preceding year, and shall make any recommendations with reference to any additional legislation or other action that may be necessary in order to carry out the purposes of this Article. (1935, c. 456, s. 27.)

§ 157-28. Restriction on right of eminent domain; right of appeal preserved; investigation by Utilities Commission.

Notwithstanding any finding of public convenience and necessity, either in general or specific, by the terms of this Article, the right of eminent domain shall not be exercised unless and until a certificate of public convenience and necessity for such project has been issued by the Utilities Commission of North

Carolina, and the proceedings leading up to the issuing of such certificate of public convenience and necessity, and the right to appeal therefrom shall be as now provided by law and said rights are hereby expressly reserved to all interested parties in said proceedings. In addition to the powers now granted by law to the Utilities Commission of North Carolina, the said Utilities Commission is hereby vested with full power and authority to investigate and examine all projects set up or attempted to be set up under the provisions of this Article and determine the question of the public convenience and necessity for said project. (1935, c. 456, s. 28.)

§ 157-29. Rentals; tenant selections; and summary ejectments.

(a) It is hereby declared to be the policy of this State that each housing authority shall manage and operate its housing projects in an efficient manner so as to enable it to fix the cost of dwelling accommodations for persons of low income at the lowest possible rates consistent with its providing decent, safe, and sanitary dwelling accommodations. No housing authority may construct or operate its housing projects so as to provide revenues for other activities of the city.

(b) In the operation or management of housing projects, portions of projects, or other housing assistance programs for persons of low income, an authority shall at all times observe the following duties with respect to rentals and tenant selection:

(1) It may rent or lease dwelling accommodations set aside for persons of low income only to persons who lack the amount of income that is necessary (as determined by the housing authority undertaking the project) to enable them, without financial assistance, to live in decent, safe, and sanitary dwellings, without overcrowding; and

(2) It may rent or lease dwelling accommodations to persons of low income only at rentals within the financial reach of such persons.

(3) Repealed by Session Laws 2006-219, s. 1, effective August 8, 2006.

(3a) It shall comply with the following targeting requirements:

a. Not less than forty percent (40%) of the families admitted to its public housing program from its waiting list in its fiscal year shall be extremely low-income families with incomes at or below thirty percent (30%) of the area median income. For purposes of this section, this shall be known as the "basic targeting requirement".

b. To the extent provided in sub-subdivisions c. and d. of this subdivision, the admission of extremely low-income families to its Section 8 voucher program during the same fiscal year shall be credited against the basic targeting requirement. For purposes of this section, "Section 8" refers to Section 8 of the U.S. Housing Act of 1937 as amended.

c. If admissions of extremely low-income families to its Section 8 voucher program during its fiscal year exceed the seventy-five percent (75%) minimum targeting requirement for its Section 8 voucher program, the excess shall be credited against its basic targeting requirement for the same fiscal year.

d. The fiscal year credit for Section 8 voucher program admissions that exceeded the minimum Section 8 voucher program targeting requirement shall not exceed the lower of any of the following:

1. Ten percent (10%) of its waiting list admissions during its fiscal year.

2. Ten percent (10%) of waiting list admissions to its Section 8 tenant-based assistance program during its fiscal year.

3. The number of qualifying low-income families who, during the fiscal year, commence occupancy of its public housing units that are located in census tracts with a poverty rate of thirty percent (30%) or more. For purposes of this sub-sub-subdivision, qualifying low-income family means a low-income family other than an extremely low-income family.

(4) Repealed by Session Laws 2006-219, s. 1, effective August 8, 2006.

(4a) Its targeting requirement for tenant-based assistance shall ensure that not less than seventy-five percent (75%) of the families admitted to its tenant-based voucher program from its waiting list during its fiscal year shall be extremely low-income families with incomes at or below thirty percent (30%) of the area median income.

(c) An authority may terminate or refuse to renew a rental agreement for a serious or repeated violation of a material term of the rental agreement such as (i) failure to make payments due under the rental agreement, if such payments were properly and promptly calculated according to applicable HUD regulation, whether or not such failure was the fault of the tenant, (ii) failure to fulfill the tenant obligations set forth in 24 C.F.R. Section 966.4(f) or other applicable provisions of federal law as they may be amended from time to time, or (iii) other good cause. Except in the case of failure to make payments due under a rental agreement, fault on the part of a tenant may be considered in determining whether good cause exists to terminate a rental agreement.

(d) The receipt or acceptance of rent by an authority, with or without knowledge of a prior default or failure by the tenant under a rental agreement, shall not constitute a waiver of that default or failure unless (i) the authority expressly agrees to such waiver in writing, or (ii) within 120 days after obtaining knowledge of the default or failure, the authority fails either to notify the tenant that a violation of the rental agreement has occurred or to exercise one of the authority's remedies for such violation.

(e) In any summary ejectment action wherein a housing authority alleges that a tenant's lease has been terminated because the tenant, a household member, or a guest has engaged in a criminal activity that threatens the health and safety of others or the peaceful enjoyment of the premises by others, or has engaged in activity involving illegal drugs, as defined in 24 C.F.R. § 966.4, the housing authority may bring an action under Article 7 of Chapter 42 of the General Statutes. (1939, c. 150; 1985, c. 741, s. 2; 1987, c. 464, s. 5; 1989, c. 272; 1995, c. 520, s. 1; 1997-473, s. 1; 2005-423, s. 8; 2006-219, s. 1; 2006-259, s. 39.)

§ 157-29.1. Fraudulent misrepresentation.

(a) Any person whether provider or recipient, or person representing himself as such, who willfully and knowingly and with intent to deceive makes a false statement or representation or who willfully and knowingly and with intent to deceive fails to disclose a material fact and as a result of making a false statement or representation or failing to disclose a material fact obtains, for himself or another person, attempts to obtain for himself or another person, or continues to receive housing assistance in the amount or value of not more than four hundred dollars ($400.00) is guilty of a Class 1 misdemeanor.

(b) Any person whether provider or recipient, or person representing himself as such, who willfully and knowingly and with intent to deceive makes a false statement or representation or who willfully and knowingly and with intent to deceive fails to disclose a material fact and as a result of making a false statement or representation or failing to disclose a material fact obtains, for himself or another person, or continues to receive housing assistance in the amount or value of more than four hundred dollars ($400.00) is guilty of a Class I felony.

(c) As used in this section the word "person" means person, association, consortium, body politic, partnership, or other group, entity, or organization. (1985, c. 741, s. 1; 1993, c. 539, s. 1080; 1994, Ex. Sess., c. 24, s. 14(c).)

§ 157-30. Creation and establishment validated.

The creation and establishment of housing authorities under the provisions of Chapter 456, Public Laws of 1935, as amended by Chapter 2, Public Laws of 1938, Extra Session, and as further amended by Chapter 150, Public Laws of 1939, and any additional amendments thereto, known as the Housing Authorities Law [G.S. 157-1 et seq.], together with all proceedings, acts and things heretofore undertaken, performed or done with reference thereto, are hereby validated, ratified, confirmed, approved and declared legal in all respects, notwithstanding any want of statutory authority or any defect or irregularity therein. (1939, c. 118, s. 1; 1941, c. 62, s. 1.)

§ 157-31. Contracts, agreements, etc., validated.

All contracts, agreements, obligations and undertakings of such housing authorities heretofore entered into relating to financing or aiding in the development, construction, maintenance or operation of any housing project or projects or to obtaining aid therefor from the United States Housing Authority, including (without limiting the generality of the foregoing) loan and annual contributions contracts and leases with the United States Housing Authority, agreements with municipalities or other public bodies (including those which are pledged or authorized to be pledged for the protection of the holders of any notes or bonds issued by such housing authorities or which are otherwise made a part of the contract with such holders of notes or bonds) relating to cooperation and contributions in aid of housing projects, payments (if any) in lieu of taxes, furnishing of municipal services and facilities, and the elimination of unsafe and insanitary dwellings, and contracts for the construction of housing projects, together with all proceedings, acts and things heretofore undertaken, performed or done with reference thereto, are hereby validated, ratified, confirmed, approved and declared legal in all respects, notwithstanding any want of statutory authority or any defect or irregularity therein. (1939, c. 118, s. 2; 1941, c. 62, s. 2.)

§ 157-32. Proceedings for issuance, etc., of bonds and notes validated.

All proceedings, acts and things heretofore undertaken, performed or done in or for the authorization, issuance, execution and delivery of notes and bonds by housing authorities for the purpose of financing or aiding in the development or construction of a housing project or projects, and all notes and bonds heretofore issued by housing authorities are hereby validated, ratified, confirmed, approved and declared legal in all respects, notwithstanding any want of statutory authority or any defect or irregularity therein. (1939, c. 118, s. 3; 1941, c. 62, s. 3.)

§ 157-32.1. Other validation of creation, etc.

The creation, establishment and organization of housing authorities under the provisions of the Housing Authorities Law (Chapter 456, Public Laws of 1935, as amended, codified as G.S. 157-1 et seq.), together with all proceedings, acts and things heretofore undertaken or done with reference thereto, are hereby validated and declared legal in all respects. (1943, c. 89, s. 1.)

§ 157-32.2. Other validation of contracts, agreements, etc.

All contracts, agreements and undertakings of such housing authorities heretofore entered into relating to financing, or aiding in the development or operation of any housing projects, including (without limiting the generality of the foregoing) loan and annual contributions contracts, agency contracts and leases, agreements with municipalities or other public bodies (including those which are pledged or authorized to be pledged for the protection of the holders of any notes or bonds issued by such housing authorities or which are otherwise made a part of the contract with such holders of notes or bonds) relating to cooperation in aid of housing projects, payments to public bodies in the State, furnishing of municipal services and facilities and the elimination of unsafe and insanitary dwellings, and contracts for the construction of housing projects, together with all proceedings, acts and things heretofore undertaken or done with reference thereto, are hereby validated and declared legal in all respects. (1943, c. 89, s. 2.)

§ 157-32.3. Other validation of bonds and notes.

All proceedings, acts and things heretofore undertaken or done in or for the authorization, issuance, execution and delivery of notes and bonds by housing authorities for the purpose of financing or aiding in the development or construction of a housing project or projects, and all notes and bonds heretofore issued by housing authorities are hereby validated and declared legal in all respects. (1943, c. 89, s. 3.)

§ 157-32.4. Further validation of contracts, agreements, etc.

All contracts or agreements of housing authorities heretofore entered into with the federal government or its agencies, and with municipalities or others relating to financial assistance for housing projects in which it was required that loans or advances shall bear an interest rate in excess of six per centum (6%) per annum, or in which a municipality or others had agreed to pay funds equal to the interest in excess of six per centum (6%) per annum are hereby validated, ratified, confirmed, approved and declared legal with respect to the payment of interest in excess of six per centum (6%), and all things done or performed in reference thereto. The housing authorities are hereby authorized to assume the full obligation of the municipalities under the contracts or agreements with reference to interest in excess of six per centum (6%), and to reimburse any municipality which has made any interest payment under such contracts or agreements. (1971, c. 87, s. 2.)

§ 157-33. Notice, hearing and creation of authority for a county.

Any 25 residents of a county may file a petition with the clerk of the board of county commissioners setting forth that there is a need for an authority to function in the county. Upon the filing of such a petition such clerk shall give notice of the time, place and purposes of a public hearing at which the board of county commissioners will determine the need for an authority in the county. Such notice shall be given at the county's expense by publishing a notice, at least 10 days preceding the day on which the hearing is to be held, in a newspaper having a general circulation in the county or, if there be no such newspaper, by posting such a notice in at least three public places within the county, at least 10 days preceding the day on which the hearing is to be held.

Upon the date fixed for said hearing to be held upon notice as provided herein, an opportunity to be heard shall be granted to all residents and taxpayers of the county and to all other interested persons. After such a hearing, the board of county commissioners shall determine (i) whether insanitary or unsafe inhabited dwelling accommodations exist in the county and/or (ii) whether there is a lack of safe or sanitary dwelling accommodations in the county available for all the inhabitants thereof. In determining whether dwelling accommodations are unsafe or insanitary, the board of county commissioners shall take into consideration the following: the physical condition and age of the buildings; the degree of overcrowding; the percentage of the land coverage; the light and air available to the inhabitants of such dwelling accommodations; the size and arrangement of the rooms; the sanitary facilities; and the extent to which conditions exist in such buildings which endanger life or property by fire or other causes.

If it shall determine that either or both of the above enumerated conditions exist, the board of county commissioners shall adopt a resolution so finding (which need not go into any detail other than the mere finding) and shall thereupon either (i) determine that the board of county commissioners shall itself constitute and act ex officio as an authority or (ii) appoint, as hereinafter provided, not less than five nor more than nine commissioners to act as an authority. Said authority shall be a public body and a body corporate and politic upon the completion of the taking of the following proceedings:

The commissioners shall present to the Secretary of State an application signed by them, which shall set forth (without any detail other than the mere recital)

(1) That a notice has been given and public hearing has been held as aforesaid, that the board of county commissioners made the aforesaid determination after such hearing and appointed them as commissioners;

(2) The name, and official residence of each of the commissioners, together with a certified copy of the appointment evidencing their right to office, the date and place of induction into and taking oath of office, and that they desire the housing authority to become a public body and a body corporate and politic under this Article;

(3) The term of office of each of the commissioners, except where the authority consists of the board of county commissioners ex officio;

(4) The name which is proposed for the corporation; and

(5) The location of the principal office of the proposed corporation.

The application shall be subscribed and sworn to by each of said commissioners before an officer authorized by the laws of the State to take and certify oaths, who shall certify upon the application that he personally knows the commissioners and knows them to be the officers as asserted in the application, and that each subscribed and swore thereto in the officer's presence. The Secretary of State shall examine the application and if he finds that the name proposed for the corporation is not identical with that of a person or of any other corporation of this State or so nearly similar as to lead to confusion and uncertainty he shall receive and file it and shall record it in an appropriate book of record in his office.

When the application has been made, filed and recorded, as herein provided, the authority shall constitute a public body and a body corporate and politic under the name proposed in the application; the Secretary of State shall make and issue to the said commissioners, a certificate of incorporation pursuant to this Article, under the seal of the State, and shall record the same with the application.

If the board of county commissioners, after a hearing as aforesaid, shall determine that neither of the above enumerated conditions exist, it shall adopt a resolution denying the petition. After three months shall have expired from the date of the denial of any such petitions, subsequent petitions may be filed as aforesaid and new hearings and determinations made thereon.

In any suit, action or proceeding involving the validity or enforcement of, or relating to any contract of the authority, the authority shall be conclusively deemed to have been established in accordance with the provisions of this Article upon proof of the issuance of the aforesaid certificate by the Secretary of State. A copy of such certificate, duly certified by the Secretary of State, shall be admissible in evidence in any such suit, action or proceeding, and shall be conclusive proof of the filing and contents thereof. (1941, c. 78, s. 4; 1943, c. 636, s. 7; 1969, c. 785, s. 1; 1981, c. 21, s. 1.)

§ 157-34. Commissioners and powers of authority for a county.

The commissioners of a housing authority created for a county may be appointed and removed by the board of county commissioners of the county in the same manner as the commissioners of a housing authority created for a city may be appointed and removed by the mayor; provided, that the board of county commissioners may determine in the case of any authority for its county that the board of county commissioners itself shall constitute and act ex officio as the authority. The board of county commissioners may at any time by resolution or ordinance increase or decrease the membership of an authority, within the limitations prescribed in G.S. 157-33. Except as otherwise provided herein, each housing authority created for a county and the commissioners thereof shall have the same functions, rights, powers, duties and limitations provided for housing authorities created for cities and the commissioners of such housing authorities: Provided, that for such purposes the term "mayor" or "council" as used in the housing authorities law and any amendments thereto shall be construed as meaning "board of county commissioners," the term "city clerk" as used therein shall be construed as meaning "clerk of the board of county commissioners" and the term "city" as used therein shall be construed as meaning "county" unless a different meaning clearly appears from the context: Provided, further, that a housing authority created for a county shall not be subject to the limitations provided in subdivision (4) of G.S. 157-29 of the housing authorities law with respect to housing projects for farmers of low income. (1941, c. 78, s. 4; 1969, c. 785, s. 2; 1981, c. 21, s. 2.)

§ 157-35. Creation of regional housing authority.

If the board of county commissioners of each of two or more contiguous counties having an aggregate population of more than 60,000 by resolution declares that there is a need for one housing authority to be created for all of such counties to exercise powers and other functions herein prescribed for a housing authority in such counties, a public body corporate and politic to be known as a regional housing authority for all of such counties shall (after the commissioners thereof file an application with the Secretary of State as hereinafter provided) thereupon exist for and exercise its powers and other functions in such counties; and thereupon any housing authority created for any of such counties shall cease to exist except for the purpose of winding up its affairs and executing a deed to the regional housing authority as hereinafter provided: Provided, that the board of county commissioners shall not adopt a resolution as aforesaid if there is a county housing authority created for such county which has any bonds or notes outstanding unless first, all holders of such bonds and notes consent in writing to the substitution of such regional housing authority in lieu of such county housing authority on all such bonds and notes; and second, the commissioners of such county housing authority adopt a resolution consenting to the transfer of all the rights, contracts, obligations, and property, real and personal, of such county housing authority to such regional housing authority as hereinafter provided: Provided, further, that when the above conditions are complied with and such regional housing authority is created and authorized to exercise its powers and other functions, all rights, contracts, agreements, obligations, and property, real and personal, of such county housing authority shall be in the name of and vest in such regional housing authority, and all obligations of such county housing authority shall be the obligations of such regional housing authority and all rights and remedies of any person against such county housing authority may be asserted, enforced, and prosecuted against such regional housing authority to the same extent as they might have been asserted, enforced, and prosecuted against such county housing authority. When any real property of a county housing authority vests in a regional housing authority as provided above, the county housing authority shall execute a deed of such property to the regional housing authority which thereupon shall file such deed in the office provided for the filing of deeds: Provided, that nothing contained in this sentence shall affect the vesting of property in the regional housing authority as provided above.

The board of county commissioners of each of two or more said contiguous counties shall by resolution declare that there is a need for one regional housing authority to be created for all of such counties to exercise powers and other functions herein prescribed in such counties, if such board of county commissioners finds (and only if it finds)

(1) Insanitary or unsafe dwelling accommodations exist in the area of its respective county and/or there is a lack of safe or sanitary dwelling accommodations in the county available for all the inhabitants thereof and

(2) That a regional housing authority for the proposed region would be a more efficient or economical administrative unit than a housing authority for an area having a smaller population to carry out the purposes of the housing authorities law and any amendments thereto, in such county.

In determining whether dwelling accommodations are unsafe or insanitary, the board of county commissioners shall take into consideration the following: the physical condition and age of the buildings; the degree of overcrowding; the percentage of land coverage; the light and air available to the inhabitants of such dwelling accommodations; the size and arrangement of the rooms; the sanitary facilities; and the extent to which conditions exist in such buildings which endanger life or property by fire or other causes.

If it shall determine that both (1) and (2) of the above enumerated conditions exist, the board of county commissioners shall adopt a resolution so finding (which need not go into any detail other than the mere finding). After the appointment, as hereinafter provided, of the commissioners to act as the regional housing authority, said authority shall be a public body and a body corporate and politic upon the completion of the taking of the following proceedings:

The commissioners shall present to the Secretary of State an application signed by them, which shall set forth (without any detail other than the mere recital)

(1) That the boards of county commissioners made the aforesaid determination and that they have been appointed as commissioners;

(2) The name, and official residence of each of the commissioners, together with a certified copy of the appointment evidencing their right to office, the date and place of induction into and taking oath of office, and that they desire the housing authority to become a public body and a body corporate and politic under this Article;

(3) The term of office of each of the commissioners;

(4) The name which is proposed for the corporation; and

(5) The location of the principal office of the proposed corporation.

The application shall be subscribed and sworn to by each of said commissioners before an officer authorized by the laws of the State to take and certify oaths, who shall certify upon the application that he personally knows the commissioners and knows them to be the officers as asserted in the application, and that each subscribed and swore thereto in the officer's presence. The Secretary of State shall examine the application and if he finds that the name proposed for the corporation is not identical with that of a person or of any other corporation of this State or so nearly similar as to lead to confusion and uncertainty he shall receive and file it and shall record it in an appropriate book of record in his office.

When the application has been made, filed and recorded, as herein provided, the authority shall constitute a public body and a body corporate and politic under the name proposed in the application; the Secretary of State shall make and issue to the said commissioners, a certificate of incorporation pursuant to this Article, under the seal of the State, and shall record the same with the application.

In any suit, action or proceeding involving the validity or enforcement of, or relating to any contract of the regional housing authority, the regional housing authority shall be conclusively deemed to have been established in accordance with the provisions of this Article upon proof of the issuance of the aforesaid certificate by the Secretary of State. A copy of such certificate, duly certified by the Secretary of State, shall be admissible in evidence in any such suit, action or proceeding, and shall be conclusive proof of the filing and contents thereof. (1941, c. 78, s. 4; 1943, c. 636, ss. 3, 7; 1998-217, s. 20.)

§ 157-36. Commissioners of regional housing authority.

(a) The board of county commissioners of each county included in a regional housing authority shall appoint one person as a commissioner of such authority, and each such commissioner to be first appointed by the board of county commissioners of a county may be appointed at or after the time of the adoption of the resolution declaring the need for such regional housing authority or declaring the need for the inclusion of such county in the area of operation of such regional housing authority. When the area of operation of a regional housing authority is increased to include an additional county or counties as provided in this Article, the board of county commissioners of each such county shall thereupon appoint one additional person as a commissioner of the regional housing authority. The board of county commissioners of each county shall appoint the successor of the commissioner appointed by it.

(b)   The commissioners of the regional housing authority shall appoint as a commissioner at least one person who is directly assisted by the authority unless the authority's rules require that the person be elected by other persons who are assisted by the authority. However, there shall be no requirement to appoint such a person if the authority: (i) operates less than 300 public housing units, (ii) provides reasonable notice to all resident advisory boards within the authority's area of operation of the opportunity for at least one person who is directly assisted by the authority to serve as a commissioner, and (iii) within a reasonable time after receipt of the notice by the resident advisory boards, has not been notified of the intention of any such person to serve. The commissioners of the regional housing authority shall appoint successors of the commissioner appointed by them and shall fill any vacancies. A certificate of the appointment signed by the chair of the commissioners of the regional housing authority shall be conclusive evidence of the due and proper selection of the commissioner. If the commissioner directly assisted by the regional housing authority ceases to receive such assistance, the commissioner's office shall be abolished and another person who is directly assisted by the regional housing authority shall be appointed by the commissioners of the regional housing authority.

(c)   No commissioner who is also a person directly assisted by the regional housing authority shall be qualified to vote on matters affecting his or her official conduct or matters affecting his or her own individual tenancy, as distinguished from matters affecting tenants in general.

(d)   If any county is excluded from the area of operation of a regional housing authority, the office of the commissioner of such regional housing authority appointed by the board of county commissioners of such county shall be thereupon abolished. If the person appointed as a commissioner under subsection (b) of this section resides in a county that is excluded from the authority's area of operation, the office of that commissioner shall be abolished and another person residing within the authority's area of operation shall be appointed.

(e) A certificate of the appointment of any commissioner signed by the chair of the board of county commissioners (or the appointing officer) shall be conclusive evidence of the due and proper appointment of such commissioner.

(f) If the area of operation of a regional housing authority consists at any time of an even number of counties, except as provided in subsection (g) of this section, the Governor shall appoint one additional commissioner to such regional housing authority whose term of office shall be as herein provided for a commissioner of a regional housing authority, except that such term shall end at any earlier time that the area of operation of the regional housing authority shall be changed to consist of an odd number of counties. The Governor shall likewise appoint each person to succeed such additional commissioner. A certificate of the appointment of any such additional commissioner shall be signed by the Governor and filed with the Secretary of State. A copy of such certificate, duly certified by the Secretary of State, shall be conclusive evidence of the due and proper appointment of such additional commissioner.

(g) If the membership of the board of commissioners consists of an even number as a result of the appointment of a person who is directly assisted by the regional housing authority, the Governor shall appoint one additional commissioner to the authority whose term of office shall be as herein provided for a commissioner of an authority, except that such term shall end at any earlier time that the area of operation of the authority shall be changed to consist of an even number of counties. A certificate of the appointment shall be signed and filed as provided in subsection (f) of this section. The Governor shall appoint successors to the additional commissioner and shall fill any vacancies.

(h) The commissioners of a regional housing authority shall be appointed for terms of five years except that all vacancies shall be filled for the unexpired terms. Each commissioner shall hold office until his or her successor has been appointed and has qualified.

(i) For inefficiency or neglect of duty or misconduct in office, a commissioner of a regional housing authority may be removed by the appointing authority. The commissioner shall have been given a copy of the charges against him or her at least 10 days prior to the hearing thereon and shall have had an opportunity to be heard in person or by counsel.

(j) The commissioners appointed as aforesaid shall constitute the regional housing authority, and the powers of such authority shall be vested in such commissioners in office from time to time.

(k) The commissioners of a regional housing authority shall elect a chair from among the commissioners and shall have power to select or employ such other officers and employees as the regional housing authority may require. A majority of the commissioners of a regional housing authority shall constitute a quorum of such authority for the purpose of conducting its business and exercising its powers and for all other purposes. (1941, c. 78, s. 4; 1943, c. 636, s. 4; 1999-146, s. 2.)

§ 157-37. Powers of regional housing authority.

Except as otherwise provided herein, a regional housing authority and the commissioners thereof shall, within the area of operation of such regional housing authority, have the same functions, rights, powers, duties and limitations provided for housing authorities created for cities or counties and the commissioners of such housing authorities: Provided, that for such purposes the term "mayor" or "council" as used in the Housing Authorities Law and any amendments thereto shall be construed as meaning "board of county commissioners," the term "city clerk" as used therein shall be construed as meaning "clerk of the board of county commissioners" and the term "city" as used therein shall be construed as meaning "county" unless a different meaning clearly appears from the context: Provided, further, that a regional housing authority shall not be subject to the limitations provided in subdivision (4) of G.S. 157-29 of the Housing Authorities Law with respect to housing projects for farmers of low income. Except as otherwise provided in this Article, all the provisions of law applicable to housing authorities created for counties and the commissioners of such authorities shall be applicable to regional housing authorities and the commissioners thereof. (1941, c. 78, s. 4; 1943, c. 636, s. 6.)

§ 157-38. Rural housing projects.

Housing authorities created for counties and regional housing authorities are specifically empowered and authorized to borrow money, accept grants and exercise their other powers to provide housing for farmers of low income. In connection with such projects, such housing authorities may enter into such lease or purchase agreements, accept such conveyances and rent or sell dwellings forming part of such projects to or for farmers of low income, as such housing authority deems necessary in order to assure the achievement of the objectives of this Article. Such leases, agreements or conveyances may include such covenants as the housing authority deems appropriate regarding such dwellings and the tracts of land described in any such instrument, which covenants shall be deemed to run with the land where the housing authority deems it necessary and the parties to such instrument so stipulate. Nothing contained in this section shall be construed as limiting any other powers of any housing authority. (1941, c. 78, s. 4.)

§ 157-39. Housing applications by farmers.

The owner of any farm operated, or worked upon, by farmers of low income in need of safe and sanitary housing may file an application with a housing authority of a county or a regional housing authority requesting that it provide for a safe and sanitary dwelling or dwellings for occupancy by such farmers of low income. Such applications shall be received and examined by housing authorities in connection with the formulation of projects or programs to provide housing for farmers of low income. (1941, c. 78, s. 4.)

§ 157-39.1. Area of operation of city, county and regional housing authorities.

(a) The boundaries or area of operation of a housing authority created for a city shall include said city and the area within 10 miles from the territorial boundaries of said city, but in no event shall it include the whole or a part of any other city, except as otherwise provided herein. Notwithstanding the previous sentence, a housing authority created for a city may operate and perform any of its lawful functions within any other city that has a common boundary with a city creating an authority when requested to do so by resolution of the governing body of such other city. The area of operation or boundaries of a housing authority created for a county shall include all of the county for which it is created and the area of operation or boundaries of a regional housing authority shall include (except as otherwise provided elsewhere in this Article) all of the counties for which such regional housing authority is created and established: Provided, that a county or regional housing authority shall not undertake any housing project or projects within the boundaries of any city unless a resolution shall have been adopted by the governing body of such city (and also by any housing authority which shall have been theretofore established and authorized to exercise its powers in such city) declaring that there is a need for the county or regional housing authority to exercise its power within such city: Provided, that the jurisdiction of any rural housing authority to which the Secretary of State has heretofore issued a certificate of incorporation shall extend to within a distance of one mile of the town or city limits of any town or city having a population in excess of 500, located in any county now or hereafter constituting a part of the territory of such rural housing authority: Provided, further, that this provision shall not affect the jurisdiction of any city housing authority to which the Secretary of State has heretofore issued a certificate of incorporation. A housing authority created for a county may operate and perform any of its lawful functions anywhere within the municipal boundaries of any city located in whole or in part within the county for which it is created, when requested to do so by resolution of the governing body of such city.

(b)   In any county in which a city housing authority has been established, but where there are portions of the county in which the city is located which are more than 10 miles from the territorial boundaries of the city, the city housing authority is authorized to operate in areas of the county beyond such limit, which are not within another city, upon the adoption of a joint resolution by the city council and the board of county commissioners. Such joint resolution must find that in such additional area, that insanitary or unsafe inhabited dwelling accommodations exist in such area or there is a shortage of safe or sanitary dwelling accommodations in such county available to persons of low income at rentals they can afford. A public hearing on such resolution need be held only by the board of county commissioners.

(c)   A joint resolution adopted under subsection (b) of this section may, in lieu of the appointment provisions of G.S. 157-5, provide that the board of commissioners of the housing authority shall be composed of nine members, with a number (not less than five) to be appointed by the mayor, and the remainder to be appointed by the board of county commissioners. Such housing authority commissioners shall be subject to removal by the appointing person or board under the procedural requirements of G.S. 157-8. (1943, c. 636, s. 5; 1961, c. 200, s. 2; 1979, 2nd Sess., c. 1108, ss. 1, 2; 1993, c. 458.)

§ 157-39.2. Increasing area of operation of regional housing authority.

The area of operation or boundaries of a regional housing authority shall be increased from time to time to include one or more additional contiguous counties not already within a regional housing authority if the board of county commissioners of each of the counties then included in the area of operation of such regional housing authority, the commissioners of the regional housing authority and the board of county commissioners of each such additional county or counties each adopts a resolution declaring that there is a need for the inclusion of such additional county or counties in the area of operation of such regional housing authority. Upon the adoption of such resolutions, any county housing authority created for any such additional county shall cease to exist except for the purpose of winding up its affairs and executing a deed to the regional housing authority as hereinafter provided. Provided, however, that such resolutions shall not be adopted unless the commissioners of such county housing authority adopt a resolution consenting to the transfer of all the rights, contracts, bonds, and property, real and personal, of such county housing authority to such regional housing authority as hereinafter provided: Provided, further, that when the above condition is complied with and the area of operation of such regional housing authority is increased to include such additional county, as hereinabove provided, all rights, contracts, bonds, and property, real and personal, of such county housing authority shall be in the name of and vested in such regional housing authority, all contracts and bonds of such county housing authority shall be the contracts and bonds of such regional housing authority and all rights and remedies of any person against such county housing authority may be asserted, enforced, and prosecuted against such regional housing authority to the same extent as they might have been asserted, enforced, and prosecuted against such county housing authority.

When any real property of a county housing authority vests in a regional housing authority as provided above, the county housing authority shall execute a deed of such property to the regional housing authority which thereupon shall file such deed in the office provided for the filing of deeds: Provided, that nothing contained in this sentence shall affect the vesting of property in the regional housing authority as provided above.

The board of county commissioners of each of the counties in the regional housing authority, the commissioners of the regional housing authority and the board of county commissioners of each such additional county or counties shall by resolution declare that there is a need for the inclusion of such county or counties in the area of operation of the regional housing authority, only if:

(1) The board of county commissioners of each such additional county or counties find that insanitary or unsafe inhabited dwelling accommodations exist in such county or there is a shortage of safe or sanitary dwelling

accommodations in such county available to persons of low income at rentals they can afford, and

(2) The board of county commissioners of each of the counties then included in the area of operation of the regional housing authority, the commissioners of the regional housing authority and the board of county commissioners of each such additional county or counties find that the regional housing authority would be a more efficient or economical administrative unit if the area of operation of the regional housing authority is increased to include such additional county or counties. (1943, c. 636, s. 5; 1971, c. 431, s. 1.)

§ 157-39.3. Decreasing area of operation of regional housing authority.

The area of operation or boundaries of a regional housing authority shall be decreased from time to time to exclude one or more counties from such area if the board of county commissioners of each of the counties in such area and the commissioners of the regional housing authority each adopt a resolution declaring that there is a need for excluding such county or counties from such area: Provided, that if such action decreases the area of operation of the regional housing authority to only one county, such authority shall thereupon constitute and become a housing authority for such county, in the same manner as though such authority were created, and constituted a public and corporate body for such county pursuant to other provisions of this housing authority law, and the commissioners of such authority shall be thereupon appointed as provided for the appointment of commissioners of a housing authority created for a county.

The board of county commissioners of each of the counties in the area of operation of the regional housing authority and the commissioners of the regional housing authority shall adopt a resolution declaring that there is a need for excluding a county or counties from such area only if:

(1) Each such board of county commissioners of the counties to remain in the area of operation of the regional housing authority and the commissioners of the regional housing authority find that, because of facts arising or determined subsequent to the time when such area first included the county or counties to be excluded, the regional housing authority would be a more efficient or economical administrative unit if such county or counties were excluded from such area, and

(2) The board of county commissioners of each county or counties to be excluded and the commissioners of the regional housing authority each also find that another housing authority for such county or counties would be a more efficient or economical administrative unit to function in such county or counties.

Nothing contained herein shall be construed as preventing a county or counties excluded from the area of operation of a regional housing authority, as provided above, from thereafter being included within the area of operation of any housing authority in accordance with this Article.

Any property held by a regional housing authority within a county or counties excluded from the area of operation of such authority as herein provided, shall, as soon as practicable after the exclusion of said county or counties, respectively, be disposed of by such authority in the public interest. (1943, c. 636, s. 5; 1971, c. 431, s. 2.)

§ 157-39.4. Requirements of public hearings.

The board of county commissioners of a county shall not adopt any resolution authorized by G.S. 157-35, 157-39.1, 157-39.2 or 157-39.3 unless a public hearing has first been held which shall conform (except as otherwise provided herein) to the requirements of this Housing Authorities Law for hearings to determine the need for a housing authority of a county: Provided, that such hearings may be held by the board of county commissioners without a petition therefor.

In connection with the issuance of bonds, a regional housing authority may covenant as to limitations on its right to adopt resolutions relating to the increase or decrease of its area of operation. (1943, c. 636, s. 5; 1979, 2nd Sess., c. 1108, s. 3.)

§ 157-39.5. Consolidated housing authority.

If the governing body of each of two or more municipalities (with a population of less than 500, but having an aggregate population of more than 500) by resolution declares that there is a need for one housing authority for all of such municipalities to exercise in such municipalities the powers and other functions prescribed for a housing authority, a public body corporate and politic to be known as a consolidated housing authority (with such corporate name as it selects) shall thereupon exist for all of such municipalities and exercise its powers and other functions within its area of operation (as herein defined), including the power to undertake projects therein; and thereupon any housing authority created for any of such municipalities shall cease to exist except for the purpose of winding up its affairs and executing a deed of its real property to the consolidated housing authority: Provided, that the creation of a consolidated housing authority and the finding of need therefor shall be subject to the same provisions and limitations of this Housing Authorities Law as are applicable to the creation of a regional housing authority and that all of the provisions of this Housing Authorities Law applicable to regional housing authorities and the commissioners thereof shall be applicable to consolidated housing authorities and the commissioners thereof: Provided, further that the area of operation or boundaries of a consolidated housing authority shall include all of the territory within the boundaries of each municipality joining in the creation of such authority together with the territory within 10 miles of the boundaries of each such municipality, except that such area of operation may be changed to include or exclude any municipality or municipalities (with its aforesaid surrounding territory) in the same manner and under the same provisions as provided in this Article for changing the area of operation of a regional housing authority by including or excluding a contiguous county or counties: Provided, further, that for all such purposes the term "board of county commissioners" shall be construed as meaning "governing body" except in G.S. 157-36, where it shall be construed as meaning "mayor" or other executive head of the municipality, the term "county" shall be construed as meaning "municipality," the term "clerk" shall be construed as meaning "clerk of the municipality or officer with similar duties," the term "region" shall be construed as meaning "area of operation of the consolidated housing authority" and the terms "county housing authority" and "regional housing authority" shall be construed as meaning "housing authority of the city" and "consolidated housing authority," respectively, unless a different meaning clearly appears from the context.

The governing body of any such municipality for which a housing authority has not been created may adopt the above resolution if it first determines that there is a need for a housing authority to function in said municipality, which determination shall be made in the same manner and subject to the same conditions as the determination required by G.S. 157-4 for the creation of a housing authority for a city: Provided, that after notice given by the clerk (or officer with similar duties) of the municipality, the governing body of the municipality may, without a petition therefor, hold a hearing to determine the need for a housing authority to function therein.

Except as otherwise provided herein, a consolidated housing authority and the commissioners thereof shall, within the area of operation of such consolidated housing authority have the same functions, rights, powers, duties, privileges, immunities and limitations as those provided for housing authorities created for cities, counties, or groups of counties and the commissioners of such housing authorities, in the same manner as though all the provisions of law applicable to housing authorities created for cities, counties, or groups of counties were applicable to consolidated housing authorities. (1943, c. 636, s. 5; 1961, c. 200, s. 3; 1965, c. 431, s. 3.)

§ 157-39.6. Findings required for authority to operate in municipality.

No governing body of a city or other municipality shall adopt a resolution as provided in G.S. 157-39.1 declaring that there is a need for a housing authority (other than a housing authority established by such municipality) to exercise its powers within such municipality, unless a public hearing has first been held by such governing body and unless such governing body shall have found in substantially the following terms: (i) that insanitary or unsafe inhabited dwelling accommodations exist in such municipality or that there is a shortage of safe or sanitary dwelling accommodations in such municipality available to persons of low income at rentals they can afford; and (ii) that these conditions can be best remedied through the exercise of the aforesaid housing authority's powers within the territorial boundaries of such municipality: Provided, that such findings shall not have the effect of thereafter preventing such municipality from establishing a housing authority or joining in the creation of a consolidated housing authority or the increase of the area of operation of a consolidated housing authority. The clerk (or the officer with similar duties) of the city or other municipality shall give notice of the public hearing and such hearing shall be held in the manner provided in G.S. 157-4 for a public hearing by a council to determine the need for a housing authority in the city.

During the time that, pursuant to these findings, a housing authority has outstanding (or is under contract to issue) any evidences of indebtedness for a project within the city or other municipality, no other housing authority may undertake a project within such municipality without the consent of said housing authority which has such outstanding indebtedness or obligation. (1943, c. 636, s. 5.)

§ 157-39.7. Meetings and residence of commissioners.

Nothing contained in this Housing Authorities Law shall be construed to prevent meetings of the commissioners of a housing authority anywhere within the perimeter boundaries of the area of operation of the authority or within any additional area where the housing authority is authorized to undertake a housing project, nor to prevent the appointment of any person as a commissioner of the authority who resides within such boundaries or such additional area, and who is otherwise eligible for such appointment under this Housing Authorities Law. (1943, c. 636, s. 5.)

§ 157-39.8. Agreement to sell as security for obligations to federal government.

In any contract or amendatory or superseding contract for a loan and annual contributions heretofore or hereafter entered into between a housing authority and the federal government with respect to any housing project undertaken by said housing authority, any such housing authority is authorized to make such covenants (including covenants with holders of bonds issued by such authority for purposes of the project involved), and to confer upon the federal government such rights and remedies, as said housing authority deems necessary to assure the fulfillment of the purposes for which the project was undertaken. In any such contract, the housing authority may, notwithstanding any other provisions of law, agree to sell and convey the project (including all lands appertaining thereto) to which such contract relates to the federal government upon the occurrence of such conditions, or upon such defaults on bonds for which any of the annual contributions provided in said contract are pledged, as may be prescribed in such contract, and at a price (which may include the assumption by the federal government of the payment, when due, of the principal of and interest on outstanding bonds of the housing authority issued for purposes of the project involved) determined as prescribed therein and upon such other terms and conditions as are therein provided. Any such housing authority is hereby authorized to enter into such supplementary contracts, and to execute such conveyances, as may be necessary to carry out the provisions hereof. Notwithstanding any other provisions of law, any contracts or supplementary contracts or conveyances made or executed pursuant to the provisions of this section shall not be or constitute a mortgage within the meaning or for the purposes of any of the laws of the State. (1943, c. 636, s. 5.)

Article 2.

Municipal Cooperation and Aid.

§ 157-40. Finding and declaration of necessity.

It is hereby declared that insanitary or unsafe dwelling accommodations exist in various areas of the State, and that consequently many persons of low income are forced to reside in such dwelling accommodations; that these conditions cause an increase in and spread of disease and crime and constitute a menace to the health, safety, morals and welfare of the citizens of the State and impair economic values; that the clearance, replanning and reconstruction of the areas in which insanitary or unsafe housing conditions exist and the providing of safe and sanitary dwelling accommodations for persons of low income are public uses and purposes for which private property may be acquired; that it is in the public interest that work on such projects be instituted as soon as possible in order to relieve unemployment which now constitutes an emergency; and the necessity in the public interest for the provisions hereinafter enacted, is hereby declared as a matter of legislative determination. (1935, c. 408, s. 1.)

§ 157-41. Definitions.

The following terms, whenever used or referred to in this Article, shall have the following respective meanings, unless a different meaning clearly appears from the context:

(1)   "City" shall mean any city or town of the State having a population of more than 500 inhabitants according to the last federal census or any revision or amendment thereto.

(2)   "Housing authority" shall mean any housing authority organized pursuant to the Housing Authorities Law of this State.

(3) "Housing project" shall mean any undertaking (i) to demolish, clear, remove, alter or repair unsafe or insanitary housing, and/or (ii) to provide dwelling accommodations for persons of low income, and said term may also include such buildings and equipment for recreational or social assemblies for educational, health or welfare purposes, and such necessary utilities as are designed primarily for the benefit and use of the housing authority and/or the occupants of such dwelling accommodations.

(4) "Municipality" shall mean any city, town or incorporated village of the State. (1935, c. 408, s. 2; 1961, c. 200, s. 4.)

§ 157-42. Conveyance, lease or agreement in aid of housing project.

For the purpose of aiding and cooperating in the planning, construction and operation of housing projects located within their respective territorial boundaries, the State, its subdivisions and agencies, and any county, city or municipality of the State may, upon such terms, with or without considerations as it may determine:

(1) Dedicate, release, sell, convey, or lease any of its interest in any property, or grant easements, licenses or any other rights or privileges therein to a housing authority or the United States of America or any agency thereof;

(2) Cause parks, playgrounds, recreational, community, educational, water, sewer or drainage facilities, or any other works, which it is otherwise empowered to undertake, to be furnished adjacent to or in connection with housing projects;

(3) Furnish, dedicate, close, pave, install, grade, regrade, plan or replan streets, roads, roadways, alleys, sidewalks or other places, which it is otherwise empowered to undertake;

(4) Plan or replan, zone, or rezone; make exceptions from building regulations and ordinances; any city or town also may change its map;

(5) Cause services to be furnished to the housing authority of the character which it is otherwise empowered to furnish;

(6) Enter into agreements with respect to the exercise by it of its powers relating to the repair, closing or demolition of unsafe, insanitary or unfit dwellings;

(7) Enter into agreements (which may extend over any period, notwithstanding any provision or rule of law to the contrary) with a housing authority respecting action to be taken pursuant to any of the powers granted by this Article. Any law or statute to the contrary notwithstanding, any sale, conveyance, lease or agreement provided for in this section may be made by the State, a city, county, municipality, subdivision or agency of the State without appraisal, public notice, advertisement or public bidding.

(8) With respect to any housing project which a housing authority has acquired or taken over from the United States of America or any agency thereof and which the housing authority by resolution has found and declared to have been constructed in a manner that will promote the public interest and afford necessary safety, sanitation and other protection, no city or county shall require any changes to be made in the housing project or the manner of its construction or take any other action relating to such construction. (1935, c. 408, s. 3; 1939, c. 137.)

§ 157-43. Advances and donations by the city and municipality.

The council or other governing body of the city included within the territorial boundaries of such authority is authorized to make an estimate of the amount of money necessary for the administrative expenses and overhead of the housing authority during the first year following the incorporation of such housing authority, and to appropriate such amount to the authority out of any moneys in the city treasury not appropriated to some other purposes, and to cause the moneys so appropriated to be paid the authority as a donation, and moneys so appropriated and paid to a housing authority by a city shall be deemed to be a necessary expense of such city. In addition thereto, the city and any municipality located in whole or in part within the boundaries of a housing authority shall have the power annually and from time to time to make donations or advances to the authority of such sums as the city or municipality in its discretion may determine. The authority, when it has money available therefor, shall reimburse the city or municipality for all advances by way of loan made to it. (1935, c. 408, s. 5.)

§ 157-44. Action of city or municipality by resolution.

Except as otherwise provided in this Article or by the Constitution of the State, all action authorized to be taken under this Article by the council or other governing body of any city or of any municipality may be by resolution adopted by a majority of all the members of its council or other governing body, which resolution may be adopted at the meeting of the council or other governing body at which such resolution is introduced and shall take effect immediately upon such adoption, and no such resolution need be published or posted. (1935, c. 408, s. 5.)

§ 157-45. Restrictions on exercise of right of eminent domain; duties of Utilities Commission; investigation of projects.

Notwithstanding any finding of public convenience and necessity, either in general or specific, by the terms of this Article, the right of eminent domain shall not be exercised unless and until a certificate of public convenience and necessity for such project has been issued by the Utilities Commission of North Carolina, and the proceedings leading up to the issuing of such certificate of public convenience and necessity, and the right to appeal therefrom shall be as now provided by law and said rights are hereby expressly reserved to all interested parties in said proceedings. In addition to the powers now granted by law to the Utilities Commission of North Carolina, the said Utilities Commission is hereby vested with full power and authority to investigate and examine all projects set up or attempted to be set up under the provisions of this Article and determine the question of public convenience and necessity for said project. (1935, c. 408, s. 6.)

§ 157-46. Purpose of Article.

It is the purpose and intent of this Article that the State, its subdivisions and agencies, and any county, city or municipality of the State shall be authorized, and are hereby authorized, to do any and all things necessary to aid and cooperate in the planning, construction and operation of housing projects by the United States of America and by housing authorities. (1935, c. 408, s. 7.)

§ 157-47. Supplemental nature of Article.

The powers conferred by this Article shall be in addition and supplemental to the powers conferred by any other law. (1935, c. 408, s. 8.)

Article 3.

Eminent Domain.

§ 157-48. Finding and declaration of necessity.

It is hereby declared that insanitary or unsafe dwelling accommodations exist in various areas of the State and that consequently many persons of low income are forced to reside in such dwelling accommodations; that these conditions cause an increase in and spread of disease and crime and constitute a menace to the health, safety, morals and welfare of the citizens of the State and impair economic values; that the clearance, replanning and reconstruction of the areas in which insanitary or unsafe housing conditions exist and the providing of safe and sanitary dwelling accommodations for persons of low income are public uses and purposes for which private property may be acquired; that it is in the public interest that work on such projects be instituted as soon as possible in order to relieve unemployment which now constitutes an emergency; and the necessity in the public interest for the provision hereinafter enacted, is hereby declared as a matter of legislative determination. (1935, c. 409, s. 1.)

§ 157-49. Housing project.

The term "housing project" whenever used in this Article shall mean any undertaking (i) to demolish, clear, remove, alter or repair unsafe or insanitary housing and/or (ii) to provide dwelling accommodations for persons of low income, and said term may also include such buildings and equipment for recreational or social assemblies for educational, health or welfare purposes, and such necessary utilities as are designed primarily for the benefit and use of the occupants of such dwelling accommodations. (1935, c. 409, s. 2.)

§ 157-50. Eminent domain for housing projects.

Any corporation which is an agency of the United States of America shall have the right to acquire by eminent domain any real property, including improvements and fixtures thereon, which it may deem necessary for a housing project being constructed, operated or aided by it or the United States of America. Any corporation borrowing money or receiving other financial assistance from the United States of America or any agency thereof for the purpose of financing the construction or operation of any housing project or projects, the operation of which will be subject to public supervision or regulation, shall have the right to acquire by eminent domain any real property, including fixtures and improvements thereon, which it may deem necessary for such project. A housing project shall be deemed to be subject to public supervision or regulation within the meaning of this Article if the rents to be charged by it are in any way subject to the supervision, regulation or approval of the United States of America, the State or any of their subdivisions or agencies, or by a housing authority, city, municipality or county, whether such right to supervise, regulate or approve be by virtue of any law, statute, contract or otherwise.

Any such corporate agency of the United States of America or any such corporation, upon the adoption of a resolution declaring that the acquisition of the property described therein is in the public interest and necessary for public use, may exercise the power of eminent domain pursuant to the provisions of Chapter 40A. (1935, c. 409, s. 3; 1981, c. 919, s. 26.)

§ 157-51: Repealed by Session Laws 1983, c. 149.

Article 4.

National Defense Housing Projects.

§ 157-52. Purpose of Article.

It is hereby found and declared that the National Defense Program involves large increases in the military forces and personnel in this State, a great increase in the number of workers in already established manufacturing centers and the bringing of a large number of workers and their families to new centers of defense industries in the State; that there is an acute shortage of safe and sanitary dwellings available to such persons and their families in this State which impedes the National Defense Program; that it is imperative that action be taken immediately to assure the availability of safe and sanitary dwellings for such persons to enable the rapid expansion of national defense activities in this State and to avoid a large labor turnover in defense industries which would seriously hamper their production; that the provisions hereinafter enacted are necessary to assure the availability of safe and sanitary dwellings for persons engaged in national defense activities which otherwise would not be provided at this time, and that such provisions are for the public use and purpose of facilitating the National Defense Program in this State. It is further declared to be the purpose of this Article to authorize housing authorities to do any and all things necessary or desirable to secure the financial aid of the federal government, or to cooperate with or act as agent of the federal government, in the expeditious development and the administration of projects to assure the availability when needed of safe and sanitary dwellings for persons engaged in national defense activities. (1941, c. 63, s. 1.)

§ 157-53. Definitions.

(a) "Administration," as used in this Article, shall mean any and all undertakings necessary for management, operation or maintenance, in connection with any project, and shall include the leasing of any project (in whole or in part) from the federal government.

(b) "Development" as used in this Article, shall mean any and all undertakings necessary for the planning, land acquisition, demolition, financing, construction or equipment in connection with a project (including the negotiation or award of contracts therefor), and shall include the acquisition of any project (in whole or in part) from the federal government.

(c) "Federal government," as used in this Article, shall mean the United States of America or any agency or instrumentality, corporate or otherwise, of the United States of America.

(d) "Housing authority," as used in this Article, shall mean any housing authority established or hereafter established pursuant to Article 1 of this Chapter.

(e) The development of a project shall be deemed to be "initiated," within the meaning of this Article, if a housing authority has issued any bonds, notes or other obligations with respect to financing the development of such project of the authority, or has contracted with the federal government with respect to the exercise of powers hereunder in the development of such project of the federal government for which an allocation of funds has been made prior to the termination of the present war.

(f) "Persons engaged in national defense activities," as used in this Article shall include: enlisted personnel in the Armed Forces of the United States and employees of the Defense Department assigned to duty at reservations, posts or bases of the Armed Forces of the United States; and workers engaged or to be engaged in industries connected with and essential to the National Defense Program; and shall include the families of the aforesaid persons who are living with them.

(g) "Persons of low income," as used in this Article, shall mean persons or families who lack the amount of income which is necessary (as determined by the housing authority undertaking the housing project) to enable them, without financial assistance, to live in decent, safe and sanitary dwellings, without overcrowding.

(h) "State public body," as used in this Article, shall include the State, its subdivisions and agencies, and any county, city, town or incorporated village of the State. (1941, c. 63, s. 8; 1943, c. 90, s. 2; 1995, c. 379, s. 4; 2011-183, s. 108.)

§ 157-54. Rights, powers, etc., of housing authorities relative to national defense projects.

Any housing authority may undertake the development and administration of projects to assure the availability of safe and sanitary dwellings for persons engaged in national defense activities whom the housing authority determines would not otherwise be able to secure safe and sanitary dwellings within the vicinity thereof, but no housing authority shall initiate the development of any such project pursuant to this Article after the termination of the present war.

In the ownership, development or administration of such projects, a housing authority shall have all the rights, powers, privileges and immunities that such authority has under any provision of law relating to the ownership, development or administration of slum clearance and housing projects for persons of low income, in the same manner as though all the provisions of law applicable to slum clearance and housing projects for persons of low income were applicable to projects developed or administered to assure the availability of safe and sanitary dwellings for persons engaged in national defense activities as provided in this Article, and housing projects developed or administered hereunder shall constitute "housing projects" under Article 1 of this Chapter, as that term is used therein: Provided, that during the period (herein called the "national defense period") that a housing authority finds (which finding shall be conclusive in any suit, action or proceeding) that within its authorized area of operation, or any part thereof, there is an acute shortage of safe and sanitary dwellings which impedes the National Defense Program in this State and that the necessary safe and sanitary dwellings would not otherwise be provided when needed for persons engaged in national defense activities, any project developed or administered by such housing authority (or by any housing authority cooperating with it) in such area pursuant to this Article, with the financial aid of the federal government (or as agent for the federal government as hereinafter provided), shall not be subject to the limitations provided in G.S. 157-29; and provided further, that, during the national defense period, a housing authority may make payments in such amounts as it finds necessary or desirable for any services, facilities, works, privileges or improvements furnished for or in connection with any such projects. After the national defense period, any such projects owned and administered by a housing authority shall be administered for the purposes and in accordance with the provisions of Article 1 of this Chapter. (1941, c. 63, s. 2; 1943, c. 90, s. 1.)

§ 157-55. Cooperation with federal government; sale to same.

A housing authority may exercise any or all of its powers for the purpose of cooperating with, or acting as agent for, the federal government in the development or administration of projects by the federal government to assure the availability of safe and sanitary dwellings for persons engaged in national defense activities and may undertake the development or administration of any such project for the federal government. In order to assure the availability of safe and sanitary housing for persons engaged in national defense activities, a housing authority may sell (in whole or in part) to the federal government any housing projects developed for persons of low income but not yet occupied by such persons; such sale shall be at such price and upon such terms as the housing authority shall prescribe and shall include provision for the satisfaction of all debts and liabilities of the authority relating to such project. (1941, c. 63, s. 3.)

§ 157-56. Cooperation of State public bodies in developing projects.

Any State public body shall have the same rights and powers to cooperate with housing authorities, or with the federal government, with respect to the development or administration of projects to assure the availability of safe and sanitary dwellings for persons engaged in national defense activities that such State public body has pursuant to Article 2 of this Chapter, for the purpose of assisting the development or administration of slum clearance or housing projects for persons of low income. (1941, c. 63, s. 4.)

§ 157-57. Obligations issued for projects made legal investments; security for public deposits.

Bonds or other obligations issued by a housing authority for a project developed or administered pursuant to this Article shall be security for public deposits and legal investments to the same extent and for the same persons, institutions, associations, corporations, bodies and officers as bonds or other obligations issued pursuant to Article 1 of this Chapter for the development of a slum clearance or housing project for persons of low income. (1941, c. 63, s. 5.)

§ 157-58. Bonds, notes, etc., issued heretofore, validated.

All bonds, notes, contracts, agreements and obligations of housing authorities heretofore issued or entered into relating to financing or undertaking (including cooperating with or acting as agent of the federal government in) the development or administration of any project to assure the availability of safe and sanitary dwellings for persons engaged in national defense activities, are hereby validated and declared legal in all respects, notwithstanding any defect or irregularity therein or any want of statutory authority. (1941, c. 63, s. 6.)

§ 157-59. Further declaration of powers granted housing authorities.

This Article shall constitute an independent authorization for a housing authority to undertake the development or administration of projects to assure the availability of safe and sanitary dwellings for persons engaged in national defense activities as provided in this Article and for a housing authority to cooperate with, or act as agent for, the federal government in the development or administration of similar projects by the federal government. A housing authority may do any and all things necessary or desirable to cooperate with, or act as agent for, the federal government, or to secure financial aid, in the expeditious development or in the administration of projects to assure the availability of safe and sanitary dwellings for persons engaged in national defense activities and to effectuate the purposes of this Article. (1941, c. 63, s. 7.)

§ 157-60. Powers conferred by Article supplemental.

The powers conferred by this Article shall be in addition and supplemental to the powers conferred by any other law, and nothing contained herein shall be construed as limiting any other powers of a housing authority. (1941, c. 63, s. 9.)

§§ 157-61 through 157-65. Reserved for future codification purposes.

Article 5.

Indian Housing Authority.

§ 157-66. Authority created.

There is hereby created and established a public body corporate and politic to be known as the North Carolina Indian Housing Authority which shall be governed by the provisions of law controlling housing authorities as set out in this Chapter as well as other applicable provisions of the General Statutes. It is the intent of the General Assembly that the North Carolina Indian Housing Authority not be treated as a State agency for any purpose, but rather that it be treated as a housing authority as set out above. (1977, c. 1112, s. 1; 1989 (Reg. Sess., 1990), c. 1066, s. 15(b); 1993, c. 201, s. 1.)

§ 157-67. Powers of Authority; applicability of certain laws; powers of Governor and Commission of Indian Affairs.

The Indian Housing Authority, hereafter referred to as the Authority, shall exercise its powers to provide housing for Indians of low income. Except as otherwise provided in this Article, all the provisions of law applicable to housing authorities created for municipalities pursuant to Chapter 157 of the General Statutes shall be applicable to this Authority, unless a different meaning clearly appears from the context. The Governor and the Commission of Indian Affairs are hereby authorized to exercise all appointing and other powers with respect to this Authority that are vested pursuant to said Chapter 157 in the chief executive officer and governing body of a municipality. (1977, c. 1112, s. 2; 1993, c. 201, s. 1.)

§ 157-68. Commissioners of Authority.

The Authority shall consist of not less than five nor more than 16 commissioners (the number to be set by the North Carolina State Commission of Indian Affairs) who shall be appointed by the Governor, after receiving nominations from the North Carolina State Commission of Indian Affairs. For each vacancy, the Governor must appoint one person from a list of two eligible persons so nominated. Commissioners shall be selected from the major groups of North Carolina Indians that elect members to the North Carolina State Commission of Indian Affairs under G.S. 143B-407. No person shall be barred from serving as a commissioner because he is a tenant or home buyer in an Indian housing project. (1977, c. 1112, s. 3; 1987 (Reg. Sess., 1988), c. 1014; 1998-155, s. 2; 2001-318, s. 2.)

§ 157-69. Area of operation.

The area of operation of the Authority shall include the entire State: Provided, that the Authority shall not undertake any housing project or projects within the area of operation of any city, county or regional housing authority unless a resolution shall have been adopted by such city, county or regional housing authority declaring that there is a need for the Indian Housing Authority to exercise its powers within such city, county or regional housing authority's area of operation. (1977, c. 1112, s. 4; 1993, c. 201, s. 1.)

§ 157-70. Rentals and tenant selection in accordance with § 157-29.

Rentals and tenant selection in connection with projects of the Authority shall be in accordance with G.S. 157-29. (1977, c. 1112, s. 5; 1983 (Reg. Sess., 1984), c. 1068.)

Chapter 157A.

Historic Properties Commissions.

§§ 157A-1 through 157A-13. Transferred to §§ 160A-399.1 to 160A-399.13 by Session Laws 1973, c. 426, s. 62.

Chapter 158.

Local Development.

Article 1.

Local Development Act of 1925.

§ 158-1. Repealed by Session Laws 1973, c. 803, s. 37.

§ 158-2. Repealed by Session Laws 1973, c. 803, s. 38.

§§ 158-3 through 158-7. Repealed by Session Laws 1973, c. 803, ss. 39-43.

§ 158-7.1. Local development.

(a) Each county and city in this State is authorized to make appropriations for the purposes of aiding and encouraging the location of manufacturing enterprises, making industrial surveys and locating industrial and commercial plants in or near such city or in the county; encouraging the building of railroads or other purposes which, in the discretion of the governing body of the city or of the county commissioners of the county, will increase the population, taxable property, agricultural industries and business prospects of any city or county. These appropriations may be funded by the levy of property taxes pursuant to

G.S. 153A-149 and 160A-209 and by the allocation of other revenues whose use is not otherwise restricted by law.

(b)   A county or city may undertake the following specific economic development activities. (This listing is not intended to limit by implication or otherwise the grant of authority set out in subsection (a) of this section). The activities listed in this subsection may be funded by the levy of property taxes pursuant to G.S. 153A-149 and G.S. 160A-209 and by the allocation of other revenues whose use is not otherwise restricted by law.

(1)   A county or city may acquire and develop land for an industrial park, to be used for manufacturing, assembly, fabrication, processing, warehousing, research and development, office use, or similar industrial or commercial purposes. A county may acquire land anywhere in the county, including inside of cities, for an industrial park, while a city may acquire land anywhere in the county or counties in which it is located. A county or city may develop the land by installing utilities, drainage facilities, street and transportation facilities, street lighting, and similar facilities; may demolish or rehabilitate existing structures; and may prepare the site for industrial or commercial uses. A county or city may convey property located in an industrial park pursuant to subsection (d) of this section.

(2)   A county or city may acquire, assemble, and hold for resale property that is suitable for industrial or commercial use. A county may acquire such property anywhere in the county, including inside of cities, while a city may acquire such property inside the city or, if the property will be used by a business that will provide jobs to city residents, anywhere in the county or counties in which it is located. A county or city may convey property acquired or assembled under this subdivision pursuant to subsection (d) of this section.

(3)   A county or city may acquire options for the acquisition of property that is suitable for industrial or commercial use. The county or city may assign such an option, following such procedures, for such consideration, and subject to such terms and conditions as the county or city deems desirable.

(4)   A county or city may acquire, construct, convey, or lease a building suitable for industrial or commercial use.

(5)   A county or city may construct, extend or own utility facilities or may provide for or assist in the extension of utility services to be furnished to an industrial facility, whether the utility is publicly or privately owned.

(6) A county or city may extend or may provide for or assist in the extension of water and sewer lines to industrial properties or facilities, whether the industrial property or facility is publicly or privately owned.

(7) A county or city may engage in site preparation for industrial properties or facilities, whether the industrial property or facility is publicly or privately owned.

(c) Any appropriation or expenditure pursuant to subsection (b) of this section must be approved by the county or city governing body after a public hearing. The county or city shall publish notice of the public hearing at least 10 days before the hearing is held. If the appropriation or expenditure is for the acquisition of an interest in real property, the notice shall describe the interest to be acquired, the proposed acquisition cost of such interest, the governing body's intention to approve the acquisition, the source of funding for the acquisition and such other information needed to reasonably describe the acquisition. If the appropriation or expenditure is for the improvement of privately owned property by site preparation or by the extension of water and sewer lines to the property, the notice shall describe the improvements to be made, the proposed cost of making the improvements, the source of funding for the improvements, the public benefit to be derived from making the improvements, and any other information needed to reasonably describe the improvements and their purpose.

(d) A county or city may lease or convey interests in real property held or acquired pursuant to subsection (b) of this section in accordance with the procedures of this subsection. A county or city may convey or lease interests in property by private negotiation and may subject the property to such covenants, conditions, and restrictions as the county or city deems to be in the public interest or necessary to carry out the purposes of this section. Any such conveyance or lease must be approved by the county or city governing body, after a public hearing. The county or city shall publish notice of the public hearing at least 10 days before the hearing is held; the notice shall describe the interest to be conveyed or leased, the value of the interest, the proposed consideration for the conveyance or lease, and the governing body's intention to approve the conveyance or lease. Before such an interest may be conveyed, the county or city governing body shall determine the probable average hourly wage to be paid to workers by the business to be located at the property to be conveyed and the fair market value of the interest, subject to whatever covenants, conditions, and restrictions the county or city proposes to subject it to. The consideration for the conveyance may not be less than the value so determined.

(d1) Repealed by Session Laws 1993, c. 497, s. 22.

(d2) In arriving at the amount of consideration that it receives, the Board may take into account prospective tax revenues from improvements to be constructed on the property, prospective sales tax revenues to be generated in the area, as well as any other prospective tax revenues or income coming to the county or city over the next 10 years as a result of the conveyance or lease provided the following conditions are met:

(1) The governing board of the county or city shall determine that the conveyance of the property will stimulate the local economy, promote business, and result in the creation of a substantial number of jobs in the county or city that pay at or above the median average wage in the county or, for a city, in the county where the city is located. A city that spans more than one county is considered to be located in the county where the greatest population of the city resides. For the purpose of this subdivision, the median average wage in a county is the median average wage for all insured industries in the county as computed by the Department of Commerce, Division of Employment Security, for the most recent period for which data is available.

(2) The governing board of the county or city shall contractually bind the purchaser of the property to construct, within a specified period of time not to exceed five years, improvements on the property that will generate the tax revenue taken into account in arriving at the consideration. Upon failure to construct the improvements specified in the contract, the purchaser shall reconvey the property back to the county or city.

(e) All appropriations and expenditures pursuant to subsections (b) and (c) of this section shall be subject to the provisions of the Local Government Budget and Fiscal Control Acts of the North Carolina General Statutes, respectively, for cities and counties and shall be listed in the annual financial report the county or city submits to the Local Government Commission. The budget format for each such governing body shall make such disclosures in such detail as the Local Government Commission may by rule and regulation direct.

(f) At the end of each fiscal year, the total of the following for each county and city may not exceed one-half of one percent (0.5%) of the outstanding assessed property tax valuation for the county or city as of January 1 preceding the beginning of the fiscal year:

(1) The investment in property acquired at any time under subdivisions (b)(1) through (b)(4) of this section and owned at the end of the fiscal year.

(2) The amount expended during the fiscal year under subdivisions (b)(5) and (b)(7) of this section.

(3) The amount of tax revenue that was taken into account under subsection (d2) of this section and was expected to be received during the fiscal year.

The Local Government Commission shall review the annual financial reports filed by counties and cities to determine if any county or city has exceeded the limit set by this subsection. If the Commission finds that a county or city has exceeded this limit, it shall notify the county or city. A county or city that receives a notice from the Commission under this subsection must submit to the Commission for its review and approval any appropriation or expenditure the county or city proposes to make under this section during the next three fiscal years. The Commission shall not approve an appropriation or expenditure that would cause a county or city to exceed the limit set by this subsection.

(g) Repealed by Session Laws 1989, c. 374, s. 1.

(h) Each economic development agreement entered into between a private enterprise and a city or county shall clearly state their respective responsibilities under the agreement. Each agreement shall contain provisions regarding remedies for a breach of those responsibilities on the part of the private enterprise. These provisions shall include a provision requiring the recapture of sums appropriated or expended by the city or county upon the occurrence of events specified in the agreement. Events that would require the city or county to recapture funds would include the creation of fewer jobs than specified in the agreement, a lower capital investment than specified in the agreement, and failing to maintain operations at a specified level for a period of time specified in the agreement. (1973, c. 803, s. 37; 1985, c. 639, s. 1; 1985 (Reg. Sess., 1986), c. 846, s. 1; c. 848, s. 1; c. 858, s. 1; c. 911, s. 1; c. 921, s. 1; 1987, c. 577, s. 1.1; 1989, c. 374, s. 1; 1991, c. 598, s. 6; c. 659, ss. 1, 2; 1991 (Reg. Sess., 1992), c. 793, s. 1; c. 799, s. 1; c. 938, s. 1; 1993, c. 31, s. 1; c. 42, s. 1; c. 246, ss. 1(a), 1(b); c. 275, s. 2; c. 358, s. 13; c. 497, ss. 22, 24; c. 536, ss. 1, 4; 2007-515, ss. 1, 7; 2011-401, s. 3.24.)

§ 158-7.2. Accounting for expenditures.

In the event funds appropriated for the purposes of this Article are turned over to any agency or organization other than the county or city for expenditure, no such expenditure shall be made until the county or city has approved the same, and all such expenditures shall be accounted for by the agency or organization at the end of the fiscal year for which they were appropriated. (1973, c. 803, s. 38.)

§ 158-7.3. Development financing.

(a) Definitions. - The following definitions apply in this section:

(1) Development project. - A capital project that includes capital expenditures by both private persons and one or more units of local government and that increases net employment opportunities for residents of the development district or within a two-mile radius of the project, whichever is larger, and increases the local government tax base.

If the district in which such a project will occur is outside a city's central business district (as that district is defined by resolution of the city council, which definition is binding and conclusive), then, of the private development forecast for a development project by the development financing plan for the district in which the project will occur, a maximum of twenty percent (20%) of the plan's estimated square footage of floor space may be proposed for use in retail sales, hotels, banking, and financial services offered directly to consumers, and other commercial uses other than office space. The twenty percent (20%) limitation in the preceding sentence does not apply to development financing districts located in a development tier one area, as defined in G.S. 143B-437.08 and created primarily for tourism-related economic development, such as developments featuring facilities for exhibitions, athletic and cultural events, show and public gatherings, racing facilities, parks and recreation facilities, art galleries, museums, and art centers.

(2) Publish. - Insertion in a newspaper qualified under G.S. 1-597 to publish legal advertisements in the county or counties in which the unit is located.

(3) Unit or unit of local government. - A county, city, town, or incorporated village.

(b) Authorization. - A unit of local government may finance public improvements that are part of a development project with the proceeds of project development financing debt instruments, issued pursuant to Article 6 of Chapter 159 of the General Statutes, together with any other revenues that are available to the unit. Before it receives the approval of the Local Government Commission for issuance of project development financing debt instruments, the unit's governing body must define a development financing district and adopt a development financing plan for the district. The county may act jointly with a city to finance a project, define a development financing district that is within the city, and adopt a development financing plan for the district.

(c) Development Financing District. - A development financing district created pursuant to this section must be comprised of property that is one or more of the following:

(1) Blighted, deteriorated, deteriorating, undeveloped, or inappropriately developed from the standpoint of sound community development and growth.

(2) Appropriate for rehabilitation or conservation activities.

(3) Appropriate for the economic development of the community.

The total land area within development financing districts in a unit, including development financing districts created pursuant to G.S. 160A-515.1, may not exceed five percent (5%) of the total land area of the unit. For the purposes of this section, land in a district created by a county that subsequently becomes part of a city, town, or incorporated village does not count against the five-percent (5%) limit for the city, town, or incorporated village unless the city, town, or incorporated village and the county have entered into an agreement pursuant to G.S. 159-107(e). A county may not include in a district created pursuant to this section any land that, at the time the district is created, is inside a city, town, or incorporated village.

(d) Development Financing Plan. - The development financing plan must include all of the following:

(1) A description of the boundaries of the development financing district.

(2) A description of the proposed development of the district, both public and private.

(3) The costs of the proposed public activities.

(4) The sources and amounts of funds to pay for the proposed public activities.

(5) The base valuation of the development financing district.

(6) The projected incremental valuation of the development financing district.

(7) The estimated duration of the development financing district.

(8) A description of how the proposed development of the district, both public and private, will benefit the residents and business owners of the district in terms of jobs, affordable housing, or services.

(9) A description of the appropriate ameliorative activities which will be undertaken if the proposed projects have a negative impact on residents or business owners of the district in terms of jobs, affordable housing, services, or displacement.

(10) A requirement that the initial users of any new manufacturing facilities that will be located in the district and that are included in the plan will comply with the wage requirements referred to in subsection (e) of this section.

(e) Wage Requirements. - A development financing plan shall include a requirement that the initial users of a new manufacturing facility to be located in the district and included in the plan must pay its employees an average weekly manufacturing wage that is either above the average manufacturing wage paid in the county in which the district will be located or not less than ten percent (10%) above the average weekly manufacturing wage paid in the State. The plan may include information on the wages to be paid by the initial users of a new manufacturing facility to its employees and any provisions necessary to implement the wage requirement. The issuing unit's governing body shall not adopt a plan until the Secretary of Commerce certifies that the Secretary has reviewed the average weekly manufacturing wage required by the plan to be paid to the employees of a new manufacturing facility and has found either (i) that the wages proposed by the initial users of a new manufacturing facility are in compliance with the amount required by this subsection or (ii) that the plan is exempt from the requirement of this subsection. The Secretary of Commerce may exempt a plan from the requirement of this subsection if the Secretary receives a resolution from the issuing unit's governing body requesting an exemption from the wage requirement and a letter from an appropriate State official, selected by the Secretary, finding that unemployment in the county in which the proposed district is to be located is especially severe. Upon the creation of the district, the unit of local government proposing the creation of the district shall take any lawful actions necessary to require compliance with the applicable wage requirement by the initial users of any new manufacturing facility included in the plan; however, failure to take such actions or obtain such compliance shall not affect the validity of any proceedings for the creation of the district, the existence of the district, or the validity of any debt instruments issued under Article 6 of Chapter 159 of the General Statutes. All findings and determinations made by the Secretary of Commerce under this subsection shall be binding and conclusive. For purposes of this section, the term "manufacturing facility" means any facility that is used in the manufacturing or production of tangible personal property, including the processing resulting in a change in the condition of the property.

(f) County Review. - If the unit creating a development financing district and adopting a development financing plan is a city, town, or incorporated village, before adopting the plan the unit's governing body shall send notice of the plan, by first-class mail, to the board of county commissioners of the county or counties in which the development financing district is located. The person mailing the notice shall certify that fact, and the date thereof, to the governing body, and the certificate is conclusive in the absence of fraud. Unless the board of county commissioners (or either board, if the district is in two counties) by resolution disapproves the proposed plan within 28 days after the date the notice is mailed, the governing body may proceed to adopt the plan.

(g) Environmental Review. - Before adopting a plan for development financing districts, the issuing unit's governing body shall submit the plan to the Secretary of Environment and Natural Resources to review to determine if the construction and operation of any new manufacturing facility in the district will have a materially adverse effect on the environment and whether the company that will operate the facility has operated in substantial compliance with federal and State laws, regulations, and rules for the protection of the environment. If the Secretary finds that the new manufacturing facility will not have a materially adverse effect on the environment and that the company that will operate the facility has operated other facilities in compliance with environmental requirements, the Secretary shall approve the plan. In making the determination on environmental impact, the Secretary shall use the same criteria that apply to the determination under G.S. 159C-7 of whether an industrial project will have a materially adverse effect on the environment. The findings of the Secretary are conclusive and binding.

(h) Plan Adoption. - Before adopting a plan for a development financing district, the issuing unit's governing body shall hold a public hearing on the plan. The governing body shall, no more than 30 days and no less than 14 days before the day of the hearing, cause notice of the hearing to be published once and shall cause notice of the hearing to be mailed, by first-class mail, to all property owners and mailing addresses of the development financing district and to the governing body of any special district, as defined by G.S. 159-7, within which the development financing district is located. The notice shall state the time and place of the hearing, shall specify its purpose, and shall state that a copy of the proposed plan is available for public inspection in the office of the unit's clerk. At the public hearing, the governing body shall hear anyone who wishes to speak with respect to the proposed district and proposed plan. Unless a board of county commissioners or the Secretary of Environment and Natural Resources has disapproved the plan pursuant to subsection (f) or (g) of this section, the governing body may adopt the plan, with or without amendment, at any time after the public hearing. However, the plan and the district do not become effective until the unit's application to issue project development financing debt instruments has been approved by the Local Government Commission, pursuant to Article 6 of Chapter 159 of the General Statutes.

(i) Plan Modification. - Subject to the limitations of this subsection, a governing body may, after the effective date of the district, amend a development financing plan adopted for a development financing district. Before making any amendment, the governing body shall follow the procedures and meet the requirements of subsections (e) through (h) of this section. The boundaries of the district may be enlarged only during the first five years after the effective date of the district and only if the area to be added has been or is about to be developed and the development is primarily attributable to development that has occurred within the district, as certified by the Local Government Commission. The boundaries of the district may be reduced at any time, but the unit may agree with the holders of any project development financing debt instruments to restrict its power to reduce district boundaries.

(j) Plan Implementation. - In implementing a development financing plan, a unit may act directly, through one or more contracts with other public agencies, through one or more contracts with private agencies, or by any combination thereof. A private agency that enters into a contract with a unit for the implementation of a development financing plan is subject to the provisions of

Article 8 of Chapter 143 of the General Statutes only to the extent specified in the contract. (2003-403, s. 19; 2005-238, s. 1; 2005-407, s. 1; 2006-211, s. 3; 2006-252, s. 2.10.)

§ 158-7.4. Interlocal agreements concerning economic development.

(a) Any two or more units of local government may enter into contracts or agreements to execute undertakings pursuant to Part 1 of Article 20 of Chapter 160A of the General Statutes, under which each participating local government agrees to provide resources for the development of an industrial or commercial park or industrial or commercial site pursuant to G.S. 158-7.1. In consideration for that participation, the unit or units in which the park or site is located may agree to place the proceeds from some or all property taxes levied on the park or site into a common fund or transfer those proceeds to a nonprofit corporation or other entity. The proceeds placed into the common fund or transferred to the other entity may then be distributed among the participating local governments as provided in the contract or agreement.

(b) Any undertaking entered into pursuant to this section may be for that period that is agreed to by the participating local governments, up to a maximum of 99 years.

(c) Any undertaking entered into pursuant to this section is binding upon each participating local government for the duration of the contract or agreement. Any participating local government may bring an action to specifically enforce the contract or agreement. (2003-417, s. 2; 2005-72, s. 1.)

Article 2.

Economic Development Commissions.

§ 158-8. Creation of municipal, county or regional commissions authorized; composition; joining or withdrawing from regional commissions.

The governing body of any municipality or the board of county commissioners of any county may by resolution create an economic development commission for said municipality or county. The governing bodies of any two or more municipalities and/or counties may by joint resolution, adopted by separate vote of each governing body concerned, create a regional economic development commission. A municipal or county economic development commission shall consist of from three to nine members, named for terms and compensation (if any) fixed by its respective governing body. The membership, compensation (if any), and terms of a regional economic development commission, and the formula for its financial support, shall be fixed by the joint resolution creating the commission. Additional governmental units may join a regional commission with the consent of all existing members. Any governmental unit may withdraw from a regional commission on two years' notice to the other members. The resolution creating a municipal, county, or regional economic development commission may be modified, amended, or repealed in the same manner as it was originally adopted. (1961, c. 722, s. 2; 2013-360, s. 15.28(a); 2013-363, s. 5.7(a).)

§ 158-8.1. (Repealed effective June 30, 2014) Creation of Western North Carolina Regional Economic Development Commission.

(a) There is created the Western North Carolina Regional Economic Development Commission to serve Buncombe, Cherokee, Clay, Graham, Haywood, Henderson, Jackson, McDowell, Macon, Madison, Polk, Rutherford, Swain, Transylvania, and Yancey Counties, and any other county assigned to the Commission by the Department of Commerce as authorized by law. The Commission shall be located administratively in the Department of Commerce but shall exercise its statutory powers and duties independently of the Department of Commerce. Funds appropriated for the Commission by the General Assembly shall be disbursed directly to the Commission at the beginning of each fiscal year.

(b) The Commission shall consist of 19 members appointed as follows:

(1) Three members shall be appointed by the Governor;

(2) Two members shall be appointed by the Lieutenant Governor;

(3) Seven members shall be appointed by the General Assembly upon the recommendation of the Speaker of the House of Representatives in accordance with G.S. 120-121; and

(4) Seven members shall be appointed by the General Assembly upon the recommendation of the President Pro Tempore of the Senate in accordance with G.S. 120-121.

(b1) The members of the State Board of Education appointed to represent the seventh and eighth education districts shall serve as nonvoting ex officio members of the Commission.

(c) The appointing authority shall designate two of the initial appointees pursuant to subdivision (b)(1), one of the initial appointees pursuant to subdivision (b)(2), two of the initial appointees pursuant to subdivision (b)(3), and two of the initial appointees pursuant to subdivision (b)(4) to serve for terms ending June 30, 1995; the remainder of the initial appointees shall serve for terms ending June 30, 1997. Their successors shall serve for four-year terms ending on June 30 quadrennially thereafter. The appointing authority shall designate the additional appointees under subsections (b3) and (b4) that were added to the Commission membership pursuant to an act of the 1995 General Assembly to serve for terms ending June 30, 1999.

Any appointment to fill a vacancy on the Commission shall be for the balance of the unexpired term. Vacancies in appointments made by the General Assembly shall be in accordance with G.S. 120-122.

(c1) The initial meeting shall be called by the Secretary of the Department of Commerce.

(d) Members of the Commission who are State employees shall receive travel expenses as provided in G.S. 138-6. Other Commission members shall receive per diem of one hundred dollars ($100.00) a day for each day of service when the Commission meets and shall be reimbursed for travel and subsistence as provided in G.S. 138-5. The Commission may adopt policies authorizing additional per diem of one hundred dollars ($100.00) a day for non-State employee members' additional days of service including Commission subcommittee meetings or other Commission activities, plus reimbursement for related travel and subsistence as provided in G.S. 138-5.

(e) In addition to the powers and duties granted to economic development commissions in this Article, the Western North Carolina Regional Economic Development Commission shall:

(1) Survey Western North Carolina and determine the assets, liabilities, and resources that the region contributes to the economic development process.

(2) Develop and evaluate alternatives for Western North Carolina economic development.

(3) Develop a preferred economic development plan for the region and establish strategies for implementing the plan.

(4) Coordinate activities with and enter into contracts with any nonprofit corporation created to assist the Commission in carrying out its powers and duties.

(5) Repealed by Session Laws 1999-237, s. 16.5(a), effective July 1, 1999. (1993, c. 321, s. 309(a); c. 561, s. 17(a); 1993 (Reg. Sess., 1994), c. 769, ss. 28.7(j), 28.8(a), 28.8(b); 1995, c. 488, s. 49(a), (b); c. 507, s. 25.5(a); c. 509, ss. 103-105; 1999-237, s. 16.5(a); 2010-184, s. 1; 2013-360, s. 15.28(a); 2013-363, s. 5.7(a).)

§ 158-8.2. (Repealed effective June 30, 2014) Creation of North Carolina's Northeast Commission.

(a) There is created the North Carolina's Northeast Commission to facilitate economic development in Beaufort, Bertie, Camden, Chowan, Currituck, Dare, Gates, Halifax, Hertford, Hyde, Martin, Northampton, Pasquotank, Perquimans, Tyrrell, and Washington Counties, and any other county assigned to the Commission by the Department of Commerce as authorized by law. The Commission shall be located administratively in the Department of Commerce but shall exercise its statutory powers and duties independently of the Department of Commerce. Funds appropriated for the Commission by the General Assembly shall be disbursed directly to the Commission at the beginning of each fiscal year.

(b) The Commission shall consist of 18 appointed members and one ex officio member, as provided below. Each appointed member shall be an experienced business person who resides for most of the year in one or more of the counties that are members of the Commission.

(1) Six members shall be appointed by the Governor.

(2) Six members shall be appointed by the General Assembly upon the recommendation of the President Pro Tempore of the Senate in accordance with G.S. 120-121.

(3) Six members shall be appointed by the General Assembly upon the recommendation of the Speaker of the House of Representatives in accordance with G.S. 120-121.

(4) The Secretary of Commerce, or a designee.

(5) Repealed by Session Laws 1999-237, s. 16.6(a).

Any person appointed to the Commission who is also a county commissioner may hold that office in addition to the offices permitted by G.S. 128-1.1. The appointing authorities are encouraged to discuss and coordinate their appointments in an effort to ensure as many counties served by the Commission are represented among the membership of the Commission.

(b1) The member of the State Board of Education appointed to represent the first education district shall serve as a nonvoting ex officio member of the Commission.

(c) All members shall serve staggered two-year terms ending on June 30 biennially.

(d) Any appointment to fill a vacancy on the Commission shall be for the balance of the unexpired term. Vacancies in appointments made by the General Assembly shall be in accordance with G.S. 120-122.

(d1) The initial meeting shall be called by the Secretary of the Department of Commerce. The Commission shall meet no less than quarterly.

(e) The Commission shall elect annually from among its membership a four-member executive committee consisting of a chair, a vice-chair, a secretary, and a treasurer. Members shall serve one-year terms on the executive committee. The executive committee shall meet no less than quarterly.

(f) In addition to the powers and duties granted to economic development commissions in this Article, the North Carolina's Northeast Commission shall:

(1) Adopt and implement an economic development program, with the assistance of the economic development advisory board, as follows:

a. Survey northeastern North Carolina and determine the assets, liabilities, and resources that the region contributes to the economic development process;

b. Enhance economic development activities that use the area's natural resources;

c. Develop and evaluate alternatives for northeastern North Carolina economic development;

d. Develop a preferred economic development plan for the region and establish strategies for implementing the plan;

e. Conduct feasibility studies to determine the nature and placement of economic developments for maximum economic impact;

f. Identify potential sites for economic development; and

g. Carry out other activities to develop and promote economic development.

(2) Repealed by Session Laws 1999-237, s. 16.6(a).

(3) Coordinate activities with and enter into contracts with any nonprofit corporation created to assist the Commission in carrying out its powers and duties.

(4) Repealed by Session Laws 1999-237, s. 16.5(b).

(g) Within the limits of funds available, the Commission may hire and fix the compensation of any personnel necessary to its operations, contract with consultants for any services as it may require, and contract with the State of North Carolina or the federal government, or any agency or department thereof, for any services as may be provided by those agencies. The Commission shall hire an employee to serve as president and chief executive officer. The Commission may carry out the provisions of any contracts it may enter.

Within the limits of funds available, the Commission may lease, rent, purchase, or otherwise obtain suitable quarters and office space for its staff, and may lease, rent, or purchase necessary furniture, fixtures, and other equipment.

(h) Members of the Commission who are State employees shall receive travel expenses as provided in G.S. 138-6. Other Commission members shall receive per diem of one hundred dollars ($100.00) a day for each day of service when the Commission meets and shall be reimbursed for travel and subsistence as provided in G.S. 138-5. (1993, c. 321, s. 309.1(a); c. 561, s. 17(b); 1993 (Reg. Sess., 1994), c. 769, ss. 28.7(k), 28.7(l), 28.8(c), 28.8(d), 28.9; 1995, c. 509, ss. 106-109; 1997-443, s. 11A.119(a); 1997-495, s. 87(a); 1999-237, ss. 16.5(b), 16.6(a); 2007-93, s. 3; 2010-184, s. 2; 2013-360, s. 15.28(a); 2013-363, s. 5.7(a).)

§ 158-8.3. (Repealed effective June 30, 2014) Creation of Southeastern North Carolina Regional Economic Development Commission.

(a) There is created the Southeastern North Carolina Regional Economic Development Commission to serve Anson, Bladen, Brunswick, Columbus, Cumberland, Hoke, Montgomery, New Hanover, Pender, Richmond, Robeson, Sampson, and Scotland Counties, and any other county assigned to the Commission by the Department of Commerce as authorized by law. The Commission shall be located administratively in the Department of Commerce but shall exercise its statutory powers and duties independently of the Department of Commerce. Funds appropriated for the Commission by the General Assembly shall be disbursed directly to the Commission at the beginning of each fiscal year.

(b) The Commission shall consist of 15 members appointed as follows:

(1) Three members shall be appointed by the Governor;

(2) Two members shall be appointed by the Lieutenant Governor;

(3) Five members shall be appointed by the General Assembly upon the recommendation of the Speaker of the House of Representatives in accordance with G.S. 120-121; and

(4) Five members shall be appointed by the General Assembly upon the recommendation of the President Pro Tempore of the Senate in accordance with G.S. 120-121.

(b1) The member of the State Board of Education appointed to represent the fourth education district shall serve as a nonvoting ex officio member of the Commission.

(c) The appointing authority shall designate two of the initial appointees pursuant to subdivision (b)(1) of this section, one of the initial appointees pursuant to subdivision (b)(2) of this section, two of the initial appointees pursuant to subdivision (b)(3) of this section, and two of the initial appointees pursuant to subdivision (b)(4) of this section to serve for terms ending June 30, 1995; the remainder of the initial appointees shall serve for terms ending June 30, 1997. Their successors shall serve for four-year terms ending on June 30 quadrennially thereafter.

Any appointment to fill a vacancy on the Commission shall be for the balance of the unexpired term. Vacancies in appointments made by the General Assembly shall be filled in accordance with G.S. 120-122.

(c1) The initial meeting shall be called by the Secretary of the Department of Commerce.

(d) Members of the Commission who are State employees shall receive travel expenses as provided in G.S. 138-6. Other Commission members shall receive per diem of one hundred dollars ($100.00) a day for each day of service when the Commission meets and shall be reimbursed for travel and subsistence as provided in G.S. 138-5. The Commission may adopt policies authorizing additional per diem of one hundred dollars ($100.00) a day for non-State employee members' additional days of service including Commission subcommittee meetings or other Commission activities, plus reimbursement for related travel and subsistence as provided in G.S. 138-5.

(e) In addition to the powers and duties granted to economic development commissions in this Article, the Southeastern North Carolina Regional Economic Development Commission shall:

(1) Survey southeastern North Carolina and determine the assets, liabilities, and resources that the region contributes to the economic development process;

(2) Develop and evaluate alternatives for southeastern North Carolina economic development;

(3) Develop a preferred economic development plan for the region and establish strategies for implementing the plan; and

(4) Coordinate activities with and enter into contracts with any nonprofit corporation created to assist the Commission in carrying out its powers and duties.

(5) Repealed by Session Laws 1999-237, s. 16.5(c), effective July 1, 1999.

(f) Within the limits of funds available, the Commission may hire and fix the compensation of any personnel necessary to its operations, contract with consultants for any services as it may require, and contract with the State of North Carolina or the federal government, or any agency or department thereof, for any services as may be provided by those agencies. With the approval of any unit of local government, the Commission may contract to use officers, employees, agents, and facilities of the unit of local government. The Commission may carry out the provisions of any contracts it may enter.

Within the limits of funds available, the Commission may lease, rent, purchase, or otherwise obtain suitable quarters and office space for its staff, and may lease, rent, or purchase necessary furniture, fixtures, and other equipment. (1993, c. 321, s. 309.2(a); c. 561, s. 17(c); 1993 (Reg. Sess., 1994), c. 769, ss. 28.7(m), 28.8(e), 28.8(f); 1995, c. 509, ss. 110, 111; 1997-155, s. 1; 1999-237, s. 16.5(c); 2010-184, s. 3; 2013-360, ss. 15.28(a), 15.28B; 2013-363, s. 5.7(a).)

§ 158-8.4. (Repealed effective June 30, 2014) Removal of commission members.

A commission created under G.S. 158-8.1, 158-8.2, or 158-8.3 may, by majority vote, remove a member of the commission if that member does not attend at least eighty percent (80%) of the regularly scheduled meetings of the commission during any full year of service of that member on the board, except that absences excused by the commission due to serious medical or family circumstances shall not be considered. If the commission votes to remove a member under this section, the vacancy will be filled in the same manner as the original appointment. (1997-495, s. 86; 2013-360, s. 15.28(a); 2013-363, s. 5.7(a).)

§ 158-8.4A. (Repealed effective June 30, 2014) State Board of Education members as ex officio commission members.

As a condition on the receipt of State funds, the member of the State Board of Education appointed to represent the designated education district shall serve as a member of the following Commissions:

(1) Charlotte Regional Partnership, Inc. - The State Board of Education member appointed to represent the sixth education district shall serve as a nonvoting ex officio member of the Commission.

(2) Piedmont Triad Regional Partnership. - The State Board of Education member appointed to represent the fifth education district shall serve as a nonvoting ex officio member of the Commission.

(3) Research Triangle Regional Partnership. - The State Board of Education member appointed to represent the third education district shall serve as a nonvoting ex officio member of the Commission. (2010-184, s. 4; 2013-360, s. 15.28(a); 2013-363, s. 5.7(a).)

§ 158-8.5. (Repealed effective June 30, 2014) Annual reporting requirement.

By February 15 of each year, the commissions created pursuant to G.S. 158-8.1, 158-8.2, 158-8.3, and 158-33 shall publish a report containing the information required by this section. As a condition on the receipt of State funds, the Charlotte Regional Partnership, Inc., the Piedmont Triad Regional Partnership, and the Research Triangle Regional Partnership shall, by February 15 of each year, publish a report containing the information required by this section. The commissions and partnerships shall also submit a copy of the report to the Department of Commerce, the Office of State Budget and Management, the Joint Legislative Commission on Governmental Operations, the Joint Legislative Economic Development Oversight Committee, and the Fiscal Research Division of the General Assembly. The report shall include all of the following:

(1) A summary of the preceding year's program activities, objectives, and accomplishments.

(2) The preceding fiscal year's itemized expenditures and fund sources. Itemized expenditures shall be reported separately for each fund source.

(3) A demonstration of how the commission's or partnership's regional economic development and marketing strategy aligns with the State's overall economic development and marketing strategies.

(4) A demonstration of how the commission's or partnership's involvement in promotion activities has generated leads.

(5) The most recent audited annual financial statement regarding State funds.

(6) A demonstration of the commission's efforts to obtain funds from local, private, and federal sources. (2006-263, s. 1; 2007-323, s. 13.7(g); 2013-360, s. 15.28(a); 2013-363, s. 5.7(a).)

§ 158-8.6. (Repealed effective June 30, 2014) Uniform standards.

The Department of Commerce, in consultation with the commissions created pursuant to G.S. 158-8.1, 158-8.2, 158-8.3, and 158-33, the Charlotte Regional Partnership, Inc., the Piedmont Triad Partnership, and the Research Triangle Regional Partnership, shall develop uniform standards for the use of State funds related to accounting procedures, personnel practices, and purchasing and contracts procedures. The commissions created pursuant to G.S. 158-8.1, 158-8.2, 158-8.3, and 158-33 shall follow these standards. As a condition on the receipt of State funds, the Charlotte Regional Partnership, Inc., the Piedmont Triad Partnership, and the Research Triangle Regional Partnership shall follow these standards. (2006-263, s. 1; 2013-360, s. 15.28(a); 2013-363, s. 5.7(a).)

§ 158-8.7. (Repealed effective June 30, 2014) Use of State funds.

The commissions created pursuant to G.S. 158-8.1, 158-8.2, 158-8.3, and 158-33, the Charlotte Regional Partnership, Inc., the Piedmont Triad Partnership, and the Research Triangle Regional Partnership, are subject to all of the provisions of G.S. 143-6.2. (2006-263, s. 1; 2013-360, s. 15.28(a); 2013-363, s. 5.7(a).)

§ 158-8.8. (Repealed effective June 30, 2014) Orientation for board members.

The commissions created pursuant to G.S. 158-8.1, 158-8.2, 158-8.3, and 158-33 shall hold an orientation session for all newly appointed commission members. The orientation shall provide information on the duties and responsibilities of commission members and shall include information on the commission's policies and State law regarding conflicts of interest, financial disclosure, and ethical behavior. At least once a year, each of these commissions shall distribute to all commission members information on the commission's policies and State law regarding conflicts of interest, financial disclosure, and ethical behavior. (2006-263, s. 1; 2013-360, s. 15.28(a); 2013-363, s. 5.7(a).)

§ 158-9. Organization of commission; rules and regulations; committees; meetings.

Upon its appointment, the economic development commission shall promptly meet and elect from among its members a chairman and such other officers as it may choose, for such terms as it shall prescribe in its rules and regulations. The commission shall adopt such rules and regulations not inconsistent herewith as it may deem necessary for the proper discharge of its duties. The chairman may appoint such committees as the work of the commission may require. The commission shall meet regularly, at least once every three months, at places and dates specified in the rules. Special meetings may be called as specified in the rules. (1961, c. 722, s. 2.)

§ 158-10. Staff and personnel; contracts for services.

Within the limits of appropriated funds, the commission may hire and fix the compensation of any personnel necessary to its operations, contract with consultants for such services as it may require, and contract with the State of North Carolina or the federal government, or any agency or department thereof, for such services as may be provided by such agencies; and it is hereby empowered to carry out the provisions of such contracts as it may enter. (1961, c. 722, s. 2.)

§ 158-11. Office and equipment.

Within the limits of appropriated funds, the commission may lease, rent, or purchase, or otherwise obtain suitable quarters and office space for its staff, and may lease, rent, or purchase necessary furniture, fixtures, and other equipment. (1961, c. 722, s. 2.)

§ 158-12. Fiscal affairs generally; appropriations.

The commission may accept, receive, and disburse in furtherance of its functions any funds, grants, and services made available by the federal government and its agencies, the State government and its agencies, any municipalities or counties, and by private and civic sources.

Each municipality or county shall have authority to appropriate funds to any local or regional economic development commission which it may have created. These appropriations may be funded by levy of property taxes pursuant to G.S. 153A-149 and G.S. 160A-209 and by the allocation of other revenues whose use is not otherwise restricted by law. (1961, c. 722, s. 2; 1973, c. 803, s. 44; c. 1446, s. 26.)

§ 158-12.1. (Repealed effective June 30, 2014) Commission funds secured.

The Western North Carolina Regional Economic Development Commission, Research Triangle Regional Partnership, Southeastern North Carolina Regional Economic Development Commission, Piedmont Triad Partnership, North

Carolina's Northeast Commission, North Carolina's Eastern Region Development Commission, and Carolinas Partnership, Inc., may deposit money at interest in any bank, savings and loan association, or trust company in this State in the form of savings accounts, certificates of deposit, or such other forms of time deposits as may be approved for county governments. Investment deposits and money deposited in an official depository or deposited at interest shall be secured in the manner prescribed in G.S. 159-31(b). When deposits are secured in accordance with this section, no public officer or employee may be held liable for any losses sustained by an institution because of the default or insolvency of the depository. This section applies to the regional economic development commissions listed in this section only for as long as the commissions are receiving State funds. (2000-67, s. 14.9; 2005-364, s. 3; 2007-93, s. 4; 2008-134, s. 77; 2013-360, s. 15.28(a); 2013-363, s. 5.7(a).)

§ 158-13. Powers and duties.

Any economic development commission created pursuant to this Article shall:

(1)   Receive from any municipal, county, joint, or regional planning board or commission with jurisdiction within its area an economic development program for part or all of the area;

(2)   Formulate projects for carrying out such economic development program, through attraction of new industries, encouragement of existing industries, encouragement of agricultural development, encouragement of new business and industrial ventures by local as well as foreign capital, and other activities of a similar nature;

(3)   Conduct industrial surveys as needed, advertise in periodicals or other communications media, furnish advice and assistance to business and industrial prospects which may locate in its area, furnish advice and assistance to existing businesses and industries, furnish advice and assistance to persons seeking to establish new businesses or industries, and engage in related activities;

(4)   Encourage the formation of private business development corporations or associations which may carry out such projects as securing and preparing sites for industrial development, constructing industrial buildings, or rendering financial or managerial assistance to businesses and industries; furnish advice and assistance to such corporations or associations;

(4a) Use grant funds to make loans for purposes permitted by the federal government, by the grant agreement and in furtherance of economic development; the economic development commission may delegate to another organization or agency the implementation of the grant's purposes, subject to approval by the federal agency involved and the commission's board of directors.

(5) Carry on such other activities as may be necessary in the proper exercise of the functions described herein. (1961, c. 722, s. 2; 1979, c. 775.)

§ 158-14. Regional planning and economic development commissions authorized.

Any municipalities and/or counties desiring to exercise the powers granted by this Article may, at their option, create a regional planning and economic development commission, which shall have and exercise all of the powers and duties granted to a regional economic development commission under this Article and in addition the powers and duties granted to a regional planning commission under Article 23 of Chapter 153. In the event that such a combined commission is created, it shall keep separate books of accounts for appropriations and expenditures made pursuant to this Article and for appropriations and expenditures made pursuant to Article 23 of Chapter 153. The financial limitations set forth in each such Article shall govern expenditures made pursuant to such Article. (1961, c. 722, s. 2; 1965, c. 431, s. 2.)

§ 158-15. Powers granted herein supplementary.

The powers granted to counties and municipalities by this Article shall be deemed supplementary to any powers heretofore or hereafter granted by any general or local act for the same or similar purposes, and in any case where the provisions of this Article conflict with or are different from the provisions of any other act, the board of county commissioners or the municipal governing board may in its discretion proceed in accordance with the provisions of this Article or, as an alternative method, in accordance with the provisions of such other act. (1961, c. 722, s. 2.)

Article 2A.

Multi-County Water Conservation and Infrastructure District.

§ 158-15.1. Multi-County Water Conservation and Infrastructure District.

(a) There is established the Multi-County Water Conservation and Infrastructure District, which is a public authority for the purpose of the Local Government Budget and Fiscal Control Act.

(b) The member counties of the Multi-County Water Conservation and Infrastructure District are Bertie, Caswell, Forsyth, Granville, Guilford, Halifax, Martin, Northampton, Person, Rockingham, Stokes, Surry, Vance, Warren, and Washington.

(c) The governing body of the Multi-County Water Conservation and Infrastructure District is the Multi-County Water Commission. One member of this Commission shall be appointed for a three-year term by the board of commissioners of each member county.

(d) All monies received by the State of North Carolina for sale of water under the Roanoke River Basin Compact, if enacted, shall be paid to the Multi-County Water Conservation and Infrastructure District.

(e) The District may accept for any of its purposes and functions any and all donations, grants of money, equipment, supplies, materials and services (conditional or otherwise) from any state or the United States or any subdivision or agency thereof, or interstate agency, or from any political subdivision of this State or any other state, or from any institution, person, firm or corporation, and may receive, utilize and dispose of the same. The nature, amount and condition, if any, attendant upon any donation or grant accepted pursuant to this subsection together with the identity of the donor or grantor, shall be detailed in the annual audit of the District.

(f) At times specified by the Multi-County Water Commission, net revenues after operating expenses of the District shall be paid to each of the fifteen member counties according to the following formula: (i) one-half pro-rata based on the population located within the Roanoke River basin area of each member county; and (ii) one-half pro-rata based on the land area located within the Roanoke River Basin area of each county.

(g) Member counties may use funds received under this section for public purposes relating to infrastructure development, economic development, and water conservation.

(h) The Commission may adopt such rules as may be needful for operation of its affairs, and shall employ and terminate personnel as if it were a county. (1995, c. 507, s. 26.12; 1996, 2nd Ex. Sess., c. 18, s. 24.22(a); 1997-443, s. 15.48(a).)

§§ 158-15.2 through 158-15.9. Reserved for future codification purposes.

Article 3.

Tax Elections for Industrial Development Purposes.

§ 158-16. Board of commissioners may call tax election; rate and purposes of tax.

The board of county commissioners in any county is authorized and empowered to call a special election to determine whether it be the will of the qualified voters of said county that they levy and cause to be collected annually, at the same time and in the same manner as the general county taxes are levied and collected, a special tax at a rate not to exceed five cents (5¢) on each one hundred dollars ($100.00) valuation of property in said county, to be known as an "industrial development tax," the funds therefrom, if the levy be authorized by the voters of said county, to be used for the purpose of attracting new and diversified industries to said county, and for the encouragement of new business and industrial ventures by local as well as foreign capital, and for the purpose of aiding and encouraging the location of manufacturing enterprises, making industrial surveys and locating industrial plants in said county, and for the purpose of encouraging agricultural development in said county. Any special election shall be conducted in accordance with G.S. 163-287. (1959, c. 212, s. 1; 2013-381, s. 10.25.)

§ 158-17. Registration of voters; election under supervision of county board of elections.

There shall be no new registration of voters for such an election. Registration shall be open for registration of new voters in said county and registration of any and all legal residents of said county, who are or could legally be enfranchised as qualified voters for regular general elections, shall be carried out in accordance with the general election laws of the State of North Carolina as provided for local elections. Notice of such registration of new voters shall be published in a newspaper circulated in said county, once, not less than 55 days before and not more than 65 days before the election, stating the hours and days for registration. The special election, if called, shall be under the control and supervision of the county board of elections. (1959, c. 212, s. 1; 1993 (Reg. Sess., 1994), c. 762, s. 11.)

§ 158-18. Form of ballot; when ballots supplied; designation of ballot box.

The form of the question shall be substantially the words "For Industrial Development Tax," and "Against Industrial Development Tax," which alternates shall appear separated from each other on one ballot containing opposite, and to the left of each alternate, squares of appropriate size in one of which squares the voters may make a mark "X" to designate the voter's choice for or against such tax. Such ballot shall be printed on white paper and each polling place shall be supplied with a sufficient number of ballots not later than the day before the election. At such special election the election board shall cause to be placed at each voting precinct in said county a ballot box marked "Industrial Development Tax Election." (1959, c. 212, s. 1.)

§ 158-19. Counting of ballots; canvassing, certifying and announcing results of elections.

The duly appointed judges and other election officials who are named and fixed by the county board of elections shall count the ballots so cast in such election and the results of the election shall be officially canvassed, certified and announced by the proper officials of the board of elections, according to the manner of canvassing, certifying and announcing the elections held under the general election laws of the State. Except as herein otherwise provided, the registration and election herein provided for shall be conducted in accordance with the general election laws of the State as provided for local elections. (1959, c. 212, s. 1.)

§ 158-20. Authorized tax rate.

If a majority of those voting in such election favor the levying of such a tax, the board of commissioners of said county are authorized to levy a special tax at a rate not to exceed five cents (5¢) on each one hundred dollars ($100.00) of assessed value of real and personal property taxable in said county, and the General Assembly does hereby give its special approval for the levy of such special tax. (1959, c. 212, s. 1.)

§ 158-21. Creation of industrial development commission; membership and terms of office; vacancies; meetings; selection of officers; bylaws and procedural rules and policies; authority of treasurer and required bond; subsidy or investment in business or industry forbidden.

If the majority of the qualified voters voting in such election favor the levying of such a tax, then and in that event, the county commissioners may create a commission to be known as the "Industrial Development Commission" for said county. Such commission shall be composed of nine members. The terms of office of the members of the commission shall be three years, with the exception of the first two years' existence of the commission, in which three shall be appointed to serve for a period of one year, three for a period of two years, and three for a period of three years; thereafter, all members shall be appointed for three years, and shall serve until their successors have been appointed and qualified. All appointments for unexpired terms resulting from resignation, death or other causes, shall be made by the county board of commissioners. The commission shall hold its first meeting within 30 days after its appointment as provided for in this Article, and the beginning date of all terms of office of the commissioners shall be the date on which the commission holds its first meeting. After the members of the commission shall have been appointed and at the time of the holding of the first meeting, they shall, by a majority vote, name and select from their membership their own chairman, vice-chairman, secretary and treasurer, and shall draw up and ratify their own bylaws and procedural rules and policies. The commission member who shall be named treasurer shall have supervision of all funds administered by the commission in any way whatsoever; shall sign and countersign all checks, drafts, bills of exchange, or any and all other negotiable instruments which shall properly be issued under his supervision; and shall furnish such surety bond as shall be designated by the board of county commissioners. No money, property or funds of the commission herein created shall be used directly or indirectly as a subsidy or investment in capital assets in any business, industry or business venture. (1959, c. 212, s. 1.)

§ 158-22. Bureau set up under supervision and control of industrial development commission; furnishing county commissioners with proposed budget.

Under the supervision and jurisdiction of the industrial development commission for said county there shall be set up a bureau, the purpose of which shall be as set forth in G.S. 158-16. The commission shall have charge of the activities of this bureau, full supervision of its operations, and full responsibility for its actions. The commission shall employ personnel for the bureau, supervise its purchases and expense accounts, and administer all the tax funds which shall be turned over to the commission by county authorities from the industrial development tax and any and all other funds which may come into its hands. The commission shall be empowered to lease, rent or purchase, or otherwise obtain suitable quarters and office space for an industrial development bureau, to lease, rent, or purchase necessary furniture, fixtures, and other equipment, to purchase advertising space in periodicals which may be selected for that purpose, and to otherwise engage in any and all activities which shall, in its discretion, promote the business and industrial development and general economic welfare of said county; and it shall have full power to exercise any and all other proper authority in connection with its duties and not expressly mentioned herein. Provided, that said commission shall provide the board of county commissioners 30 days prior to July 1 a proposed budget for the fiscal year commencing on July 1 and shall provide the board of county commissioners an audit by a certified public accountant within 60 days after the expiration of the fiscal year ending on June 30. (1959, c. 212, s. 1.)

§ 158-23. Board of county commissioners may function and carry out duties of industrial development commission.

Nothing herein shall prevent the board of county commissioners itself from functioning and carrying out the duties of the industrial development commission as provided for herein. (1959, c. 212, s. 1.)

§ 158-24. Counties to which Article applies.

The provisions of this Article shall apply only to the following counties: Alexander, Burke, Caswell, Chowan, Edgecombe, Franklin, Harnett, Haywood, Hertford, Mitchell, Northampton, Onslow, Pasquotank, Perquimans, Person, Polk, Rockingham, Rutherford, Tyrrell, Vance and Warren. (1959, c. 212, s. 2; 1961, cc. 208, 228, 339, 560, 683, 701, 1011, 1058; 1963, c. 157, s. 2; cc. 443, 504, 506, 613, 1101; 1965, cc. 189, 523, 622.)

§§ 158-25 through 158-29. Reserved for future codification purposes.

Article 4.

North Carolina's Eastern Region.

§ 158-30. (Repealed effective June 30, 2014) Title.

This Article shall be known as the "North Carolina's Eastern Region Act". (1993, c. 544, s. 1; 2005-364, s. 1; 2013-360, s. 15.28(a); 2013-363, s. 5.7(a).)

§ 158-31. (Repealed effective June 30, 2014) Purpose.

The purpose of this Article is to allow the following counties, which have the potential to derive direct economic benefits from the North Carolina Global TransPark, to create a special economic development district, to be known as North Carolina's Eastern Region: Carteret, Craven, Duplin, Edgecombe, Greene, Jones, Lenoir, Nash, Onslow, Pamlico, Pitt, Wayne, and Wilson.

The purpose of North Carolina's Eastern Region is to promote the development of the North Carolina Global TransPark and to promote and encourage economic development within the territorial jurisdiction of the Region by fostering or sponsoring development projects to provide land, buildings, facilities, programs, information and data systems, and infrastructure requirements for business and industry in the North Carolina Global TransPark outside of the Global TransPark Complex, and elsewhere in the Region. (1993, c. 544, s. 1; 1993 (Reg. Sess., 1994), c. 751, s. 1; 2005-364, s. 1; 2013-360, s. 15.28(a); 2013-363, s. 5.7(a).)

§ 158-32. (Repealed effective June 30, 2014) Definitions.

The following definitions apply in this Article:

(1)   Authority. - The North Carolina Global TransPark Authority created under Chapter 63A of the General Statutes.

(2)   Commission. - North Carolina's Eastern Region Development Commission, the governing body of North Carolina's Eastern Region.

(3)   Global TransPark Complex. - The approximately four to six thousand acre site designated by the Authority for a cargo airport and related facilities in Lenoir County. The site will contain a modern airport large enough to handle the largest aircraft and will be dedicated to the rapid movement of freight and passengers by air with intermodal connecting links with rail, highway, and water transportation facilities.

(4)   North Carolina Global TransPark. - A large area surrounding and including the Global TransPark Complex, which will contain commercial and industrial sites providing attractive locations for business and industry of differing sizes and varying kinds.

(4a)   Region. - North Carolina's Eastern Region, an economic development district created pursuant to this Article.

(5)   Unit of Local Government. - A local subdivision or unit of government or a local public corporate entity, including any type of special district or public authority.

(6)   Repealed by Session Laws 2005-364, s. 1, effective October 1, 2005. (1993, c. 544, s. 1; 2005-364, s. 1; 2013-360, s. 15.28(a); 2013-363, s. 5.7(a).)

§ 158-33. (Repealed effective June 30, 2014) Creation of North Carolina's Eastern Region.

(a)   Resolution to Create Region. - Any three or more of the counties listed in G.S. 158-31 may create North Carolina's Eastern Region as provided in this section. In order to create the Region, the governing bodies of the counties creating the Region must first adopt, on or before October 1, 1993, substantially similar resolutions stating their intent to organize the Region pursuant to this Article. Each resolution shall include articles of incorporation for the Region that shall set forth the following:

(1) The name of the Region, which shall be "North Carolina's Eastern Region."

(2) A statement that the Region is organized under this Article.

(3) The names of the organizing counties known to the county adopting the resolution.

(b) Public Hearing. - Each resolution may be adopted only after a public hearing on the question, notice of which hearing has been given by publication at least once after July 25, 1993, and not less than 10 days before the date set for the hearing, in a newspaper having a general circulation in the county. The notice shall contain a brief statement of the substance of the proposed resolution, set forth the proposed articles of incorporation of the Region, and state the time and place of the public hearing to be held on the resolution. No other publication or notice of the resolution is required.

(c) Incorporation of Region. - Each county that adopts a resolution as provided in this section shall file a certified copy of the resolution with the Secretary of State on or before October 15, 1993, together with proof of publication of notice of the hearing on the resolution. Each resolution must contain the county clerk's attestation that it was adopted by the board of commissioners. If the Secretary of State finds that the resolutions, including the articles of incorporation, conform to the provisions of this Article and that notices of the hearings were properly published, the Secretary of State shall file the resolutions and proofs of publication and shall issue a certificate of incorporation for the Region under the seal of the State. The Secretary of State shall record the certificate of incorporation in an appropriate book of record in the Secretary of State's office.

(d) Effect of Incorporation. - The issuance of the certificate of incorporation by the Secretary of State shall constitute North Carolina's Eastern Region a public body and body politic and corporate of the State. The certificate of incorporation shall be conclusive evidence that the Region has been duly created and established under this Article. (1993, c. 544, s. 1; 2005-364, s. 1; 2006-226, s. 26; 2006-264, s. 76.8; 2013-360, s. 15.28(a); 2013-363, s. 5.7(a).)

§ 158-33.1. (Repealed effective June 30, 2014) Addition of counties to Region.

(a) Authority. - The Region shall allow an eligible county to participate in the Region as provided in this section. A county is eligible to participate in the Region under this section if G.S. 158-31 authorizes the county to create the Region, but the county failed to adopt a resolution stating its intent to create the Region by the October 1, 1993, deadline set in G.S. 158-33(b).

(b) Application. - The governing body of an eligible county may apply to participate in the Region under this section by adopting a resolution to participate in the Region. The resolution must comply with all the requirements of G.S. 158-33(a) and (b) except that it may be adopted at any time before October 1, 1994. After adopting the resolution, the county shall file a certified copy of the resolution with the Commission.

(c) Approval of Application. - Within one month after receipt of an application to join the Region pursuant to this section, the Commission shall meet to consider the application. At the meeting, the Commission shall approve the application if all of the following conditions are met:

(1) The applicant is an eligible county and has adopted a resolution that complies with subsection (b) of this section.

(2) The applicant agrees to pay a fee equal to the initiation fee paid by each of the counties that originally created the Region.

(3) The applicant agrees to make monthly payments in lieu of taxes as provided in subsection (f) of this section.

(d) Commission Resolution. - After the Commission votes to add a county to the Region, the Commission shall adopt a resolution that states its intent to add the county and includes amended articles of incorporation for the Region which set forth the name of the county to be added to the Region. The Commission shall file certified copies of this resolution with the Secretary of State.

(e) Effect of Amendment. - If the Secretary of State finds that the resolution conforms to the requirements of this Article, the Secretary of State shall file the resolution, issue an amended certificate of incorporation for the Region including the additional county, and record the amended certificate of incorporation. The amended certificate of incorporation for the Region shall become effective on the first day of the second month after it is issued. Upon the effective date of the amended certificate of incorporation for the Region, the new county becomes a fully participating member of the Region. If the Commission has levied a tax in the Region pursuant to G.S. 158-42, that tax applies within the new county beginning on the date the amended certificate of incorporation becomes effective.

(f)   Payments in Lieu of Taxes. - A county that participates in the Region under this section is required to make monthly payments in lieu of taxes to the Region after the expiration of the tax levied pursuant to G.S. 158-42. Each payment shall be equal to the estimated net amount of tax that would have been collected in the county under G.S. 158-42 for that month if the tax were still in effect. Each payment is due within 15 days after the end of the month in which it accrues. The county is required to make monthly payments for a period equal to the number of months that the county was not participating in the Region while the tax was levied under G.S. 158-42. The requirement that a county make payments in lieu of taxes expires, however, on the effective date of a withdrawal from the Region by the county. For the purposes of this Article, payments in lieu of taxes shall be considered proceeds of the tax levied in G.S. 158-42 collected in the county making the payment. (1993 (Reg. Sess., 1994), c. 751, s. 2; 2005-364, s. 1; 2013-360, s. 15.28(a); 2013-363, s. 5.7(a).)

§ 158-34. (Repealed effective June 30, 2014) Territorial jurisdiction of Region.

The territorial jurisdiction of the Region created pursuant to this Article shall be coterminous with the boundaries of the counties participating in the Region. (1993, c. 544, s. 1; 2005-364, s. 1; 2013-360, s. 15.28(a); 2013-363, s. 5.7(a).)

§ 158-35. (Repealed effective June 30, 2014) Commission membership, officers, compensation.

(a)   Commission Membership. - The governing body of the Region is the Commission. The members of the Commission must be residents of the Region and shall be appointed as follows:

(1)   The board of commissioners of each county participating in the Region shall, in consultation with the county's local business community, appoint one member.

(2), (3) Repealed by Session Laws 2005-364, s. 1, effective October 1, 2005.

(4) The General Assembly shall appoint two members to the Commission on the recommendation of the Speaker of the House of Representatives and two members on the recommendation of the President Pro Tempore of the Senate in accordance with G.S. 120-121. The Governor shall appoint two members to the Commission. No two members appointed under this subdivision may be residents of the same county. The President Pro Tempore of the Senate, Speaker of the House of Representatives, and the Governor shall consult to assist in geographic diversity in those six appointments. In order to be eligible for appointment under this subdivision, a person must be a resident of the region. No person appointed under this subdivision is eligible to be chairperson or vice-chairperson.

(a1) Ex Officio Member. - The member of the State Board of Education appointed to represent the second education district shall serve as a nonvoting ex officio member of the Commission.

(b) Terms. - Members of the Commission shall serve for staggered four-year terms. Three of the members initially appointed by the boards of county commissioners pursuant to subdivision (a)(1) of this section shall serve an initial term of two years. The three members to serve initial terms of two years shall be determined by lot at the organizational meeting of the Commission. Each of the initial appointees by the General Assembly and Governor pursuant to subdivision (a)(4) of this section shall serve an initial term of two years.

(c) Removal; Vacancies. - A member of the Commission may be removed with or without cause by the appointing body. In addition, a majority of the Commission members may, by majority vote, remove a member of the Commission if that member does not attend at least three-quarters of the regularly scheduled meetings of the Commission during any consecutive 12-month period of service of that member on the Commission, except that absences excused by the Commission due to serious medical or family circumstances shall not be considered. If the Commission votes to remove a member under this subsection, the vacancy shall be filled in the same manner as the original appointment. Appointments to fill vacancies shall be made for the remainder of the unexpired term by the respective appointing authority. All members shall serve until their successors are appointed and qualified, unless removed from office.

(d) Dual Office Holding. - Service on the Commission may be in addition to any other office a person is entitled to hold.

(e) Officers. - The Commission shall annually elect from its membership a chairperson and a vice-chairperson, and shall annually elect a secretary and a treasurer. After the Commission has been duly organized and its officers elected as provided in this section, the secretary of the Commission shall certify to the Secretary of State the names and addresses of the officers as well as the address of the principal office of the Commission.

(f) Compensation. - The members of the Commission shall receive no compensation other than travel, subsistence, and reasonable per diem expenses determined by the Commission for attendance at Commission meetings and other official Region functions. (1993, c. 544, s. 1; 1998-217, s. 48; 2001-424, ss. 20.13(a), (b); 2001-496, s. 3.5; 2003-94, s. 1; 2005-364, s. 1; 2010-184, s. 5; 2013-360, s. 15.28(a); 2013-363, s. 5.7(a).)

§ 158-36. (Repealed effective June 30, 2014) Voting.

A majority of the Commission members constitutes a quorum for the transaction of business. Each voting member of the Commission shall have one vote. Except as otherwise provided in this Article, the Commission may transact business only by majority vote of the members present and voting. (1993, c. 544, s. 1; 2005-364, s. 1; 2013-360, s. 15.28(a); 2013-363, s. 5.7(a).)

§ 158-37. (Repealed effective June 30, 2014) Powers of the Region.

(a) The general powers of the Region include the following:

(1) The powers of a corporate body, including the power to sue and be sued and to adopt and use a common seal.

(2) To adopt bylaws and resolutions in accordance with this Article for its organization and internal management, including the power to create and appoint an executive and other committees and to vest authority in the executive and other committees, as the Commission deems advisable.

(3) To employ persons as necessary and to fix their compensation within the limit of available funds.

(4) With the approval of the unit of local government's chief administrative official, to use officers, employees, agents, and facilities of a unit of local government for purposes and upon terms agreed upon with the unit of local government.

(5) To make contracts, deeds, leases with or without option to purchase, conveyances, and other instruments, including contracts with the United States, the State of North Carolina, and units of local government.

(6) To acquire, lease as lessee with or without option to purchase, hold, own, and use any franchise or property or any interest in a franchise or property, within the limit of available funds.

(7) To transfer, lease as lessor with or without option to purchase, exchange, or otherwise dispose of any franchise or property or any interest in a franchise or property, within the limit of available funds.

(8) To surrender to the State of North Carolina any property no longer required by the Region.

(b) The economic development powers of the Region include the following, to the extent appropriate to carry out its purposes as provided in this Article:

(1) To levy a temporary annual motor vehicle registration tax on vehicles with a tax situs within the Region, as provided in G.S. 158-42.

(2) To acquire, construct, improve, maintain, repair, operate, or administer any component part of a public infrastructure system or facility within the Region, directly or by contract with a third party.

(3) Except as otherwise provided in this Article, to exercise the powers granted to a local government for development by G.S. 158-7.1, except the power to levy a property tax.

(4) To make grants and loans to support economic development projects authorized by this Article within the Region.

(5) To promote travel and tourism, and natural resource-based attractions, within the Region.

(6) To contract with units of local government within the Region to administer the issuance of permits and approvals required of businesses.

(7) To provide employee training programs to prepare workers for employment in the Region.

(8) To gather and maintain information of an economic, a business, or a commercial character that would be useful to businesses within the Region.

(9) To prepare specific site studies to assess the appropriateness of any area within the Region for use or development by a business and to provide opportunities for businesses to examine sites.

(10) To exercise the powers of a regional planning commission as provided in G.S. 153A-395 and the powers of a regional economic development commission as provided in Article 2 of this Chapter, but the Region does not have the authority to establish land-use zoning in any county.

(11) To carry out the purposes of a consolidation and governmental study commission as provided in Article 20 of Chapter 153A of the General Statutes.

(12) To enter in a reasonable manner land, water, or premises within the Region to make surveys, soundings, drillings, or examinations. Such an entry shall not constitute trespass, but the Region shall be liable for actual damages resulting from such an entry.

(13) To monitor and encourage the use of utility corridors adjacent to intrastate and interstate highways within the Region that are four-lane, divided, limited-access highways.

(14) To plan for and assist in the extension of natural gas within the Region.

(15) To assist in the placement of an information highway within the Region.

(16) To do all other things necessary or appropriate to carry out its purposes as provided in this Article. (1993, c. 544, s. 1; 1993 (Reg. Sess., 1994), c. 745, ss. 30, 31; 2005-364, s. 1; 2013-360, s. 15.28(a); 2013-363, s. 5.7(a).)

§ 158-38. (Repealed effective June 30, 2014) Fiscal accountability.

The Region is a public authority subject to the provisions of Chapter 159 of the General Statutes. (1993, c. 544, s. 1; 2005-364, s. 1; 2013-360, s. 15.28(a); 2013-363, s. 5.7(a).)

§ 158-39. (Repealed effective June 30, 2014) Funds.

The establishment and operation of the Region are governmental functions and constitute a public purpose. The State of North Carolina and any unit of local government may appropriate or otherwise provide funds to support the establishment and operation of the Region. The State of North Carolina and any unit of local government may also dedicate, sell, convey, donate, or lease any of their interests in property to the Region. The Region may apply for grants from the State of North Carolina, the United States, or any department, agency, or instrumentality of the State or the United States. Any department of State government may allocate to the Region any funds the use of which is not restricted by law. (1993, c. 544, s. 1; 2005-364, s. 1; 2013-360, s. 15.28(a); 2013-363, s. 5.7(a).)

§ 158-40. (Repealed effective June 30, 2014) Tax exemption.

Property owned by the Region is exempt from taxation. This tax exemption does not apply to the lease, or other arrangement that amounts to a leasehold interest, of Region property to a private party, or to the income of the lessee, unless the property is leased solely for the purpose of the Region, in which case the activities of the lessee are considered the activities of the Region. (1993, c. 544, s. 1; 2005-364, s. 1; 2013-360, s. 15.28(a); 2013-363, s. 5.7(a).)

§ 158-41. (Repealed effective June 30, 2014) Withdrawal; termination.

(a)   (Repealed for Carteret, Craven, Duplin, Edgecombe, Greene, Jones, Lenoir, Nash, Onslow, Pamlico, Pitt, Wayne, and Wilson Counties - see Editor's note) Withdrawal. - A county participating in the Region may, by resolution, withdraw from the Region. A resolution withdrawing from the Region may not become effective before the end of the fiscal year in which it is adopted. Upon adoption of a resolution withdrawing from the Region, the board of commissioners of the county shall provide a copy of the resolution to the Secretary of State, the Commission, the Authority, and every other county participating in the Region. Withdrawal does not entitle a county to early distribution of its beneficial interest in Region assets, but a county that has withdrawn retains its right to any distributions that may be made to participating counties pursuant to subsection (b) of this section on the same basis as if it had not withdrawn. For all other purposes, a county that has withdrawn from the Region no longer participates in the Region.

(b) Termination. - The Commission may dissolve the Region and terminate its existence at any time. If the Region is dissolved and terminated or is otherwise unable to expend the tax proceeds received pursuant to G.S. 158-42, the Commission shall liquidate the assets of the Region to the extent possible and distribute all Region assets to the counties of the Region in proportion to the amount of tax collected in each county. The assets of the Region that exceed the amount of tax collected by the counties and are attributable to an appropriation made to the Region by the General Assembly shall revert to the General Fund and may not be distributed to the counties. A county may use funds distributed to it pursuant to this subsection only for economic development projects and infrastructure construction projects. In calculating the amount to be refunded to each county, the Region shall first allocate amounts loaned and not yet repaid as follows:

(1) Amounts loaned for a project in a county will be allocated to that county to the extent of its beneficial ownership of the principal of the trust account created under G.S. 158-42 and the county will become the owner of the right to repayment of the amount loaned to the extent of its beneficial ownership of the principal of the trust account created under G.S. 158-42.

(2) Amounts not allocated pursuant to subdivision (1) shall be allocated among the remaining counties in proportion to the amount of tax collected in each county under G.S. 158-42, and the remaining counties shall become the owners of the right to repayment of the amounts loaned in proportion to the amount of tax collected in each county under G.S. 158-42.

Notes and other instruments representing the right to repayment shall, upon dissolution of the Region, be held and collected by the State Treasurer, who shall disburse the collections to the counties as provided in this subsection.

The Commission shall distribute those assets that it is unable to liquidate among the Region counties insofar as practical on an equitable basis, as determined by the Commission. Upon termination, the State of North Carolina shall succeed to any remaining rights, obligations, and liabilities of the Region not assigned to the Region counties. (1993, c. 544, s. 1; 2005-364, s. 1; 2013-256, ss. 2, 2.1; 2013-360, s. 15.28(a); 2013-363, s. 5.7(a).)

§ 158-42. (Repealed effective June 30, 2014) Temporary Region vehicle registration tax.

(a)   Levy. - The Commission may, by resolution, after not less than 10 days' public notice and a public hearing, levy an annual registration tax of five dollars ($5.00) on motor vehicles with a tax situs within the Region. A tax levied under this section is in addition to any other motor vehicle license or registration tax.

The tax applies to vehicles required to pay a tax under G.S. 20-88, except trailers, and G.S. 20-87(1), (2), (4), (5), (6), and (7). The tax situs of a motor vehicle for the purpose of this section is its ad valorem tax situs. If the vehicle is not subject to ad valorem tax, its tax situs for the purpose of this section is the ad valorem tax situs it would have if it were subject to ad valorem tax.

(b)   Effective Date; Expiration. - The effective date of a tax levied under this section shall be no earlier than July 1, 1994. The effective date of a tax levied under this section must be the first day of a calendar month set by the Commission in the resolution levying the tax, and shall be no earlier than the first day of the third calendar month after the adoption of the resolution.

The authority of the Region to levy a tax under this section expires five years after the effective date of the first tax levied under this section. A tax levied under this section expires when the Region's authority to levy the tax expires. The expiration of the tax does not affect the rights or liabilities of the Region, a taxpayer, or another person arising under this section before the expiration of the tax; nor does it affect the right to any refund or credit of a tax that would otherwise have been available under this section before the expiration of the tax.

(c)   Repeal of Tax. - The Commission may, by resolution, repeal a tax levied under this section. The effective date of the repeal must be the first day of a calendar month set by the Commission in the resolution repealing the tax, and shall be no earlier than the first day of the third calendar month after the adoption of the resolution. Repeal of the tax does not affect the date the Region's authority to levy the tax expires under subsection (b) of this section. Repeal of the tax does not affect the rights or liabilities of the Region, a taxpayer, or another person arising under this section before the effective date of the repeal; nor does it affect the right to any refund or credit of a tax that would otherwise have been available under this section before the effective date of the repeal.

(d) Administration. - The Division of Motor Vehicles of the Department of Transportation shall collect and administer a tax levied under this section. Immediately after adopting a resolution levying or repealing a tax under this section, the Commission shall deliver a certified copy of the resolution to the Division of Motor Vehicles. If the Secretary of State issues an amended certificate of incorporation adding a county to the Region pursuant to G.S. 158-33.1, the Commission shall deliver a certified copy of the amended certificate immediately to the Division of Motor Vehicles. If the Commission receives a resolution from a county withdrawing from the Region pursuant to G.S. 158-41, the Commission shall deliver a certified copy of the resolution immediately to the Division of Motor Vehicles.

A tax levied under this section is due at the same time and subject to the same restrictions as the tax levied in G.S. 20-87 and G.S. 20-88. The tax shall be prorated in accordance with G.S. 20-95. The Commissioner of Motor Vehicles may adopt rules necessary to administer the tax.

(e) Distribution of Tax Proceeds. - The Commissioner of Motor Vehicles shall credit the proceeds of the tax levied under this section to a special account and distribute the net proceeds on a quarterly basis to the Region. Interest on the special account shall be credited quarterly to the Highway Fund to reimburse the Division of Motor Vehicles for the cost of collecting and administering the tax. The Commissioner of Motor Vehicles shall provide the Region with an accounting of the percentage of proceeds collected in each county of the Region in each quarter.

(f) Use of Tax Proceeds. - The Region may use the proceeds of the tax levied under this section only for economic development projects and infrastructure construction projects that are within the territorial jurisdiction of the Region but not within the Global TransPark Complex. The Region shall use the tax proceeds only for public purposes authorized by this Article.

The Region shall place fifteen percent (15%) of the tax proceeds distributed to it under this section in a general funds account and the remaining eighty-five percent (85%) in an interest-bearing trust account. Each county shall be the beneficial owner of a share of the principal of the trust account in proportion to the amount of tax proceeds collected in that county.

The Region may not disburse the principal of the trust account except pursuant to a contract that provides that, within a reasonable time not to exceed 20 years, the Region will recover or be repaid the amount disbursed. The Region may, in its discretion, set reasonable terms and conditions for the repayment of the principal disbursed, including provisions for securing the debt and the payment of interest.

(g) Disbursement of Tax Proceeds. - Upon receipt of a resolution adopted by a participating county's board of county commissioners, the Region shall disburse to the county its net share of tax proceeds placed in trust under this section. A participating county's net share of tax proceeds is the total amount in the trust fund attributable to that county less the total amount of outstanding loans from the Region to the county and less any amount attributable to an appropriation made to the Region by the General Assembly. If this calculation results in a negative amount, the county is not entitled to a disbursement under this subsection. Funds disbursed under this subsection may be used only for economic development purposes. For purposes of this subsection, "economic development purposes" includes the provision of land, buildings, facilities, programs, information and data systems, or infrastructure required to promote business or industry in the county.

This subsection applies only to Carteret, Craven, Duplin, Edgecombe, Greene, Jones, Lenoir, Nash, Onslow, Pamlico, Pitt, Wayne, and Wilson Counties. (1993, c. 544, s. 1; 1993 (Reg. Sess., 1994), c. 751, s. 3; c. 761, s. 33; 1995, c. 465, s. 1; 2005-364, s. 1; 2013-256, ss. 1, 2.1; 2013-360, s. 15.28(a); 2013-363, s. 5.7(a).)

Chapter 159.

Local Government Finance.

SUBCHAPTER I. SHORT TITLE AND DEFINITIONS.

Article 1.

Short Title and Definitions.

§ 159-1. Short title and definitions.

(a) This Chapter may be cited as "The Local Government Finance Act."

(b) The words and phrases defined in this section have the meanings indicated when used in this Chapter, unless the context clearly requires another meaning, or unless the word or phrase is given a more restrictive meaning by definition in another Article herein.

(1) "Chairman" means the chairman of the Local Government Commission.

(2) "City" includes towns and incorporated villages.

(3) "Clerk" means an officer or employee of a local government or public authority charged by law or direction of the governing board with the duty of keeping the minutes of board meetings and conserving records evidencing official actions of the board.

(4) "Commission" means the Local Government Commission.

(5) "Publish," "publication," and other forms of the word "publish" mean insertion in a newspaper qualified under G.S. 1-597 to publish legal advertisements.

(6) "Secretary" means the secretary of the Local Government Commission.

(c) Words in the singular number include the plural, and in the plural include the singular. Words of the masculine gender include the feminine and the neuter, and when the sense so indicates, words of the neuter gender may refer to any gender. (1927, c. 81, s. 2; 1931, c. 60, s. 2; 1971, c. 780, s. 1.)

§ 159-2. Computation of time.

(a) Notwithstanding any other provisions of law, whenever in this Chapter an act is to be done within a given period of time, the period of time shall be computed according to the rules set out in this section.

(b)   When an act is to be done within a given number of days before or after a given day, the period is computed by counting forward beginning with the day following the given day, or counting backward beginning with the day next before the given day. Saturdays, Sundays, and holidays are counted as any other day.

(c)   The word "month" means 30 days, unless the words "calendar month" are used, in which case the number of days in the month may vary according to the calendar.

(d)   The word "year" means the calendar year.

(e)   The word "day," when used to denote a period of time within which an act may be done, means a period of 24 hours beginning at 12:00 midnight.

(f)   When a time of day is given, the time is local time in the City of Raleigh, North Carolina. (1971, c. 780, s. 1.)

SUBCHAPTER II. LOCAL GOVERNMENT COMMISSION.

Article 2.

Local Government Commission.

§ 159-3. Local Government Commission established.

(a)   The Local Government Commission consists of nine members. The State Treasurer, the State Auditor, the Secretary of State, and the Secretary of Revenue each serve ex officio; the remaining five members are appointed to four-year terms as follows: three by the Governor, one by the General Assembly upon the recommendation of the President Pro Tempore in accordance with G.S. 120-121, and one by the General Assembly upon the recommendation of the Speaker of the House in accordance with G.S. 120-121. Of the three members appointed by the Governor, one shall be or have been the mayor or a member of the governing board of a city and one shall be or have been a member of a county board of commissioners. The State Treasurer is chairman ex officio of the Local Government Commission. Membership on the Commission is an office that may be held concurrently with one other office, as permitted by G.S. 128-1.1.

(b) The Commission shall meet at least quarterly in the City of Raleigh, and may hold special meetings at any time or place upon notice to each member given in person or by mail not later than the fifth day before the meeting. The notice need not state the purpose of the meeting.

Action of the Commission shall be taken by resolution adopted by majority vote of those present and voting. A majority of the Commission constitutes a quorum.

(c) The appointed members of the Commission are entitled to the per diem compensation and allowances prescribed by G.S. 138-5. All members are entitled to reimbursement for necessary travel and other expenses.

(d) The Commission may call upon the Attorney General for legal advice in relation to its powers and duties.

(e) The Local Government Commission shall operate as a division of the Department of the State Treasurer.

(f) The Commission may adopt rules and regulations to carry out its powers and duties. (1931, c. 60, s. 7; c. 296, s. 8; 1933, c. 31, s. 1; 1957, c. 541, s. 18; 1963, c. 1130; 1969, c. 445, s. 1; 1971, c. 780, s. 1; 1973, c. 474, s. 2; c. 476, s. 193; 1995, c. 490, s. 30(a).)

§ 159-4. Executive committee; appeal.

(a) The State Auditor, the State Treasurer, the Secretary of State, and the Secretary of Revenue shall constitute the executive committee of the Local Government Commission. The executive committee is vested with all the powers of the Commission when it is not in session, except that the executive committee may not overrule, reverse, or disregard any action of the full Commission. Action of the executive committee shall be taken by resolution adopted by a majority of those present and voting. Any three members of the executive committee constitute a quorum. The chairman may call meetings of the executive committee at any time.

(b) Any member of the Commission or any person affected by an action of the executive committee may appeal to the full Commission by filing a request for review with the chairman within five days after the action is taken. Review of executive committee action by the full Commission shall be de novo. (1931, c.

60, ss. 8, 10; 1933, c. 31, s. 2; 1953, c. 675, s. 27; 1971, c. 780, s. 1; 1973, c. 476, s. 193.)

§ 159-5. Secretary and staff of the Commission.

The chairman shall appoint a secretary of the Commission, and may appoint such other deputies and assistants as may be necessary, who shall be responsible to the chairman through the secretary. The secretary and his deputies and assistants shall have and may exercise any power that the chairman himself may exercise. All actions taken by the secretary, including the signing of any documents and papers provided for in this Chapter, shall be effective as though the chairman himself had taken such action or signed such documents or papers. (1931, c. 60, s. 7; c. 296, s. 8; 1933, c. 31, s. 1; 1957, c. 541, s. 18; 1963, c. 1130; 1969, c. 445, s. 1; 1971, c. 780, s. 1; 1983, c. 717, s. 91.)

§ 159-6. Fees of the Commission.

(a) The Commission may charge and collect fees for services rendered and for all expenses incurred by the Commission in connection with approving or denying an application for an issue of other than general obligation bonds or notes, participating in the sale, award or delivery of such issue or carrying out any other of its powers and duties with respect to such issue or the issuer thereof, pursuant to the laws of the State of North Carolina.

(b) The Commission shall establish rules and regulations concerning the setting and collection of such fees. In establishing the amount of or method of determining such fees, the Commission shall take into account, among other things, the scope of its statutory responsibilities and the nature and extent of its services for such issue or issuer or class thereof.

(c) Such fees collected by the Commission shall be incorporated into the budget of the State Treasurer and shall be expended for costs incurred by the Commission in carrying out its statutory responsibilities in the issuance of revenue bonds.

(d) Apart from the above fees, the Commission is authorized to receive reimbursement for all expenses incurred in the sale or issuance of general obligation bonds and notes by assessing and collecting fees.

(e) In addition to any other fees authorized by this section, the Commission may charge and collect fees for services rendered and expenses incurred in reviewing and processing petitions of counties or cities concerning use of local sales and use tax revenue in accordance with G.S. 105-487(c). (1981 (Reg. Sess., 1982), c. 1175; 1983, c. 908, s. 2.)

SUBCHAPTER III. BUDGETS AND FISCAL CONTROL.

Article 3.

The Local Government Budget and Fiscal Control Act.

Part 1. Budgets.

§ 159-7. Short title; definitions; local acts superseded.

(a) This Article may be cited as "The Local Government Budget and Fiscal Control Act."

(b) The words and phrases defined in this section have the meanings indicated when used in this Article, unless the context clearly requires another meaning.

(1) "Budget" is a proposed plan for raising and spending money for specified programs, functions, activities or objectives during a fiscal year.

(2) "Budget ordinance" is the ordinance that levies taxes and appropriates revenues for specified purposes, functions, activities, or objectives during a fiscal year.

(3) "Budget year" is the fiscal year for which a budget is proposed or a budget ordinance is adopted.

(4) "Debt service" is the sum of money required to pay installments of principal and interest on bonds, notes, and other evidences of debt accruing within a fiscal year, to maintain sinking funds, and to pay installments on debt

instruments issued pursuant to Chapter 159G of the General Statutes or Chapter 159I of the General Statutes accruing within a fiscal year.

(5), (6) Repealed by Session Laws 1975, c. 514, s. 2.

(7) "Fiscal year" is the annual period for the compilation of fiscal operations, as prescribed in G.S. 159-8(b).

(8) "Fund" is a fiscal and accounting entity with a self-balancing set of accounts recording cash and other resources, together with all related liabilities and residual equities or balances, and changes therein, for the purpose of carrying on specific activities or attaining certain objectives in accordance with special regulations, restrictions, or limitations.

(9) Repealed by Session Laws 1975, c. 514, s. 2.

(10) "Public authority" is a municipal corporation (other than a unit of local government) that is not subject to the State Budget Act (Chapter 143C of the General Statutes) or a local governmental authority, board, commission, council, or agency that (i) is not a municipal corporation, (ii) is not subject to the State Budget Act, and (iii) operates on an area, regional, or multi-unit basis, and the budgeting and accounting systems of which are not fully a part of the budgeting and accounting systems of a unit of local government.

(11) Repealed by Session Laws 1975, c. 514, s. 2.

(12) "Sinking fund" means a fund held for the retirement of term bonds.

(13) "Special district" is a unit of local government (other than a county, city, town, or incorporated village) that is created for the performance of limited governmental functions or for the operation of a particular utility or public service enterprises.

(14) "Taxes" do not include special assessments.

(15) "Unit," "unit of local government," or "local government" is a municipal corporation that is not subject to the State Budget Act (Chapter 143C of the General Statutes) and that has the power to levy taxes, including a consolidated city-county, as defined by G.S. 160B-2(1), and all boards, agencies, commissions, authorities, and institutions thereof that are not municipal corporations.

(16) "Vending facilities" has the same meaning as it does in G.S. 111-42(d), but also means any mechanical or electronic device dispensing items or something of value or entertainment or services for a fee, regardless of the method of activation, and regardless of the means of payment, whether by coin, currency, tokens, or other means.

(c) It is the intent of the General Assembly by enactment of this Article to prescribe for local governments and public authorities a uniform system of budget adoption and administration and fiscal control. To this end and except as otherwise provided in this Article, all provisions of general laws, city charters, and local acts in effect as of July 1, 1973 and in conflict with the provisions of Part 1 or Part 3 of this Article are repealed. No general law, city charter, or local act enacted or taking effect after July 1, 1973, may be construed to modify, amend, or repeal any portion of Part 1 or Part 3 of this Article unless it expressly so provides by specific reference to the appropriate section.

(d) Except as expressly provided herein, this Article does not apply to school administrative units. The adoption and administration of budgets for the public school system and the management of the fiscal affairs of school administrative units are governed by the School Budget and Fiscal Control Act, Chapter 115, Article 9. However, this Article and the School Budget and Fiscal Control Act shall be construed together to the end that the administration of the fiscal affairs of counties and school administrative units may be most effectively and efficiently administered. (1927, c. 146, ss. 1, 2; 1955, c. 724; 1971, c. 780, s. 1; 1973, c. 474, ss. 3, 4; 1975, c. 437, s. 12; c. 514, s. 2; 1981, c. 685, s. 1; 1983 (Reg. Sess., 1984), c. 1034, s. 173; 1987, c. 282, ss. 30, 31; c. 796, s. 3(1); 1989, c. 756, s. 3; 1995, c. 461, s. 9; 2006-203, s. 125.)

§ 159-8. Annual balanced budget ordinance.

(a) Each local government and public authority shall operate under an annual balanced budget ordinance adopted and administered in accordance with this Article. A budget ordinance is balanced when the sum of estimated net revenues and appropriated fund balances is equal to appropriations. Appropriated fund balance in any fund shall not exceed the sum of cash and investments minus the sum of liabilities, encumbrances, and deferred revenues arising from cash receipts, as those figures stand at the close of the fiscal year next preceding the budget year. It is the intent of this Article that, except for moneys expended pursuant to a project ordinance or accounted for in an intragovernmental service fund or a trust and agency fund excluded from the budget ordinance under G.S. 159-13(a), all moneys received and expended by a local government or public authority should be included in the budget ordinance. Therefore, notwithstanding any other provision of law, no local government or public authority may expend any moneys, regardless of their source (including moneys derived from bond proceeds, federal, state, or private grants or loans, or special assessments), except in accordance with a budget ordinance or project ordinance adopted under this Article or through an intragovernmental service fund or trust and agency fund properly excluded from the budget ordinance.

(b) The budget ordinance of a unit of local government shall cover a fiscal year beginning July 1 and ending June 30. The budget ordinance of a public authority shall cover a fiscal year beginning July 1 and ending June 30, except that the Local Government Commission, if it determines that a different fiscal year would facilitate the authority's financial operations, may enter an order permitting an authority to operate under a fiscal year other than from July 1 to June 30. If the Commission does permit an authority to operate under an altered fiscal year, the Commission's order shall also modify the budget calendar set forth in G.S. 159-10 through 159-13 so as to provide a new budget calendar for the altered fiscal year that will clearly enable the authority to comply with the intent of this Part. (1971, c. 780, s. 1; 1973, c. 474, s. 5; 1975, c. 514, s. 3; 1979, c. 402, s. 1; 1981, c. 685, s. 2.)

§ 159-9. Budget officer.

Each local government and public authority shall appoint a budget officer to serve at the will of the governing board. In counties or cities having the manager form of government, the county or city manager shall be the budget officer. Counties not having the manager form of government may impose the duties of budget officer upon the county finance officer or any other county officer or employee except the sheriff, or in counties having a population of more than 7,500, the register of deeds. Cities not having the manager form of government may impose the duties of budget officer on any city officer or employee, including the mayor if he agrees to undertake them. A public authority or special district may impose the duties of budget officer on the chairman or any member of its governing board or any other officer or employee. (1971, c. 780, s. 1; 1973, c. 474, s. 6.)

§ 159-10. Budget requests.

Before April 30 of each fiscal year (or an earlier date fixed by the budget officer), each department head shall transmit to the budget officer the budget requests and revenue estimates for his department for the budget year. The budget request shall be an estimate of the financial requirements of the department for the budget year, and shall be made in such form and detail, with such supporting information and justifications, as the budget officer may prescribe. The revenue estimate shall be an estimate of all revenues to be realized by department operations during the budget year. At the same time, the finance officer or department heads shall transmit to the budget officer a complete statement of the amount expended for each category of expenditure in the budget ordinance of the immediately preceding fiscal year, a complete statement of the amount estimated to be expended for each category of expenditure in the current year's budget ordinance by the end of the current fiscal year, the amount realized from each source of revenue during the immediately preceding fiscal year, and the amount estimated to be realized from each source of revenue by the end of the current fiscal year, and such other information and data on the fiscal operations of the local government or public authority as the budget officer may request. (1927, c. 146, s. 5; 1955, cc. 698, 724; 1971, c. 780, s. 1.)

§ 159-11. Preparation and submission of budget and budget message.

(a) Upon receipt of the budget requests and revenue estimates and the financial information supplied by the finance officer and department heads, the budget officer shall prepare a budget for consideration by the governing board in such form and detail as may have been prescribed by the budget officer or the governing board. The budget shall comply in all respects with the limitations imposed by G.S. 159-13(b), and unless the governing board shall have authorized or requested submission of an unbalanced budget as provided in subsection (c) of this section, the budget shall be balanced.

(b) The budget, together with a budget message, shall be submitted to the governing board not later than June 1. The budget and budget message should, but need not, be submitted at a formal meeting of the board. The budget message should contain a concise explanation of the governmental goals fixed by the budget for the budget year, should explain important features of the activities anticipated in the budget, should set forth the reasons for stated changes from the previous year in program goals, programs, and appropriation levels, and should explain any major changes in fiscal policy.

(c) The governing board may authorize or request the budget officer to submit a budget containing recommended appropriations in excess of estimated revenues. If this is done, the budget officer shall present the appropriations recommendations in a manner that will reveal for the governing board the nature of the activities supported by the expenditures that exceed estimated revenues.

(d) The budget officer shall include in the budget a proposed financial plan for each intragovernmental service fund, as required by G.S. 159-13.1, and information concerning capital projects and grant projects authorized or to be authorized by project ordinances, as required by G.S. 159-13.2.

(e) In each year in which a general reappraisal of real property has been conducted, the budget officer shall include in the budget, for comparison purposes, a statement of the revenue-neutral property tax rate for the budget. The revenue-neutral property tax rate is the rate that is estimated to produce revenue for the next fiscal year equal to the revenue that would have been produced for the next fiscal year by the current tax rate if no reappraisal had occurred. To calculate the revenue-neutral tax rate, the budget officer shall first determine a rate that would produce revenues equal to those produced for the current fiscal year and then increase the rate by a growth factor equal to the average annual percentage increase in the tax base due to improvements since the last general reappraisal. This growth factor represents the expected percentage increase in the value of the tax base due to improvements during the next fiscal year. The budget officer shall further adjust the rate to account for any annexation, deannexation, merger, or similar event. (1927, c. 146, s. 6; 1955, cc. 698, 724; 1969, c. 976, s. 1; 1971, c. 780, s. 1; 1975, c. 514, s. 4; 1979, c. 402, s. 2; 2003-264, s. 1.)

§ 159-12. Filing and publication of the budget; budget hearings.

(a) On the same day that he submits the budget to the governing board, the budget officer shall file a copy of it in the office of the clerk to the board where it shall remain available for public inspection until the budget ordinance is adopted. The clerk shall make a copy of the budget available to all news media in the county. He shall also publish a statement that the budget has been submitted to the governing board, and is available for public inspection in the office of the clerk to the board. The statement shall also give notice of the time and place of the budget hearing required by subsection (b) of this section.

(b) Before adopting the budget ordinance, the board shall hold a public hearing at which time any persons who wish to be heard on the budget may appear. (1927, c. 146, s. 7; 1955, cc. 698, 724; 1971, c. 780, s. 1.)

§ 159-13. The budget ordinance; form, adoption, limitations, tax levy, filing.

(a) Not earlier than 10 days after the day the budget is presented to the board and not later than July 1, the governing board shall adopt a budget ordinance making appropriations and levying taxes for the budget year in such sums as the board may consider sufficient and proper, whether greater or less than the sums recommended in the budget. The budget ordinance shall authorize all financial transactions of the local government or public authority except

(1) Those authorized by a project ordinance,

(2) Those accounted for in an intragovernmental service fund for which a financial plan is prepared and approved, and

(3) Those accounted for in a trust or agency fund established to account for moneys held by the local government or public authority as an agent or common-law trustee or to account for a retirement, pension, or similar employee benefit system.

The budget ordinance may be in any form that the board considers most efficient in enabling it to make the fiscal policy decisions embodied therein, but it shall make appropriations by department, function, or project and show revenues by major source.

(b) The following directions and limitations shall bind the governing board in adopting the budget ordinance:

(1) The full amount estimated by the finance officer to be required for debt service during the budget year shall be appropriated.

(2) The full amount of any deficit in each fund shall be appropriated.

(3)   A contingency appropriation shall not exceed five percent (5%) of the total of all other appropriations in the same fund, except there is no limit on contingency appropriations for public assistance programs required by Chapter 108A. Each expenditure to be charged against a contingency appropriation shall be authorized by resolution of the governing board, which resolution shall be deemed an amendment to the budget ordinance setting up an appropriation for the object of expenditure authorized. The governing board may authorize the budget officer to authorize expenditures from contingency appropriations subject to such limitations and procedures as it may prescribe. Any such expenditures shall be reported to the board at its next regular meeting and recorded in the minutes.

(4)   No appropriation may be made that would require the levy of a tax in excess of any constitutional or statutory limitation, or expenditures of revenues for purposes not permitted by law.

(5)   The total of all appropriations for purposes which require voter approval for expenditure of property tax funds under Article V, Sec. 2(5), of the Constitution shall not exceed the total of all estimated revenues other than the property tax (not including such revenues required by law to be spent for specific purposes) and property taxes levied for such purposes pursuant to a vote of the people.

(6)   The estimated percentage of collection of property taxes shall not be greater than the percentage of the levy actually realized in cash as of June 30 during the preceding fiscal year. For purposes of the calculation under this subdivision only, the levy for the registered motor vehicle tax under Article 22A of Chapter 105 of the General Statutes shall be based on the nine-month period ending March 31 of the preceding fiscal year, and the collections realized in cash with respect to this levy shall be based on the 12-month period ending June 30 of the preceding fiscal year.

(7)   Estimated revenues shall include only those revenues reasonably expected to be realized in the budget year, including amounts to be realized from collections of taxes levied in prior fiscal years.

(8)   Repealed by Session Laws 1975, c. 514, s. 6.

(9)   Appropriations made to a school administrative unit by a county may not be reduced after the budget ordinance is adopted, unless the board of education

of the administrative unit agrees by resolution to a reduction, or unless a general reduction in county expenditures is required because of prevailing economic conditions. Before a board of county commissioners may reduce appropriations to a school administrative unit as part of a general reduction in county expenditures required because of prevailing economic conditions, it must do all of the following:

a. Hold a public meeting at which the school board is given an opportunity to present information on the impact of the reduction.

b. Take a public vote on the decision to reduce appropriations to a school administrative unit.

(10) Appropriations made to another fund from a fund established to account for property taxes levied pursuant to a vote of the people may not exceed the amount of revenues other than the property tax available to the fund, except for appropriations from such a fund to an appropriate account in a capital reserve fund.

(11) Repealed by Session Laws 1975, c. 514, s. 6.

(12) Repealed by Session Laws 1981, c. 685, s. 4.

(13) No appropriation of the proceeds of a bond issue may be made from the capital project fund account established to account for the proceeds of the bond issue except (i) for the purpose for which the bonds were issued, (ii) to the appropriate debt service fund, or (iii) to an account within a capital reserve fund consistent with the purposes for which the bonds were issued. The total of other appropriations made to another fund from such a capital project fund account may not exceed the amount of revenues other than bond proceeds available to the account.

(14) No appropriation may be made from a utility or public service enterprise fund to any other fund than the appropriate debt service fund unless the total of all other appropriations in the fund equal or exceed the amount that will be required during the fiscal year, as shown by the budget ordinance, to meet operating expenses, capital outlay, and debt service on outstanding utility or enterprise bonds or notes. A county may, upon a finding that a fund balance in a utility or public service enterprise fund used for operation of a landfill exceeds the requirements for funding the operation of that fund, including closure and post-closure expenditures, transfer excess funds accruing due to imposition of a

surcharge imposed on another local government located within the State for use of the disposal facility, as authorized by G.S. 153A-292(b), to support the other services supported by the county's general fund.

(15) Sufficient funds to meet the amounts to be paid during the fiscal year under continuing contracts previously entered into shall be appropriated unless such contract reserves to the governing board the right to limit or not to make such appropriation.

(16) The sum of estimated net revenues and appropriated fund balance in each fund shall be equal to appropriations in that fund. Appropriated fund balance in a fund shall not exceed the sum of cash and investments minus the sum of liabilities, encumbrances, and deferred revenues arising from cash receipts, as those figures stand at the close of the fiscal year next preceding the budget year.

(17) No appropriations may be made from a county reappraisal reserve fund except for the purposes for which the fund was established.

(18) No appropriation may be made from a service district fund to any other fund except (i) to the appropriate debt service fund or (ii) to an appropriate account in a capital reserve fund unless the district has been abolished.

(19) No appropriation of the proceeds of a debt instrument may be made from the capital project fund account established to account for such proceeds except for the purpose for which such debt instrument was issued. The total of other appropriations made to another fund from such a capital project fund account may not exceed the amount of revenues other than debt instrument proceeds available to the account.

Notwithstanding subdivisions (9), (10), (12), (14), (17), or (18) of this subsection, any fund may contain an appropriation to another fund to cover the cost of (i) levying and collecting the taxes and other revenues allocated to the fund, and (ii) building maintenance and other general overhead and administrative expenses properly allocable to functions or activities financed from the fund.

(c) The budget ordinance of a local government shall levy taxes on property at rates that will produce the revenue necessary to balance appropriations and revenues, after taking into account the estimated percentage of the levy that will not be collected during the fiscal year. The budget ordinance of a public authority shall be balanced so that appropriations do not exceed revenues.

(d) The budget ordinance shall be entered in the minutes of the governing board and within five days after adoption copies thereof shall be filed with the finance officer, the budget officer, and the clerk to the governing board. (1927, c. 146, s. 8; 1955, cc. 698, 724; 1969, c. 976, s. 2; 1971, c. 780, s. 1; 1973, c. 474, ss. 7-9; c. 489, s. 3; 1975, c. 437, ss. 13, 14; c. 514, ss. 5, 6; 1981, c. 685, ss. 3-5, 10; 1987, c. 796, s. 3(2); 1989, c. 756, s. 2; 1999-261, s. 1; 2000-140, s. 80; 2002-126, s. 6.7(a); 2013-413, s. 59.4(b).)

§ 159-13.1. Financial plan for intragovernmental service funds.

(a) If a local government or public authority establishes and operates one or more intragovernmental service funds, it need not include such a fund in its budget ordinance. However, at the same time it adopts the budget ordinance, the governing board shall approve a balanced financial plan for each intragovernmental service fund. A financial plan is balanced when estimated expenditures do not exceed estimated revenues.

(b) The budget officer shall include in the budget he submits to the board, pursuant to G.S. 159-11, a proposed financial plan for each intragovernmental service fund to be operated during the budget year by the local government or public authority. The proposed financial plan shall be in such form and detail as prescribed by the budget officer or governing board.

(c) The approved financial plan shall be entered in the minutes of the governing board, as shall each amendment to the plan approved by the board. Within five days after approval, copies of the plan and copies of each amendment thereto shall be filed with the finance officer, the budget officer, and the clerk to the governing board.

(d) Any change in a financial plan must be approved by the governing board. (1975, c. 514, s. 7.)

§ 159-13.2. Project ordinances.

(a) Definitions. -

(1) In this section "capital project" means a project financed in whole or in part by the proceeds of bonds or notes or debt instruments or a project involving the construction or acquisition of a capital asset.

(2) "Grant project" means a project financed in whole or in part by revenues received from the federal and/or State government for operating or capital purposes as defined by the grant contract.

(b) Alternative Budget Methods. - A local government or public authority may, in its discretion, authorize and budget for a capital project or a grant project either in its annual budget ordinance or in a project ordinance adopted pursuant to this section. A project ordinance authorizes all appropriations necessary for the completion of the project and neither it nor any part of it need be readopted in any subsequent fiscal year. Neither a bond order nor an order authorizing any debt instrument constitutes a project ordinance.

(c) Adoption of Project Ordinances. - If a local government or public authority intends to authorize a capital project or a grant project by a project ordinance, it shall not begin the project until it has adopted a balanced project ordinance for the life of the project. A project ordinance is balanced when revenues estimated to be available for the project equal appropriations for the project. A project ordinance shall clearly identify the project and authorize its undertaking, identify the revenues that will finance the project, and make the appropriations necessary to complete the project.

(d) Project Ordinance Filed. - Each project ordinance shall be entered in the minutes of the governing board. Within five days after adoption, copies of the ordinance shall be filed with the finance officer, the budget officer, and the clerk to the governing board.

(e) Amendment. - A project ordinance may be amended in any manner so long as it continues to fulfill all requirements of this section.

(f) Inclusion of Project Information in Budget. - Each year the budget officer shall include in the budget information in such detail as he or the governing board may require concerning each grant project or capital project (i) expected to be authorized by project ordinance during the budget year and (ii) authorized by previously adopted project ordinances which will have appropriations available for expenditure during the budget year. (1975, c. 514, s. 8; 1979, c. 402, s. 3; 1987, c. 796, s. 3(3), 3(4).)

§ 159-14. Trust and agency funds; budgets of special districts.

(a) Budgets of Special Districts. - If the tax-levying power of a special district is by law exercised on its behalf by a county or city, and if the county or city governing board is vested by law with discretion as to what rate of tax it will levy on behalf of the special district, the governing board of the special district shall transmit to the governing board of the county or city on or before June 1 a request to levy taxes on its behalf for the budget year at a stated rate. The county or city governing board shall then determine what rate of tax it will approve, and shall so notify the district governing board not later than June 15. Failure of the county or city governing board to act on the district's request on or before June 15 and to so notify the district governing board by that date shall be deemed approval of the full rate requested by the district governing board. Upon receiving notification from the county or city governing board as to what rate of tax will be approved or after June 15 if no such notification is received, the district governing board shall complete its budget deliberations and shall adopt its budget ordinance.

If the tax-levying power of a special district is by law exercised on its behalf by a county or city, and if the county or city governing board has no discretion as to what rate of tax it will levy on behalf of the special district, the governing board of the district shall notify the city or county by June 15 of the rate of tax it wishes to have levied. If the district does not notify the county or city governing board on or before June 15 of the rate of tax it wishes to have levied, the county or city is not required to levy a tax for the district for the fiscal year.

If the taxes of a special district are collected on its behalf by a county or city, and if the county or city governing board has no power to approve the district tax levy, the district governing board shall adopt its budget ordinance not later than July 1 and on or before July 15 shall notify the county or city collecting its taxes of the rate of tax it has levied. If the district does not notify the county or city governing board on or before July 15 of the rate of tax it has levied, the county or city is not required to collect the district's taxes for the fiscal year.

(b) Transfers from Certain Trust and Agency Funds. - Except for transfers to the appropriate special district or public authority, a unit of local government may not transfer moneys from a fund established to account for taxes collected on behalf of a special district or from a fund established to account for special assessments collected on behalf of a public authority unless the special district or public authority has ceased to function. (1971, c. 780, s. 1; 1973, c. 474, ss. 10, 11; 1975, c. 514, s. 9.)

§ 159-15. Amendments to the budget ordinance.

Except as otherwise restricted by law, the governing board may amend the budget ordinance at any time after the ordinance's adoption in any manner, so long as the ordinance, as amended, continues to satisfy the requirements of G.S. 159-8 and 159-13. However, except as otherwise provided in this section, no amendment may increase or reduce a property tax levy or in any manner alter a property taxpayer's liability, unless the board is ordered to do so by a court of competent jurisdiction, or by a State agency having the power to compel the levy of taxes by the board.

If after July 1 the local government receives revenues that are substantially more or less than the amount anticipated, the governing body may, before January 1 following adoption of the budget, amend the budget ordinance to reduce or increase the property tax levy to account for the unanticipated increase or reduction in revenues.

The governing board by appropriate resolution or ordinance may authorize the budget officer to transfer moneys from one appropriation to another within the same fund subject to such limitations and procedures as it may prescribe. Any such transfers shall be reported to the governing board at its next regular meeting and shall be entered in the minutes. (1927, c. 146, s. 13; 1955, cc. 698, 724; 1971, c. 780, s. 1; 1973, c. 474, s. 12; 2001-308, s. 3; 2002-126, s. 30A.2.)

§ 159-16. Interim budget.

In case the adoption of the budget ordinance is delayed until after July 1, the governing board shall make interim appropriations for the purpose of paying salaries, debt service payments, and the usual ordinary expenses of the local government or public authority for the interval between the beginning of the budget year and the adoption of the budget ordinance. Interim appropriations so made shall be charged to the proper appropriations in the budget ordinance. (1927, c. 146, s. 14; 1955, cc. 698, 724; 1971, c. 780, s. 1.)

§ 159-17. Ordinance procedures not applicable to budget or project ordinance adoption.

Notwithstanding the provisions of any city charter, general law, or local act:

(1) Any action with respect to the adoption or amendment of the budget ordinance or any project ordinance may be taken at any regular or special meeting of the governing board by a simple majority of those present and voting, a quorum being present;

(2) No action taken with respect to the adoption or amendment of the budget ordinance or any project ordinance need be published or is subject to any other procedural requirement governing the adoption of ordinances or resolutions by the governing board other than the procedures set out in this Article;

(3) The adoption and amendment of the budget ordinance or any project ordinance and the levy of taxes in the budget ordinance are not subject to the provisions of any city charter or local act concerning initiative or referendum.

During the period beginning with the submission of the budget to the governing board and ending with the adoption of the budget ordinance, the governing board may hold any special meetings that may be necessary to complete its work on the budget ordinance. Except for the notice requirements of G.S. 143-318.12, which continue to apply, no provision of law concerning the call of special meetings applies during that period so long as (i) each member of the board has actual notice of each special meeting called for the purpose of considering the budget, and (ii) no business other than consideration of the budget is taken up. This section does not allow the holding of closed meetings or executive sessions by any governing board otherwise prohibited by law from holding such a meeting or session, and may not be construed to do so.

No general law, city charter, or local act enacted or taking effect after July 1, 1973, may be construed to modify, amend, or repeal any portion of this section unless it expressly so provides by specific reference to this section. (1971, c. 780, s. 1; 1973, c. 474, s. 13; 1979, c. 402, ss. 4, 5; c. 655, s. 2.)

§ 159-17.1. Vending facilities.

Moneys received by a public authority, special district, or unit of local government on account of operation of vending facilities shall be deposited, budgeted, appropriated, and expended in accordance with the provisions of this Article. (1983 (Reg. Sess., 1984), c. 1034, s. 174.)

Part 2. Capital Reserve Funds.

§ 159-18. Capital reserve funds.

Any local government or public authority may establish and maintain a capital reserve fund for any purposes for which it may issue bonds. A capital reserve fund shall be established by resolution or ordinance of the governing board which shall state (i) the purposes for which the fund is created, (ii) the approximate periods of time during which the moneys are to be accumulated for each purpose, (iii) the approximate amounts to be accumulated for each purpose, and (iv) the sources from which moneys for each purpose will be derived. (1943, c. 593, ss. 3, 5; 1957, c. 863, s. 1; 1967, c. 1189; 1971, c. 780, s. 1.)

§ 159-19. Amendments.

The resolution or ordinance may be amended from time to time in the same manner in which it was adopted. Amendments may, among other provisions, authorize the use of moneys accumulated or to be accumulated in the fund for capital outlay purposes not originally stated. (1943, c. 593, s. 7; 1967, c. 1189; 1971, c. 780, s. 1; 1973, c. 474, s. 14.)

§ 159-20. Funding capital reserve funds.

Capital reserve funds may be funded by appropriations from any other fund consistent with the limitations imposed in G.S. 159-13(b). When moneys or investment securities, the use of which is restricted by law, come into a capital reserve fund, the identity of such moneys or investment securities shall be maintained by appropriate accounting entries. (1943, c. 593, s. 4; 1945, c. 464, s. 2; 1957, c. 863, s. 1; 1967, c. 1189; 1971, c. 780, s. 1; 1973, c. 474, s. 15.)

§ 159-21. Investment.

The cash balances, in whole or in part, of capital reserve funds may be deposited at interest or invested as provided by G.S. 159-30. (1957, c. 863, s. 1; 1967, c. 1189; 1971, c. 780, s. 1.)

§ 159-22. Withdrawals.

Withdrawals from a capital reserve fund may be authorized by resolution or ordinance of the governing board of the local government or public authority. No withdrawal may be authorized for any purpose not specified in the resolution or ordinance establishing the fund or in a resolution or ordinance amending it. The withdrawal resolution or ordinance shall authorize an appropriation from the capital reserve fund to an appropriate appropriation in one of the funds maintained pursuant to G.S. 159-13(a). No withdrawal may be made which would result in an appropriation for purposes for which an adequate balance of eligible moneys or investment securities is not then available in the capital reserve fund. (1943, c. 593, ss. 11, 16; 1945, c. 464, s. 2; 1949, c. 196, s. 3; 1957, c. 863, s. 1; 1967, c. 1189; 1971, c. 780, s. 1; 1973, c. 474, s. 16.)

§ 159-23. Reserved for future codification purposes.

Part 3. Fiscal Control.

§ 159-24. Finance officer.

Each local government and public authority shall appoint a finance officer to hold office at the pleasure of the appointing board or official. The finance officer may be entitled "accountant," "treasurer," "finance director," "finance officer," or any other reasonably descriptive title. The duties of the finance officer may be imposed on the budget officer or any other officer or employee on whom the duties of budget officer may be imposed. (1971, c. 780, s. 1; 1973, c. 474, s. 17.)

§ 159-25. Duties of finance officer; dual signatures on checks; internal control procedures subject to Commission regulation.

(a) The finance officer shall have the following powers and duties:

(1) He shall keep the accounts of the local government or public authority in accordance with generally accepted principles of governmental accounting and the rules and regulations of the Commission.

(2) He shall disburse all funds of the local government or public authority in strict compliance with this Chapter, the budget ordinance, and each project ordinance and shall preaudit obligations and disbursements as required by this Chapter.

(3) As often as may be requested by the governing board or the manager, he shall prepare and file with the board a statement of the financial condition of the local government or public authority.

(4) He shall receive and deposit all moneys accruing to the local government or public authority, or supervise the receipt and deposit of money by other duly authorized officers or employees.

(5) He shall maintain all records concerning the bonded debt and other obligations of the local government or public authority, determine the amount of money that will be required for debt service or the payment of other obligations during each fiscal year, and maintain all sinking funds.

(6) He shall supervise the investment of idle funds of the local government or public authority.

(7) He shall perform such other duties as may be assigned to him by law, by the manager, budget officer, or governing board, or by rules and regulations of the Commission.

All references in other portions of the General Statutes, local acts, or city charters to county, city, special district, or public authority accountants, treasurers, or other officials performing any of the duties conferred by this section on the finance officer shall be deemed to refer to the finance officer.

(b) Except as otherwise provided by law, all checks or drafts on an official depository shall be signed by the finance officer or a properly designated deputy finance officer and countersigned by another official of the local government or public authority designated for this purpose by the governing board. If the board makes no other designation, the chairman of the board or chief executive officer of the local government or public authority shall countersign these checks and drafts. The governing board of a unit or authority may waive the requirements of this subsection if the board determines that the internal control procedures of the unit or authority will be satisfactory in the absence of dual signatures.

(c) The Local Government Commission has authority to issue rules and regulations having the force of law governing procedures for the receipt, deposit, investment, transfer, and disbursement of money and other assets by units of local government and public authorities, may inquire into and investigate the internal control procedures of a local government or public authority, and may require any modifications in internal control procedures which, in the opinion of the Commission, are necessary or desirable to prevent embezzlements or mishandling of public moneys. (1971, c. 780, s. 1; 1973, c. 474, ss. 18-20; 1975, c. 514, s. 10; 1987, c. 796, s. 3(5).)

§ 159-26. Accounting system.

(a) System Required. - Each local government or public authority shall establish and maintain an accounting system designed to show in detail its assets, liabilities, equities, revenues, and expenditures. The system shall also be designed to show appropriations and estimated revenues as established in the budget ordinance and each project ordinance as originally adopted and subsequently amended.

(b) Funds Required. - Each local government or public authority shall establish and maintain in its accounting system such of the following funds and ledgers as are applicable to it. The generic meaning of each type of fund or ledger listed below is that fixed by generally accepted accounting principles.

(1) General fund.

(2) Special Revenue Funds. - One or more separate funds shall be established for each of the following classes: (i) functions or activities financed in whole or in part by property taxes voted by the people, (ii) service districts established pursuant to the Municipal or County Service District Acts, and (iii) grant project ordinances. If more than one function is accounted for in a voted

tax fund, or more than one district in a service district fund, or more than one grant project in a project fund, separate accounts shall be established in the appropriate fund for each function, district, or project.

(3) Debt service funds.

(4) A Fund for Each Utility or Enterprise Owned or Operated by the Unit or Public Authority. - If a water system and a sanitary sewerage system are operated as a consolidated system, one fund may be established and maintained for the consolidated system.

(5) Internal service funds.

(6) Capital Project Funds. - Such a fund shall be established to account for the proceeds of each bond order or order authorizing any debt instrument and for all other resources used for the capital projects financed by the bond or debt instrument proceeds. A unit or public authority may account for two or more bond orders or orders authorizing any debt instrument in one capital projects fund, but the proceeds of each such order and the other revenues associated with that order shall be separately accounted for in the fund.

(7) Trust and agency funds, including a fund for each special district, public authority, or school administrative unit whose taxes or special assessments are collected by the unit.

(8) A ledger or group of accounts in which to record the details relating to the general fixed assets of the unit or public authority.

(9) A ledger or group of accounts in which to record the details relating to the general obligation bonds and notes and other long-term obligations of the unit.

In addition, each unit or public authority shall establish and maintain any other funds required by other statutes or by State or federal regulations.

(c) Basis of Accounting. - Except as otherwise provided by regulation of the Commission, local governments and public authorities shall use the modified accrual basis of accounting in recording transactions.

(d) Encumbrance Systems. - Except as otherwise provided in this subsection, no local government or public authority is required to record or show encumbrances in its accounting system. Each city or town with a population over 10,000 and each county with a population over 50,000 shall maintain an accounting system that records and shows the encumbrances outstanding against each category of expenditure appropriated in its budget ordinance. Any other local government or any public authority may record and show encumbrances in its accounting system. In determining a unit's population, the most recent federal decennial census shall be used.

(e)   Commission Regulations. - The Commission may prescribe rules and regulations having the force of law as to:

(1)   Features of accounting systems to be maintained by local governments and public authorities.

(2)   Bases of accounting, including identifying in detail the characteristics of a modified accrual basis, identifying what revenues are susceptible to accrual, and permitting or requiring use of a basis other than modified accrual in a fund that does not account for the receipt of a tax.

(3)   Definitions of terms not clearly defined in this Article.

The Commission may vary these rules and regulations according to any other criteria reasonably related to the purpose or complexity of the financial operations involved. (1971, c. 780, s. 1; 1975, c. 514, ss. 11, 16; 1979, c. 402, s. 6; 1981, c. 685, ss. 6, 7; 1987, c. 796, s. 3(6).)

§ 159-27. Distribution of tax collections among funds according to levy.

(a)   The finance officer shall distribute property tax collections among the appropriate funds, according to the budget ordinance, at least monthly.

(b)   Taxes collected during the current fiscal year, that were levied in any one of the two immediately preceding fiscal years, shall be distributed to the appropriate funds according to the levy of the fiscal year in which they were levied. If any fund for which such taxes were levied is not being maintained in the current fiscal year, the proportionate share of the tax that would have been distributed to the discontinued fund shall be allocated (i) to the fund from which the activity or function for which the tax was levied is then being financed, or (ii) to the general fund if the activity or function for which the tax was levied is no longer being performed.

(c)   Taxes collected during the current fiscal year, that were levied in any prior fiscal year other than one of the two immediately preceding fiscal years, may be distributed in the discretion of the governing board either (i) to the general fund, or (ii) in accordance with subsection (b) of this section. This subsection shall not repeal any portion of a local act or city charter inconsistent herewith and in effect on July 1, 1973.

(d)   This section applies to taxes levied by a unit of local government on behalf of another unit, including school administrative units. (1971, c. 780, s. 1; 1973, c. 474, s. 21; 1975, c. 437, s. 15.)

§ 159-27.1. Use of revenue bond project reimbursements; restrictions.

The finance officer of a unit shall deposit any funds received by the unit as a reimbursement of a loan or advance made by the unit pursuant to G.S. 159-83(a)(8a) in the fund from which the unit originally derived the funds to make the loan or advance.

If the funds originally loaned or advanced were proceeds of a bond issue, any funds received as reimbursement shall be applied as required by this section. The funds shall be applied as provided in the instrument securing payment of the bond issue if the instrument contains applicable provisions. Otherwise, the funds shall be applied to either (i) the same general purposes as those for which the bond issue was authorized, or (ii) payment of debt service on the bond issue, including principal, interest, and premium, if any, upon redemption, or payment of the purchase price of bonds for retirement at not more than their face value and accrued interest. After all the bonds of the issue have been paid or satisfied in full, any funds received as reimbursement shall be deposited in the general fund of the unit and may be used for any general fund purpose. (1991, c. 508, s. 3, c. 761, s. 29.)

§ 159-28. Budgetary accounting for appropriations.

(a) Incurring Obligations. - No obligation may be incurred in a program, function, or activity accounted for in a fund included in the budget ordinance unless the budget ordinance includes an appropriation authorizing the obligation and an unencumbered balance remains in the appropriation sufficient to pay in the current fiscal year the sums obligated by the transaction for the current fiscal year. No obligation may be incurred for a capital project or a grant project authorized by a project ordinance unless that project ordinance includes an appropriation authorizing the obligation and an unencumbered balance remains in the appropriation sufficient to pay the sums obligated by the transaction. If an obligation is evidenced by a contract or agreement requiring the payment of money or by a purchase order for supplies and materials, the contract, agreement, or purchase order shall include on its face a certificate stating that the instrument has been preaudited to assure compliance with this subsection unless the obligation or a document related to the obligation has been approved by the Local Government Commission, in which case no certificate shall be required. The certificate, which shall be signed by the finance officer or any deputy finance officer approved for this purpose by the governing board, shall take substantially the following form:

"This instrument has been preaudited in the manner required by the Local Government Budget and Fiscal Control Act.

_____

(Signature of finance officer)."

Certificates in the form prescribed by G.S. 153-130 or 160-411 as those sections read on June 30, 1973, or by G.S. 159-28(b) as that section read on June 30, 1975, are sufficient until supplies of forms in existence on June 30, 1975, are exhausted.

An obligation incurred in violation of this subsection is invalid and may not be enforced. The finance officer shall establish procedures to assure compliance with this subsection.

(b) Disbursements. - When a bill, invoice, or other claim against a local government or public authority is presented, the finance officer shall either approve or disapprove the necessary disbursement. If the claim involves a program, function, or activity accounted for in a fund included in the budget ordinance or a capital project or a grant project authorized by a project ordinance, the finance officer may approve the claim only if

(1) He determines the amount to be payable and

(2) The budget ordinance or a project ordinance includes an appropriation authorizing the expenditure and either (i) an encumbrance has been previously created for the transaction or (ii) an unencumbered balance remains in the appropriation sufficient to pay the amount to be disbursed.

The finance officer may approve a bill, invoice, or other claim requiring disbursement from an intragovernmental service fund or trust or agency fund not included in the budget ordinance, only if the amount claimed is determined to be payable. A bill, invoice, or other claim may not be paid unless it has been approved by the finance officer or, under subsection (c) of this section, by the governing board. The finance officer shall establish procedures to assure compliance with this subsection.

(c) Governing Board Approval of Bills, Invoices, or Claims. - The governing board may, as permitted by this subsection, approve a bill, invoice, or other claim against the local government or public authority that has been disapproved by the finance officer. It may not approve a claim for which no appropriation appears in the budget ordinance or in a project ordinance, or for which the appropriation contains no encumbrance and the unencumbered balance is less than the amount to be paid. The governing board shall approve payment by formal resolution stating the board's reasons for allowing the bill, invoice, or other claim. The resolution shall be entered in the minutes together with the names of those voting in the affirmative. The chairman of the board or some other member designated for this purpose shall sign the certificate on the check or draft given in payment of the bill, invoice, or other claim. If payment results in a violation of law, each member of the board voting to allow payment is jointly and severally liable for the full amount of the check or draft given in payment.

(d) Payment. - A local government or public authority may not pay a bill, invoice, salary, or other claim except by a check or draft on an official depository, a bank wire transfer from an official depository, or an electronic payment or an electronic funds transfer originated by the local government or public authority through an official depository. Except as provided in this subsection each check or draft on an official depository shall bear on its face a certificate signed by the finance officer or a deputy finance officer approved for this purpose by the governing board (or signed by the chairman or some other member of the board pursuant to subsection (c) of this section). The certificate shall take substantially the following form:

"This disbursement has been approved as required by the Local Government Budget and Fiscal Control Act.

_____

(Signature of finance officer)."

An electronic payment or electronic funds transfer must be subjected to the pre-audit process. Execution of the electronic payment or electronic funds transfer shall indicate that the finance officer or duly appointed deputy finance officer has performed the pre-audit process as required by G.S. 159-28(a).

Certificates in the form prescribed by G.S. 153-131 or 160-411.1 as those sections read on June 30, 1973, or by G.S. 159-28(a) as that section read on June 30, 1975, are sufficient until supplies in existence on June 30, 1975, are exhausted.

No certificate is required on payroll checks or drafts on an imprest account in an official depository, if the check or draft depositing the funds in the imprest account carried a signed certificate.

As used in this subsection, the term "electronic payment" means payment by charge card, credit card, debit card, or by electronic funds transfer, and the term "electronic funds transfer" means a transfer of funds initiated by using an electronic terminal, a telephone, a computer, or magnetic tape to instruct or authorize a financial institution or its agent to credit or debit an account.

(e)   Penalties. - If an officer or employee of a local government or public authority incurs an obligation or pays out or causes to be paid out any funds in violation of this section, he and the sureties on his official bond are liable for any sums so committed or disbursed. If the finance officer or any properly designated deputy finance officer gives a false certificate to any contract, agreement, purchase order, check, draft, or other document, he and the sureties on his official bond are liable for any sums illegally committed or disbursed thereby. (1971, c. 780, s. 1; 1973, c. 474, ss. 22, 23; 1975, c. 514, s. 12; 1979, c. 402, ss. 7, 8; 2010-99, s. 1; 2012-156, s. 1.)

§ 159-28.1. Facsimile signatures.

The governing board of a local government or public authority may provide by appropriate resolution or ordinance for the use of facsimile signature machines, signature stamps, or similar devices in signing checks and drafts and in signing the preaudit certificate on contracts or purchase orders. The board shall charge the finance officer or some other bonded officer or employee with the custody of the necessary machines, stamps, plates, or other devices, and that person and the sureties on his official bond are liable for any illegal, improper, or unauthorized use of them. (1975, c. 514, s. 13.)

§ 159-29. Fidelity bonds.

(a) The finance officer shall give a true accounting and faithful performance bond with sufficient sureties in an amount to be fixed by the governing board, not less than fifty thousand dollars ($50,000). The premium on the bond shall be paid by the local government or public authority.

(b) Each officer, employee, or agent of a local government or public authority who handles or has in his custody more than one hundred dollars ($100.00) of the unit's or public authority's funds at any time, or who handles or has access to the inventories of the unit or public authority, shall, before being entitled to assume his duties, give a faithful performance bond with sufficient sureties payable to the local government or public authority. The governing board shall determine the amount of the bond, and the unit or public authority may pay the premium on the bond. Each bond, when approved by the governing board, shall be deposited with the clerk to the board.

If another statute requires an officer, employee, or agent to be bonded, this subsection does not require an additional bond for that officer, employee, or agent.

(c) A local government or public authority may adopt a system of blanket faithful performance bonding as an alternative to individual bonds. If such a system is adopted, statutory requirements of individual bonds, except for elected officials and for finance officers and tax collectors by whatever title known, do not apply to an officer, employee, or agent covered by the blanket bond. However, although an individual bond is required for an elected official, a tax collector, or finance officer, such an officer or elected official may also be included within the coverage of a blanket bond if the blanket bond protects against risks not protected against by the individual bond. (1971, c. 780, s. 1; 1975, c. 514, s. 14; 1987 (Reg. Sess., 1988), c. 975, s. 32; 2005-238, s. 2.)

§ 159-30. Investment of idle funds.

(a) A local government or public authority may deposit at interest or invest all or part of the cash balance of any fund. The finance officer shall manage investments subject to whatever restrictions and directions the governing board may impose. The finance officer shall have the power to purchase, sell, and exchange securities on behalf of the governing board. The investment program shall be so managed that investments and deposits can be converted into cash when needed.

(b) Moneys may be deposited at interest in any bank, savings and loan association, or trust company in this State in the form of certificates of deposit or such other forms of time deposit as the Commission may approve. Investment deposits, including investment deposits of a mutual fund for local government investment established under subdivision (c)(8) of this section, shall be secured as provided in G.S. 159-31(b).

(b1) In addition to deposits authorized by subsection (b) of this section, the finance officer may deposit any portion of idle funds in accordance with all of the following conditions:

(1) The funds are initially deposited through a bank or savings and loan association that is an official depository and that is selected by the finance officer.

(2) The selected bank or savings and loan association arranges for the redeposit of funds in deposit accounts of the local government or public authority in one or more federally insured banks or savings and loan associations wherever located, provided that no funds shall be deposited in a bank or savings and loan association that at the time holds other deposits from the local government or public authority.

(3) The full amount of principal and any accrued interest of each deposit account are covered by federal deposit insurance.

(4) The selected bank or savings and loan association acts as custodian for the local government or public authority with respect to the deposit in the local government's or public authority's account.

(5) On the same date that the local government or public authority funds are redeposited, the selected bank or savings and loan association receives an amount of federally insured deposits from customers of other financial institutions wherever located equal to or greater than the amount of the funds invested by the local government or public authority through the selected bank or savings and loan association.

(c) Moneys may be invested in the following classes of securities, and no others:

(1) Obligations of the United States or obligations fully guaranteed both as to principal and interest by the United States.

(2) Obligations of the Federal Financing Bank, the Federal Farm Credit Bank, the Bank for Cooperatives, the Federal Intermediate Credit Bank, the Federal Land Banks, the Federal Home Loan Banks, the Federal Home Loan Mortgage Corporation, Fannie Mae, the Government National Mortgage Association, the Federal Housing Administration, the Farmers Home Administration, the United States Postal Service.

(3) Obligations of the State of North Carolina.

(4) Bonds and notes of any North Carolina local government or public authority, subject to such restrictions as the secretary may impose.

(5) Savings certificates issued by any savings and loan association organized under the laws of the State of North Carolina or by any federal savings and loan association having its principal office in North Carolina; provided that any principal amount of such certificate in excess of the amount insured by the federal government or any agency thereof, or by a mutual deposit guaranty association authorized by the Commissioner of Banks of the Department of Commerce of the State of North Carolina, be fully collateralized.

(6) Prime quality commercial paper bearing the highest rating of at least one nationally recognized rating service and not bearing a rating below the highest by any nationally recognized rating service which rates the particular obligation.

(7) Bills of exchange or time drafts drawn on and accepted by a commercial bank and eligible for use as collateral by member banks in borrowing from a federal reserve bank, provided that the accepting bank or its holding company is

either (i) incorporated in the State of North Carolina or (ii) has outstanding publicly held obligations bearing the highest rating of at least one nationally recognized rating service and not bearing a rating below the highest by any nationally recognized rating service which rates the particular obligations.

(8) Participating shares in a mutual fund for local government investment; provided that the investments of the fund are limited to those qualifying for investment under this subsection (c) and that said fund is certified by the Local Government Commission. The Local Government Commission shall have the authority to issue rules and regulations concerning the establishment and qualifications of any mutual fund for local government investment.

(9) A commingled investment pool established and administered by the State Treasurer pursuant to G.S. 147-69.3.

(10) A commingled investment pool established by interlocal agreement by two or more units of local government pursuant to G.S. 160A-460 through G.S. 160A-464, if the investments of the pool are limited to those qualifying for investment under this subsection (c).

(11) Evidences of ownership of, or fractional undivided interests in, future interest and principal payments on either direct obligations of the United States government or obligations the principal of and the interest on which are guaranteed by the United States, which obligations are held by a bank or trust company organized and existing under the laws of the United States or any state in the capacity of custodian.

(12) Repurchase agreements with respect to either direct obligations of the United States or obligations the principal of and the interest on which are guaranteed by the United States if entered into with a broker or dealer, as defined by the Securities Exchange Act of 1934, which is a dealer recognized as a primary dealer by a Federal Reserve Bank, or any commercial bank, trust company or national banking association, the deposits of which are insured by the Federal Deposit Insurance Corporation or any successor thereof if:

a. Such obligations that are subject to such repurchase agreement are delivered (in physical or in book entry form) to the local government or public authority, or any financial institution serving either as trustee for the local government or public authority or as fiscal agent for the local government or public authority or are supported by a safekeeping receipt issued by a depository satisfactory to the local government or public authority, provided that such repurchase agreement must provide that the value of the underlying obligations shall be maintained at a current market value, calculated at least daily, of not less than one hundred percent (100%) of the repurchase price, and, provided further, that the financial institution serving either as trustee or as fiscal agent for the local government or public authority holding the obligations subject to the repurchase agreement hereunder or the depository issuing the safekeeping receipt shall not be the provider of the repurchase agreement;

b.   A valid and perfected first security interest in the obligations which are the subject of such repurchase agreement has been granted to the local government or public authority or its assignee or book entry procedures, conforming, to the extent practicable, with federal regulations and satisfactory to the local government or public authority have been established for the benefit of the local government or public authority or its assignee;

c.   Such securities are free and clear of any adverse third party claims; and

d.   Such repurchase agreement is in a form satisfactory to the local government or public authority.

(13)   In connection with funds held by or on behalf of a local government or public authority, which funds are subject to the arbitrage and rebate provisions of the Internal Revenue Code of 1986, as amended, participating shares in tax-exempt mutual funds, to the extent such participation, in whole or in part, is not subject to such rebate provisions, and taxable mutual funds, to the extent such fund provides services in connection with the calculation of arbitrage rebate requirements under federal income tax law; provided, the investments of any such fund are limited to those bearing one of the two highest ratings of at least one nationally recognized rating service and not bearing a rating below one of the two highest ratings by any nationally recognized rating service which rates the particular fund.

(d)   Investment securities may be bought, sold, and traded by private negotiation, and local governments and public authorities may pay all incidental costs thereof and all reasonable costs of administering the investment and deposit program. Securities and deposit certificates shall be in the custody of the finance officer who shall be responsible for their safekeeping and for keeping accurate investment accounts and records.

(e)   Interest earned on deposits and investments shall be credited to the fund whose cash is deposited or invested. Cash of several funds may be combined for deposit or investment if not otherwise prohibited by law; and when such joint deposits or investments are made, interest earned shall be prorated and credited to the various funds on the basis of the amounts thereof invested, figured according to an average periodic balance or some other sound accounting principle. Interest earned on the deposit or investment of bond funds shall be deemed a part of the bond proceeds.

(f) Registered securities acquired for investment may be released from registration and transferred by signature of the finance officer.

(g) A local government, public authority, an entity eligible to participate in the Local Government Employee's Retirement System, or a local school administrative unit may make contributions to a Local Government Other Post-Employment Benefits Trust established pursuant to G.S. 159-30.1.

(h) A unit of local government employing local law enforcement officers may make contributions to the Local Government Law Enforcement Special Separation Allowance Fund established in G.S. 147-69.5. (1957, c. 864, s. 1; 1967, c. 798, ss. 1, 2; 1969, c. 862; 1971, c. 780, s. 1; 1973, c. 474, ss. 24, 25; 1975, c. 481; 1977, c. 575; 1979, c. 717, s. 2; 1981, c. 445, ss. 1-3; 1983, c. 158, ss. 1, 2; 1987, c. 672, s. 1; 1989, c. 76, s. 31; c. 751, s. 7(46); 1991 (Reg. Sess., 1992), c. 959, s. 77; c. 1007, s. 40; 1993, c. 553, s. 55; 2001-193, s. 16; 2001-487, s. 14(o); 2005-394, s. 2; 2007-384, ss. 4, 9; 2010-175, s. 1; 2013-305, s. 1.)

§ 159-30.1. Trust for other post-employment benefits.

(a) Trust. - A local government, a public authority, an entity eligible to participate in the Local Government Employee's Retirement System, or a local school administrative unit may establish and fund an irrevocable trust for the purpose of paying post-employment benefits for which the entity is liable. The irrevocable trust must be established by resolution or ordinance of the entity's governing board. The resolution or ordinance must state the purposes for which the trust is created and the method of determining and selecting the Fund's trustees. The resolution or ordinance establishing the trust may be amended from time to time, but an amendment may not authorize the use of monies in the trust for a purpose not stated in the resolution or ordinance establishing the trust.

(b) Restrictions. - Monies in an irrevocable trust established under subsection (a) of this section may be appropriated only for the purposes for which the trust was established. Monies in the trust are not subject to the claims of creditors of the entity that established the trust. An entity that establishes a trust may not deposit money in the trust if the total amount held in trust would exceed the entity's actuarial liability, determined in accordance with the standards of the Governmental Accounting Standards Board, for the purposes for which the trust was established. A trust established pursuant to subsection (a) of this section shall be referred to as a Local Government Other Post-Retirement Benefits Trust, and the assets of that trust may be invested as provided in G.S. 159-30(c) or deposited with the State Treasurer for investment pursuant to G.S. 147-69.2(b4). (2007-384, s. 5; 2010-175, s. 2.)

§ 159-30.2. Trust for law enforcement special separation allowance benefits.

(a) Trust. - A unit of local government employing local law enforcement officers may establish and fund an irrevocable trust for the purpose of paying law enforcement special separation allowance benefits for which the unit of local government is liable. The irrevocable trust must be established by resolution or ordinance of the unit's governing board. The resolution or ordinance must state the purposes for which the trust is created and the method of determining and selecting the Fund's trustees. The resolution or ordinance establishing the trust may be amended from time to time, but an amendment may not authorize the use of monies in the trust for a purpose not stated in the resolution or ordinance establishing the trust.

(b) Restrictions. - Monies in an irrevocable trust established under subsection (a) of this section may be appropriated only for the purposes for which the trust was established. Monies in the trust are not subject to the claims of creditors of the entity that established the trust. A unit of local government that establishes a trust may not deposit money in the trust if the total amount held in trust would exceed the unit's actuarial liability, determined in accordance with the standards of the Governmental Accounting Standards Board, for the purpose for which the trust was established. (2007-384, s. 10.)

§ 159-31. Selection of depository; deposits to be secured.

(a) The governing board of each local government and public authority shall designate as its official depositories one or more banks, savings and loan associations, or trust companies in this State or, with the written permission of the secretary, a national bank located in another state. In addition, a unit or public authority, with the written permission of the secretary, may designate a state bank or trust company located in another state as an official depository for the purpose of acting as fiscal agent for the unit or public authority. The names and addresses of the depositories shall be reported to the secretary. It shall be unlawful for any public moneys to be deposited in any place, bank, or trust company other than an official depository, except as permitted by G.S. 159-30(b); however, public moneys may be deposited in official depositories in Negotiable Order of Withdrawal (NOW) accounts.

(b) The amount of funds on deposit in an official depository or deposited at interest pursuant to G.S. 159-30(b) shall be secured by deposit insurance, surety bonds, letters of credit issued by a Federal Home Loan Bank, or investment securities of such nature, in a sufficient amount to protect the local government or public authority on account of deposit of funds made therein, and in such manner, as may be prescribed by rule or regulation of the Local Government Commission. When deposits are secured in accordance with this subsection, no public officer or employee may be held liable for any losses sustained by a local government or public authority because of the default or insolvency of the depository. No security is required for the protection of funds remitted to and received by a bank, savings and loan association, or trust company acting as fiscal agent for the payment of principal and interest on bonds or notes, when the funds are remitted no more than 60 days prior to the maturity date. (1927, c. 146, s. 19; 1929, c. 37; 1931, c. 60, s. 32; c. 296, s. 7; 1935, c. 375, s. 1; 1939, c. 129, s. 1; c. 134; 1953, c. 675, s. 28; 1955, cc. 698, 724; 1971, c. 780, s. 1; 1973, c. 474, s. 26; 1979, c. 637, s. 1; 1981, c. 447, s. 2; 1983, c. 158, s. 3; 1999-74, s. 1.)

§ 159-32. Daily deposits.

Except as otherwise provided by law, all taxes and other moneys collected or received by an officer or employee of a local government or public authority shall be deposited in accordance with this section. Each officer and employee of a local government or public authority whose duty it is to collect or receive any taxes or other moneys shall deposit his collections and receipts daily. If the governing board gives its approval, deposits shall be required only when the moneys on hand amount to as much as two hundred fifty dollars ($250.00), but in any event a deposit shall be made on the last business day of the month. All deposits shall be made with the finance officer or in an official depository. Deposits in an official depository shall be immediately reported to the finance officer by means of a duplicate deposit ticket. The finance officer may at any time audit the accounts of any officer or employee collecting or receiving taxes or other moneys, and may prescribe the form and detail of these accounts. The accounts of such an officer or employee shall be audited at least annually. (1927, c. 146, s. 19; 1929, c. 37; 1939, c. 134; 1955, cc. 698, 724; 1971, c. 780, s. 1; 1973, c. 474, s. 27.)

§ 159-32.1. Electronic payment.

A unit of local government, public hospital, or public authority may, in lieu of payment by cash or check, accept payment by electronic payment as defined in G.S. 147-86.20 for any tax, assessment, rate, fee, charge, rent, interest, penalty, or other receivable owed to it. A unit of local government, public hospital, or public authority may pay any negotiated discount, processing fee, transaction fee, or other charge imposed by a credit card, charge card, or debit card company, or by a third-party merchant bank, as a condition of contracting for the unit's or the authority's acceptance of electronic payment. A unit of local government, public hospital, or public authority may impose the fee or charge as a surcharge on the amount paid by the person using electronic payment. (1999-434, s. 5.)

§ 159-33. Semiannual reports on status of deposits and investments.

Each officer having custody of any funds of any local government or public authority shall report to the secretary of the Local Government Commission on January 1 and July 1 of each year (or such other dates as he may prescribe) the amounts of funds then in his custody, the amounts of deposits of such funds in depositories, and a list of all investment securities and time deposits held by the local government or public authority. In like manner, each bank or trust company acting as the official depository of any unit of local government or public authority may be required to report to the secretary a description of the surety bonds or investment securities securing such public deposits. If the secretary finds at any time that any funds of any unit or authority are not properly deposited or secured, or are invested in securities not eligible for investment, he shall notify the officer or depository in charge of the funds of the failure to comply with law or applicable regulations of the Commission. Upon such notification, the officer or depository shall comply with the law or regulations within 30 days, except as to the sale of securities not eligible for investment which shall be sold within nine months at a price to be approved by the secretary. The Commission may extend the time for sale of ineligible securities, but no one extension may cover a period of more than one year. (1931, c. 60, s. 33; 1971, c. 780, s. 1; 1979, c. 637, s. 2.)

§ 159-33.1. Semiannual reports of financial information.

The finance officer of each unit and public authority shall submit to the secretary on January 1 and July 1 of each year (or such other dates as the secretary may prescribe) a statement of financial information concerning the unit or public authority. The secretary may prescribe the information to be included in the statement and may prescribe the form of the statement. (1973, c. 474, s. 28.)

§ 159-34. Annual independent audit; rules and regulations.

(a) Each unit of local government and public authority shall have its accounts audited as soon as possible after the close of each fiscal year by a certified public accountant or by an accountant certified by the Commission as qualified to audit local government accounts. When specified by the secretary, the audit shall evaluate the performance of a unit of local government or public authority with regard to compliance with all applicable federal and State agency regulations. This audit, combined with the audit of financial accounts, shall be deemed to be the single audit described by the "Federal Single Audit Act of 1984". The auditor shall be selected by and shall report directly to the governing board. The audit contract or agreement shall (i) be in writing, (ii) include the entire entity in the scope of the audit, except that an audit for purposes other than the annual audit required by this section should include an accurate description of the scope of the audit, (iii) require that a typewritten or printed report on the audit be prepared as set forth herein, (iv) include all of its terms and conditions, and (v) be submitted to the secretary for his approval as to form, terms, conditions, and compliance with the rules of the Commission. As a minimum, the required report shall include the financial statements prepared in accordance with generally accepted accounting principles, all disclosures in the public interest required by law, and the auditor's opinion and comments relating to financial statements. The audit shall be performed in conformity with generally accepted auditing standards. The finance officer shall file a copy of the audit report with the secretary, and shall submit all bills or claims for audit fees and costs to the secretary for his approval. Before giving his approval the secretary shall determine that the audit and audit report substantially conform to the requirements of this section. It shall be unlawful for any unit of local government or public authority to pay or permit the payment of such bills or claims without this approval. Each officer and employee of the local government or local public authority having custody of public money or responsibility for keeping records of public financial or fiscal affairs shall produce all books and records requested by the auditor and shall divulge such information relating to fiscal affairs as he may request. If any member of a governing board or any other public officer or employee shall conceal, falsify, or refuse to deliver or divulge any books, records, or information, with an attempt thereby to mislead the auditor or impede or interfere with the audit, he is guilty of a Class 1 misdemeanor.

(b) The Local Government Commission has authority to issue rules and regulations for the purpose of improving the quality of auditing and the quality and comparability of reporting pursuant to this section or any similar section of the General Statutes. The rules and regulations may consider the needs of the public for adequate information and the performance that the auditor has demonstrated in the past, and may be varied according to the size, purpose or function of the unit, or any other criteria reasonably related to the purpose or substance of the rules or regulation.

(c) Notwithstanding any other provision of law, except for Article 5A of Chapter 147 of the General Statutes pertaining to the State Auditor, all State departments and agencies shall rely upon the single audit accepted by the secretary as the basis for compliance with applicable federal and State regulations. All State departments and agencies which provide funds to local governments and public authorities shall provide the Commission with documents that the Commission finds are in the prescribed format describing standards of compliance and suggested audit procedures sufficient to give adequate direction to independent auditors retained by local governments and public authorities to conduct a single audit as required by this section. The secretary shall be responsible for the annual distribution of all such standards of compliance and suggested audit procedures proposed by State departments and agencies and any amendments thereto. Further, the Commission with the cooperation of all affected State departments and agencies shall be responsible for the following:

(1) Procedures for the timely distribution of compliance standards developed by State departments and agencies, reviewed and approved by the Commission to auditors retained by local governments and public authorities.

(2) Procedures for the distribution of single audits for local governments and public authorities such that they are available to all State departments and agencies which provide funds to local units.

(3) The acceptance of single audits on behalf of all State departments and agencies; provided that, the secretary may subsequently revoke such acceptance for cause, whereupon affected State departments and agencies shall no longer rely upon such audit as the basis for compliance with applicable federal and State regulations. (1971, c. 780, s. 1; 1975, c. 514, s. 15; 1979, c. 402, s. 9; 1981, c. 685, ss. 8, 9; 1987, c. 287; 1993, c. 257, s. 20; c. 539, s. 1081; 1994, Ex. Sess., c. 24, s. 14(c); 2001-160, s. 1.)

§ 159-35. Secretary of Local Government Commission to notify units of debt service obligations.

(a) The secretary shall mail to each local government and public authority not later than May 1 of each year a statement of its debt service obligations for the coming fiscal year, including sums to be paid into sinking funds.

(b) The secretary shall mail to each local government and public authority not later than 30 days prior to the due date of each installment of principal or interest on outstanding debt, a statement of the amount of principal and interest so payable, the due date, the place to which the payments should be sent, and a summary of the legal penalties for failing to meet debt service obligations.

(c) The secretary shall mail to each unit of local government not later than 30 days prior to the due date of each payment due to the State under debt instruments issued pursuant to Chapter 159G of the General Statutes or Chapter 159I of the General Statutes a statement of the amount so payable, the due date, the amount of any moneys due to the unit of local government that will be withheld by the State and applied to the payment, the amount due to be paid by the unit of local government from local sources, the place to which payment should be sent, and a summary of the legal penalties for failing to honor the debt instrument according to its terms. Failure of the secretary timely to mail such statement or otherwise comply with the provisions of this subsection (c) shall not affect in any manner the obligation of a unit of local government to make payments to the State in accordance with any such debt instrument. (1931, c. 60, ss. 36, 37; 1971, c. 780, s. 1; 1987, c. 796, s. 3(7); 1989, c. 756, s. 4.)

§ 159-36. Failure of local government to levy debt service taxes or provide for payment of debt.

(a) If any local government or public authority fails or refuses to levy taxes or allocate other revenues in an amount sufficient to meet all installments of principal and interest falling due on its debt during the budget year, or to adequately maintain its sinking funds, the Commission shall enter an order directing and commanding the governing board of the local government or public authority to enact a budget ordinance levying the necessary taxes or raising the necessary revenue by whatever means are legally available. If the governing board shall fail or refuse to comply with the Commission's order within 10 days, the order shall have the same legal force and effect as if the actions therein commanded had been taken by the governing board, and the appropriate officers and employees of the local government or public authority shall proceed to collect the tax levy or implement the plan for raising the revenue to the same extent as if such action had been authorized and directed by the governing board. Any officer, employee, or member of the governing board of any local government or public authority who willfully fails or refuses to implement an order of the Local Government Commission issued pursuant to this section forfeits his office or position.

(b) This section does not apply to contractual obligations undertaken by a unit of local government in a debt instrument issued pursuant to Chapter 159G of the General Statutes unless such debt instrument is secured by a pledge of the faith and credit of the unit of local government. (1971, c. 780, s. 1; 1987, c. 796, s. 3(8).)

§ 159-37. Reports on status of sinking funds.

Each unit or public authority maintaining any sinking fund shall transmit to the secretary upon his request financial reports on the status of the fund and the means by which moneys are obtained for deposit therein. The secretary shall determine from this information whether the sinking funds are being properly maintained, and if he shall find that they are not, he shall order the unit to take such action as may be necessary to maintain the funds in accordance with law. (1931, c. 60, s. 31; 1971, c. 780, s. 1.)

§ 159-38. Local units authorized to accept their bonds in payment of certain claims and judgments.

Any unit of local government or public authority may accept its own bonds, at par, in settlement of any claim or judgment that it may have against any person, firm, corporation, or association due to funds held in an insolvent bank, trust company, or savings and loan association. (1933, c. 376; 1971, c. 780, s. 1.)

Part 4. Public Hospitals.

§ 159-39. Special regulations pertaining to public hospitals.

(a)   For the purposes of this Part, "public hospital" means any hospital that

(1)   Is operated by a county, city, hospital district, or hospital authority, or

(2)   Is owned by a county, city, hospital district or hospital authority and operated by a nonprofit corporation or association, a majority of whose board of directors or trustees are appointed by the governing body of a county, city, hospital district, or hospital authority, or

(3)   On whose behalf a county or city has issued and has outstanding general obligation or revenue bonds, or to which a county or city makes current appropriations (other than appropriations for the cost of medical care to prisoners or indigents).

(b)   Except as provided in this Part, none of the provisions of Parts 1, 2, and 3 of this Article apply to public hospitals.

(c) Each public hospital shall operate under an annual balanced budget. A budget is balanced when the sum of appropriations is equal to the sum of estimated net revenues and appropriated fund balances.

(d) The governing board of each public hospital shall appoint or designate a finance officer, who shall have the following powers and duties:

(1) He shall prepare the annual budget for presentation to the governing board of the public hospital and shall administer the budget as approved by the board.

(2) He shall keep the accounts of the hospital in accordance with generally accepted principles of accounting.

(3) He shall prepare and file a statement of the financial condition of the hospital as revealed by its accounts upon the request of the hospital governing board or the governing board of any county, city, or other unit of local government that has issued on behalf of the hospital and has outstanding its general obligation or revenue bonds or makes current appropriations to the hospital (other than appropriations for the cost of medical care to prisoners or indigents).

(4) He shall receive and deposit all moneys accruing to the hospital, or supervise the receipt and deposit of money by other duly authorized officers or employees of the hospital.

(5) He shall supervise the investment of idle funds of the hospital.

(6) He shall maintain all records concerning the bonded debt of the hospital, if any, determine the amount of money that will be required for debt service during each fiscal year, and maintain all sinking funds, but shall not be responsible for records concerning the bonded debt of any county, city, or other unit of local government incurred on behalf of the hospital.

(e) The Local Government Commission has authority to issue rules and regulations governing procedures for the receipt, deposit, investment, transfer, and disbursement of money and other assets by public hospitals, may inquire into and investigate the internal control procedures of a public hospital, and may require any modifications in internal control procedures which, in the opinion of the Commission, are necessary or desirable to prevent embezzlements, mishandling of funds, or continued operating deficits.

(f) The accounting system of a public hospital shall be so designed that the true financial condition of the hospital can be determined therefrom at any time. As soon as possible after the close of each fiscal year, the accounts shall be audited by a certified public accountant or by an accountant certified by the Local Government Commission as qualified to audit local government accounts. The auditor shall be selected by and shall report directly to the hospital governing board. The audit contract or agreement shall be in writing, shall include all its terms and conditions, and shall be submitted to the secretary of the Local Government Commission for his approval as to form, terms and conditions. The terms and conditions of the audit shall include the scope of the audit, and the requirement that upon completion of the examination the auditor shall prepare a written report embodying financial statements and his opinion and comments relating thereto. The finance officer shall file a copy of the audit with the secretary of the Local Government Commission and with the finance officer of any county, city, or other unit of local government that has issued on behalf of the hospital and has outstanding its general obligation or revenue bonds or makes current appropriations to the hospital (other than appropriations for the cost of medical care to prisoners or indigents).

(g) A public hospital may deposit or invest at interest all or part of its cash balance pursuant to G.S. 159-30 and may deposit any funds held in reserves or sinking funds, or any funds not required for immediate disbursement, with the State Treasurer for investment pursuant to G.S. 147-69.2.

(h) Public hospitals are subject to G.S. 159-31 with regard to selection of an official depository and security of deposits.

(i) Public hospitals are subject to G.S. 159-32 with regard to daily deposits.

(i1) Public hospitals may accept electronic payments pursuant to G.S. 159-32.1.

(j) Public hospitals are subject to G.S. 159-33 with regard to semiannual reports to the Local Government Commission on the status of deposits and investments.

(k) Any hospital district or hospital authority having outstanding general obligation or revenue bonds is subject to G.S. 159-35, 159-36, 159-37, and 159-38. (1973, c. 474, s. 28.1; c. 1215; 1999-434, s. 5.1; 2005-417, s. 1.)

Part 5. Nonprofit Corporations Receiving Public Funds.

§ 159-40. Special regulations pertaining to nonprofit corporations receiving public funds.

(a)   If a city or county grants or appropriates one thousand dollars ($1,000) or more in any fiscal year to a nonprofit corporation or organization, the city or county may require that the nonprofit corporation or organization have an audit performed for the fiscal year in which the funds are received and may require that the nonprofit corporation or organization file a copy of the audit report with the city or county.

(b)   Any nonprofit corporation or organization which receives one thousand dollars ($1,000) or more in State funds shall, at the request of the State Auditor, submit to an audit by the office of the State Auditor for the fiscal year in which such funds were received.

(c)   Every nonprofit corporation or organization which has an audit performed pursuant to this section shall file a copy of the audit report with the office of the State Auditor.

(d)   The provisions of this section shall not apply to sheltered workshops or to Adult Development Activity Programs or to private residential facilities for the mentally retarded and developmentally disabled or to Developmental Day Care Centers or to any nonprofit corporation or organization whose sole use of public funds is to provide hospital services or operate as a volunteer fire department, rescue squad, ambulance squad, or which operates as a junior college, college or university duly accredited by the southern regional accrediting association.

(e)   Repealed by Session Laws 1979, c. 905. (1977, c. 687, s. 1; 1977, 2nd Sess., c. 1195, s. 1; 1979, c. 905.)

Part 6. Joint Municipal Power Agencies and Joint Municipal Assistance Agencies.

§ 159-41. Special regulations pertaining to joint municipal power agencies.

(a) For the purposes of this Part, "joint agency" means a public body corporate and politic organized in accordance with the provisions of Chapter 159B, or the combination or recombination of any joint agencies so organized.

(b) Except as provided in this Part, none of the provisions of Article 3 of this Chapter shall apply to joint agencies. Whenever the provisions of this Part and the provisions of Chapter 159B of the General Statutes shall conflict, the provisions of Chapter 159B shall govern.

(c) Each joint agency shall operate under an annual balanced budget resolution adopted by the governing board and entered into the minutes. A budget is balanced when the sum of the appropriations is equal to the sum of estimated net revenues and appropriated fund balances. The budget resolution of a joint agency shall cover a fiscal year beginning January 1 and ending December 31, except that the Local Government Commission, if it determines that a different fiscal year would facilitate the agency's financial operations, may enter an order permitting an agency to operate under a fiscal year other than from January 1 to December 31.

(d) The following directions and limitations shall bind the governing board in adopting the budget resolution:

(1) The full amount estimated by the finance officer to be required for debt service during the budget year shall be appropriated.

(2) The full amount of any deficit in each fund shall be appropriated.

(3) Sufficient funds to meet the amounts to be paid during the fiscal year under continuing contracts previously entered into shall be appropriated.

(4) The sum of estimated net revenue and appropriated fund balance in each fund shall be equal to appropriations in that fund. Appropriated fund balances in a fund shall not exceed the sum of cash and investments minus the sum of liabilities, encumbrances, and deferred revenue, as those figures stand at the close of the fiscal year preceding the budget year.

(e) The governing board of the joint agency may amend the budget resolution at any time after its adoption and may authorize its designated finance officer to transfer moneys from one appropriation to another, subject to such limitations and procedures as it may prescribe. All such transfers will be reported to the governing board or its executive committee at its next regular meeting and shall be entered in the minutes.

(f) Joint agencies are subject to the following sections of Article 3 of this Chapter, to the same extent as a "public authority," provided, however, the term "budget ordinance" as used in such sections shall be interpreted for the purposes of this Part to mean the budget resolution of a joint agency:

(1) G.S. 159-9, provided, however, that the governing board of an agency may designate as budget officer someone other than a member of the governing board or an officer or employee of the agency.

(2) G.S. 159-12, provided, however, that the provision relating to making the budget available to the news media of a county shall not apply to a joint agency.

(3) G.S. 159-13.2.

(4) G.S. 159-16.

(5) G.S. 159-18.

(6) G.S. 159-19.

(7) G.S. 159-21.

(8) G.S. 159-22, provided, however, that the provision restricting transfers to funds maintained pursuant to G.S. 159-13(a) shall not apply to a joint agency.

(9) G.S. 159-24.

(10) G.S. 159-25.

(11) G.S. 159-26.

(12) G.S. 159-28.

(13) G.S. 159-28.1.

(14) G.S. 159-29.

(15) G.S. 159-30.

(16) G.S. 159-31.

(17) G.S. 159-32.

(18) G.S. 159-33.

(19) G.S. 159-33.1.

(20) G.S. 159-34.

(21) G.S. 159-36.

(22) G.S. 159-38. (1979, c. 685, s. 1.)

Part 7. Public Housing Authorities.

§ 159-42. Special regulations pertaining to public housing authorities.

(a) Definition. - As used in this Part, the term "housing authority" means any entity as defined in G.S. 157-3(1) that is not subject to G.S. 157-4.2.

(b) Applicability. - Except as provided in this Part, none of the provisions of Parts 1, 2, or 3 of this Article apply to housing authorities in compliance with this Part.

(c) Annual Budget. - Each housing authority shall operate under an annual budget. The budget shall take the form of estimated revenues plus fund balances available for the program, as defined by the U.S. Department of Housing and Urban Development regulations or their successors, that are equal to or greater than estimated expenditures. The proposed budget shall be available for public inspection in a manner consistent with G.S. 159-12(a). Before adopting the budget, the housing authority governing board shall hold a public hearing at which time any persons who wish to be heard on the budget may appear. The governing board shall cause notice of the public hearing to be published in a newspaper of general circulation in the area once a week for two consecutive weeks prior to the public hearing.

(d) Project Ordinances. - The annual budget shall not include those estimated revenues and expenditures accounted for in a project ordinance. A housing authority shall adopt a project ordinance, as defined by G.S. 159-13.2, for those programs which span two or more fiscal years. The form of the project ordinance shall be in accordance with the relevant funding agency guidelines for that project. The estimated revenues plus fund balances available for a project shall be equal to or greater than the estimated expenditures. The estimated revenues and expenditures related to approved projects for a fiscal year may be included in the annual budget on an informational basis.

(e) Finance Officer. - The housing authority governing board shall appoint or designate a finance officer with the following powers and duties:

(1) Preparation of the annual budget for presentation to the governing board.

(2) Administration of the approved budget.

(3) Maintenance of the accounts and other financial records in accordance with generally accepted principles of accounting.

(4) Preparation and filing of statements of the financial condition, at least annually and at other times as requested by the governing board.

(5) Receipt and deposit, or supervision of the receipt and deposit, of all moneys accruing to the housing authority.

(6) Supervision of the investment of the idle funds of the housing authority.

(7) Maintenance of all records concerning the bonded debt of the housing authority, if any.

(8) Maintenance of any sinking funds of the housing authority.

(f) Accounting Procedures. - A housing authority must comply with federal rules and regulations issued by the U.S. Department of Housing and Urban Development pertaining to procedures for the receipt, deposit, investment, transfer, and disbursement of money and other assets. The Commission may inquire into and investigate, with reasonable cause, the internal control procedures of a housing authority. The Commission may require any modifications in internal control procedures which, in the opinion of the

Commission, are necessary or desirable to prevent embezzlement, mishandling of funds, or continued operating deficits.

(g) Audits. - The accounting system of a housing authority shall be so designed that the true financial condition of the housing authority can be determined at any time. As soon as possible after the close of each fiscal year, the accounts shall be independently audited by a certified public accountant. The auditor shall be selected by the housing authority governing board and shall report directly to that body. The audit contract or agreement shall be in writing and shall include all its terms and conditions. The terms and conditions of the audit shall include the scope of the audit and the requirement that upon completion of the examination the auditor shall prepare a written report embodying the financial statements and the auditor's opinion and comments relating thereto. The finance officer shall file a copy of the audit with the Secretary of the Commission.

(h) Bonding of Employees. - The bonding requirements of G.S. 159-29 shall apply to the finance officer and those employees of the housing authority handling or having custody of more than one hundred dollars ($100.00) at any one time or those employees who have access to the inventories of the housing authority.

(i) Investments. - A housing authority may deposit or invest, at interest, all or part of its cash balance pursuant to U.S. Department of Housing and Urban Development regulations.

(j) Official Depository. - Housing authorities shall comply with G.S. 159-31, except in those circumstances where the statute is in conflict with U.S. Department of Housing and Urban Development guidance, which shall control.

(k) Deposits and Payments. - Housing authorities shall comply with G.S. 159-32, 159-32.1, and 159-33. (2001-206, s. 1.)

SUBCHAPTER IV. LONG-TERM FINANCING.

Article 4.

Local Government Bond Act.

Part 1. Operation of Article.

§ 159-43. Short title; legislative intent.

(a) This Article may be cited as "The Local Government Bond Act."

(b) It is the intent of the General Assembly by enactment of this Article to prescribe a uniform system of limitations upon and procedures for the exercise by all units of local government in North Carolina of the power to borrow money secured by a pledge of the taxing power. To this end, all provisions of special, local, or private acts in effect as of July 1, 1973, authorizing the issuance of bonds or notes secured by a pledge of the taxing power or prescribing procedures therefor are repealed. No special, local, or private act enacted or taking effect after July 1, 1973, may be construed to modify, amend, or repeal any portion of this Article unless it expressly so provides by specific reference to the appropriate section of this Article. (1971, c. 780, s. 1; 1973, c. 494, s. 2.)

§ 159-44. Definitions.

The words and phrases defined in this section shall have the meanings indicated when used in this Article, unless the context clearly requires another meaning:

(1) "Finance officer" means the officer performing the duties of finance officer of a unit of local government pursuant to G.S. 159-24 of the Local Government Budget and Fiscal Control Act.

(2) "Governing board" or "board" means the governing body of a unit of local government.

(3) "Sinking fund" means a fund held for the retirement of term bonds.

(4) "Unit," "unit of local government," or "local government" means counties; cities, towns, and incorporated villages; consolidated city-counties, as defined by G.S. 160B-2(1); sanitary districts; mosquito control districts; hospital districts; merged school administrative units described in G.S. 115C-513; metropolitan sewerage districts; metropolitan water districts; metropolitan water and sewerage districts; county water and sewer districts; regional public transportation authorities; and special airport districts.

(5) "Utility or public service enterprise" includes:

a. Electric power transmission and distribution systems;

b. Water supply facilities and distribution systems;

c. Sewage collection and disposal systems;

d. Gas transmission and distribution systems;

e. Public transportation systems, including but not limited to bus lines, ferries, and mass transit systems;

f. Solid waste collection and disposal systems and facilities;

g. Cable television systems;

h. Off-street parking facilities and systems;

i. Public auditoriums, coliseums, stadiums and convention centers;

j. Airport;

k. Hospitals and other health-related facilities; and

l. Structural and natural stormwater and drainage systems of all types. (1971, c. 780, s. 1; 1973, c. 494, s. 3; 1977, c. 466, s. 2; 1979, c. 727, s. 2; 1989, c. 643, s. 3; c. 740, s. 3; 1991, c. 325, s. 4; 1995, c. 461, s. 10; 1997-456, s. 27; 2013-50, s. 3.)

§ 159-45. All general obligation bonds subject to Local Government Bond Act.

No unit of local government in this State shall have authority to enter into any contract or agreement, whether oral or written, whereby it borrows money and makes an express or implied pledge of its power to levy taxes as security for repayment of the loan, except by the issuance of its bonds in accordance with the limitations and procedures prescribed in this Article or by the issuance of its negotiable notes in accordance with the limitations and procedures prescribed in Article 9 of this Chapter or by the issuance of debt instruments in accordance with the limitations and procedures prescribed in Chapter 159G of the General Statutes. (1971, c. 780, s. 1; 1987, c. 796, s. 2(1).)

§ 159-46. Faith and credit pledged.

The faith and credit of the issuing unit are hereby pledged for the payment of the principal of and interest on all bonds issued under this Article and debt instruments secured by a pledge of its faith and credit in accordance with the limitations and procedures prescribed in Chapter 159G of the General Statutes according to their terms, and the power and obligation of the issuing unit to levy taxes and raise other revenues for the prompt payment of installments of principal and interest or for the maintenance of sinking funds shall be unrestricted as to rate or amount, notwithstanding any other provisions of law whether general, special, local, or private. (1971, c. 780, s. 1; 1987, c. 796, s. 2(2).)

§ 159-47. Additional security for utility or public service enterprise bonds.

(a) The revenues of a utility or public service enterprise owned or leased by a unit of local government shall be applied in accordance with the following priorities:

(1) First, to pay the operating, maintenance, and capital outlay expenses of the utility or enterprise.

(2) Second, to pay when due the interest on and principal of outstanding bonds issued for capital projects that are or were a part of the utility or enterprise.

(3) Third, for any other lawful purpose.

Notwithstanding the foregoing provisions, a county which owns or leases hospitals or other health-related facilities and has not issued any general obligation bonds during the period July 1, 1973, to July 1, 1974, for a capital project that is or was a part of such hospitals or other health-related facilities shall have the option of applying the revenues of such hospitals or other health-related facilities in accordance with a bond order adopted under the Local Government Revenue Bond Act.

(b) In the discretion of the governing board of the issuing unit, the bond order may pledge the revenues (or any portion of the revenues) of a utility or public service enterprise to the payment of the interest on and principal of bonds issued under this Article to finance capital projects that are to become a part of the utility or enterprise.

(c) In the discretion of the governing board of the issuing unit, a bond order authorizing the issuance of bonds under this Article to finance capital projects that are to become a part of a utility or public service enterprise owned or leased by the issuing unit may state that the revenues of the utility or enterprise may be pledged to the payment of the interest on and principal of the bonds if and to the extent that the governing board of the unit shall thereafter determine by resolution (prior to the issuance of the bonds), and that a tax sufficient to pay the principal of and interest on the bonds shall be annually levied and collected by the issuing unit on all taxable property within its taxing jurisdiction, but that in the event that any revenues of the utility or enterprise shall be pledged to the payment of the bonds, the tax may be reduced by the amount of utility or enterprise revenues available for the payment of the principal and interest. A pledge of utility or enterprise revenues pursuant to this subsection shall be made by resolution of the governing board of the issuing unit after the bond order is adopted and before bonds are issued thereunder.

(d) When a pledge of utility or enterprise revenues is made pursuant to this section, the issuing unit shall have, with respect to the utility or enterprise whose revenues are pledged, all of the powers set out in G.S. 159-83 and G.S. 159-89. (1971, c. 780, s. 1; 1973, c. 1326.)

§ 159-48. For what purposes bonds may be issued.

(a) Each unit of local government is authorized to borrow money and issue its bonds under this Article in evidence thereof for any one or more of the following purposes:

(1) To suppress riots, insurrections, or any extraordinary breach of law and order.

(2) To supply an unforeseen deficiency in the revenue when taxes actually received or collected during the fiscal year fall below collection estimates made in the annual budget ordinance within the limits prescribed in G.S. 159-13.

(3) To meet emergencies threatening the public health or safety, as conclusively determined in writing by the Governor.

(4) To refund outstanding revenue bonds or revenue bond anticipation notes.

(5) To refund outstanding general obligation bonds or general obligation bond anticipation notes.

(6) To fund judgments for specified sums of money entered against the unit by a court of competent jurisdiction.

(7) To fund valid, existing obligations of the unit not incurred by the borrowing of money.

(b) Each county and city is authorized to borrow money and issue its bonds under this Article in evidence thereof for the purpose of paying any capital costs of any one or more of the following:

(1) Providing airport facilities, including without limitation related land, landing fields, runways, clear zones, lighting, navigational and signal systems, hangars, terminals, offices, shops, and parking facilities.

(2) Providing armories for the North Carolina National Guard.

(3) Providing auditoriums, coliseums, arenas, stadiums, civic centers, convention centers, and facilities for exhibitions, athletic and cultural events, shows, and public gatherings.

(4) Providing beach improvements, including without limitation jetties, seawalls, groins, moles, sand dunes, vegetation, additional sand, pumps and related equipment, and drainage channels, for the control of beach erosion and the improvement of beaches.

(5) Providing cemeteries.

(6) Providing facilities for fire fighting and prevention, including without limitation headquarters buildings, station buildings, training facilities, hydrants, alarm systems, and communications systems.

(7) Providing hospital facilities, including without limitation general, tuberculosis, mental, chronic disease, and other types of hospitals and related facilities such as laboratories, outpatient departments, nurses' homes and training facilities, and central service facilities operated in connection with

hospitals; facilities for the provision of public health services, including related facilities such as laboratories, clinics, and administrative offices; facilities specially designed for the diagnosis, treatment, education, training, or custodial care of the mentally retarded, including facilities for training specialists and sheltered workshops for the mentally retarded; nursing homes; and in connection with the foregoing, laundries, nurses', doctors', or interns' residences, administrative buildings, research facilities, maintenance, storage, and utility facilities, auditoriums, dining halls, food service and preparation facilities, fire prevention facilities, mental and physical health care facilities, dental care facilities, nursing schools, mental teaching facilities, offices, parking facilities, and other supporting service structures.

(8)   Providing land for corporate purposes.

(9)   Providing facilities for law enforcement, including without limitation headquarters buildings, station buildings, jails and other confinement facilities, training facilities, alarm systems, and communications systems.

(10)   Providing library facilities, including without limitation fixed and mobile libraries.

(11)   Providing art galleries, museums, and art centers, and providing for historic properties.

(12)   Providing parking facilities, including on- and off-street parking, and in connection therewith any area or place for the parking and storing of automobiles and other vehicles open to public use, with or without charge, including without limitation meters, buildings, garages, driveways, and approaches.

(13)   Providing parks and recreation facilities, including without limitation land, athletic fields, parks, playgrounds, recreation centers, shelters, stadiums, arenas, permanent and temporary stands, golf courses, swimming pools, wading pools, marinas, and lighting.

(14)   Providing public building, including without limitation buildings housing courtrooms, other court facilities, and council rooms, office buildings, public markets, public comfort stations, warehouses, and yards.

(15) Providing public vehicles, including without limitation those for law enforcement, fire fighting and prevention, sanitation, street paving and maintenance, safety and public health, and other corporate purposes.

(16) Providing for redevelopment through the acquisition of land and the improvement thereof for assisting local redevelopment commissions.

(17) Providing sanitary sewer systems, including without limitation community sewerage facilities for the collection, treatment, and disposal of sewage or septic tank systems and other on-site collection and disposal facilities or systems.

(18) Providing solid waste disposal systems, including without limitation land for sanitary landfills, incinerators, and other structures and buildings.

(19) Providing storm sewers and flood control facilities, including without limitation levees, dikes, diversionary channels, drains, catch basins, and other facilities for storm water drainage.

(20) Providing voting machines.

(21) Providing water systems, including without limitation facilities for the supply, storage, treatment, and distribution of water.

(22) Providing for any other purpose for which it is authorized, by general laws uniformly applicable throughout the State, to raise or appropriate money, except for current expenses.

(23) Providing public transportation facilities, including without limitation equipment for public transportation, buses, surface and below-ground railways, ferries, and garage facilities.

(24) Providing industrial parks, land suitable for industrial or commercial purposes, shell buildings, in order to provide employment opportunities for citizens of the county or city.

(25) Providing property to preserve a railroad corridor.

(26) Undertaking public activities in or for the benefit of a development financing district pursuant to a development financing plan.

(c) Each county is authorized to borrow money and issue its bonds under this Article in evidence of the debt for the purpose of, in the case of subdivisions (1) through (4b) of this subsection, paying any capital costs of any one or more of the purposes and, in the case of subdivisions (5) and (6) of this subsection, to finance the cost of the purpose:

(1) Providing community college facilities, including without limitation buildings, plants, and other facilities, physical and vocational educational buildings and facilities, including in connection therewith classrooms, laboratories, libraries, auditoriums, administrative offices, student unions, dormitories, gymnasiums, athletic fields, cafeterias, utility plants, and garages.

(2) Providing courthouses, including without limitation offices, meeting rooms, court facilities and rooms, and detention facilities.

(3) Providing county homes for the indigent and infirm.

(4) Providing school facilities, including without limitation schoolhouses, buildings, plants and other facilities, physical and vocational educational buildings and facilities, including in connection therewith classrooms, laboratories, libraries, auditoriums, administrative offices, gymnasiums, athletic fields, lunchrooms, utility plants, garages, and school buses and other necessary vehicles.

(4a) Providing improvements to subdivision and residential streets pursuant to G.S. 153A-205.

(4b) Providing land for present or future county corporate, open space, community college, and public school purposes.

(5) Providing for the octennial revaluation of real property for taxation.

(6) Providing housing projects for persons of low or moderate income, including construction or acquisition of projects to be owned by a county, redevelopment commission, or housing authority and the provision of loans, grants, interest supplements, and other programs of financial assistance to such persons. A housing project may provide housing for persons of other than low or moderate income if at least forty percent (40%) of the units in the project are exclusively reserved for persons of low or moderate income. No rent subsidy may be paid from bond proceeds.

(d) Each city is authorized to borrow money and issue its bonds under this Article in evidence thereof for the purpose of paying any capital costs of any one or more of the following:

(1) Repealed by Session Laws 1977, c. 402, s. 2.

(2) Providing cable television systems.

(3) Providing electric systems, including without limitation facilities for the generation, transmission, and distribution of electric light and power.

(4) Providing gas systems, including without limitation facilities for the production, storage, transmission and distribution of gas, where systems shall also include the purchase and/or lease of natural gas fields and natural gas reserves and the purchase of natural gas supplies, and where any parts of such systems may be located either within the State or without.

(5) Providing streets and sidewalks, including without limitation bridges, viaducts, causeways, overpasses, underpasses, and alleys; paving, grading, resurfacing, and widening streets; sidewalks, curbs and gutters, culverts, and drains; traffic controls, signals, and markers; lighting; and grade crossings and the elimination thereof and grade separations.

(6) Improving existing systems or facilities for the transmission or distribution of telephone services.

(7) Providing housing projects for the benefit of persons of low income, or moderate income, or low and moderate income, including without limitation (i) construction or acquisition of projects to be owned by a city, redevelopment commission or housing authority, and (ii) loans, grants, interest supplements and other programs of financial assistance to persons of low income, or moderate income, or low and moderate income, and developers of housing for persons of low income, or moderate income, or low and moderate income. A housing project may provide housing for persons of other than low or moderate income, as long as at least twenty percent (20%) of the units in the project are set aside for housing for the exclusive use of persons of low income. No rent subsidy may be paid from bond proceeds.

(e) Each sanitary district, mosquito control district, hospital district, merged school administrative unit described in G.S. 115C-513; metropolitan sewerage district, metropolitan water district, metropolitan water and sewerage district, county water and sewer district, regional public transportation authority and special airport district is authorized to borrow money and issue its bonds under this Article in evidence thereof for the purpose of paying any capital costs of any one or more of the purposes for which it is authorized, by general laws uniformly applicable throughout the State, to raise or appropriate money, except for current expenses.

(f) For any of the purposes authorized by subsections (b), (c), (d), or (e) of this section, a unit may do any of the following that it considers necessary or convenient:

(1) Acquire, construct, erect, provide, develop, install, furnish, and equip; and

(2) Reconstruct, remodel, alter, renovate, replace, refurnish, and reequip; and

(3) Enlarge, expand, and extend; and

(4) Demolish, relocate, improve, grade, drain, landscape, pave, widen, and resurface.

(g) Bonds for two or more unrelated purposes, not of the same general class or character, shall not be authorized by the same bond order. However, bonds for any of the purposes listed in any subdivision of any subsection of this section shall be deemed to be for one purpose and may be authorized by the same bond order. In addition, nothing herein may be deemed to prohibit the combining of purposes from any of such paragraphs and the authorization of bonds therefor by the same bond order to the extent that the purposes are not unrelated.

(h) As used in this section, "capital costs" include, without limitation, the following:

(1) The costs of doing any or all of the things mentioned in subsection (f) of this section; and

(2) The costs of all property, both real and personal and both improved and unimproved, plants, works, appurtenances, structures, facilities, furnishings, machinery, equipment, vehicles, easements, water rights, franchises, and licenses used or useful in connection with the purpose authorized; and

(3) The costs of demolishing or moving structures from land acquired and acquiring any lands to which such structures are to be moved; and

(4) Financing charges, including estimated interest during construction and for six months thereafter; and

(5) The costs of plans, specifications, studies and reports, surveys, and estimates of costs and revenues; and

(6) The costs of bond printing and insurance; and

(7) Administrative and legal expenses; and

(8) Any other services, costs, and expenses necessary or incidental to the purpose authorized.

(i) This section does not authorize any unit to undertake any program, function, joint undertaking, or service not otherwise authorized by law. It is intended only to authorize the borrowing of money and the issuance of bonds within the limitations set out herein to finance programs, functions, joint undertakings, or services authorized by other portions of the General Statutes or by city charters. (1917, c. 138, s. 16; 1919, c. 178, s. 3(16); C.S., s. 2937; 1921, c. 8, s. 1; Ex. Sess. 1921, c. 106, s. 1; 1927, c. 81, s. 8; 1929, c. 171, s. 1; 1931, c. 60, ss. 48, 54; 1933, c. 259, ss. 1, 2; 1935, c. 302, ss. 1, 2; 1939, c. 231, ss. 1, 2(c); 1943, c. 13; 1945, c. 403; 1947, cc. 520, 931; 1949, c. 354; c. 766, s. 3; c. 1270; 1953, c. 1065, s. 1; 1957, c. 266, s. 1; c. 856, s. 1; c. 1098, s. 16; 1959, c. 525; c. 1250, s. 2; 1961, c. 293; c. 1001, s. 2; 1965, c. 307, s. 2; 1967, c. 987, s. 2; c. 1001, s. 1; 1971, c. 780, s. 1; 1973, c. 494, s. 4; c. 1037; 1975, c. 549, s. 1; c. 821, s. 1; 1977, c. 402, ss. 1, 2; c. 811; 1979, c. 619, s. 3; c. 624, s. 1; c. 727, s. 3; 1985, c. 639, s. 2; 1987, c. 464, s. 7; c. 564, s. 10; 1989, c. 600, s. 7; c. 740, s. 4; 1991, c. 325, s. 5; 1997-6, s. 19; 1999-366, s. 4; 1999-378, s. 1; 2003-403, s. 3; 2009-281, s. 1; 2013-50, s. 4.)

§ 159-49. When a vote of the people is required.

Bonds may be issued under this Article only if approved by a vote of the qualified voters of the issuing unit as provided in this Article, except that voter approval shall not be required for:

(1) Bonds issued for any purpose authorized by G.S. 159-48(a)(1), (2), (3), or (5).

(2) Bonds issued by a county, county water and sewer district created under Article 6 of Chapter 162A of the General Statutes, metropolitan water district created under Article 4 of Chapter 162A of the General Statutes, or city for any purpose authorized by G.S. 159-48(a)(4), (6), or (7) or G.S. 159-48(b), (c), (d), or (e) (except purposes authorized by G.S. 159-48(b)(3), (11), (16), (22), or (23) or by G.S. 159-48(d)(2)) in an aggregate principal sum not exceeding two thirds of the amount by which the outstanding indebtedness of the issuing county, county water and sewer district, metropolitan water district, or city has been reduced during the next preceding fiscal year.

Pursuant to Article V, Sec. 4(2) of the Constitution, the General Assembly hereby declares that the purposes authorized by G.S. 159-48(a)(4), (6), and (7) and by G.S. 159-48(b), (c), (d), and (e) (except purposes authorized by G.S. 159-48(b)(3), (11), (16), (22), or (23) or by G.S. 159-48(d)(2)) are purposes for which bonds may be issued without a vote of the people, to the extent of two thirds of the amount by which the outstanding indebtedness of the issuing county, county water and sewer district, metropolitan water district, or city was reduced in the last preceding fiscal year. (1971, c. 780, s. 1; 1973, c. 494, s. 5; 1977, c. 402, s. 3; 1989, c. 470.)

Part 2. Procedure for Issuing Bonds.

§ 159-50. Notice of intent to make application for issuance of voted bonds; objection by citizens and taxpayers.

When a unit of local government proposes to issue bonds that must be approved by a vote of the people, it shall first publish a notice of its intent to make application to the Commission for approval of the issue. The notice shall be published once not less than 10 days before the application is filed. The notice shall state (i) that the board intends to file an application with the Commission for approval of a bond issue, (ii) in brief and general terms the purpose of the proposed issue, (iii) the maximum amount of bonds to be issued, and (iv) that any citizen or taxpayer of the issuing unit may, within seven days after the date of the publication, file with the governing board and the Commission a statement of any objections he may have to the issue. The Commission may prescribe the form of the notice.

Any citizen or taxpayer of the issuing unit who objects to the proposed bond issue in whole or in part may, within seven days from the date of publication of the notice, file a written statement of his objections with the board and the Commission. The statement shall set forth each objection to the proposed bond issue and shall contain the name and address of the person filing it. The Commission shall consider the statement of objections along with the application and shall notify the objector and the board of its disposition of each objection.

Failure to comply with this section shall not affect the validity of any bonds otherwise issued in accordance with the law. This section shall not apply to bonds that need not be submitted to a vote of the people. (1953, c. 1121; 1971, c. 780, s. 1.)

§ 159-51. Application to Commission for approval of bond issue; preliminary conference; acceptance of application.

No bonds may be issued under this Article unless the issue is approved by the Local Government Commission. The governing board of the issuing unit shall file an application for Commission approval of the issue with the secretary of the Commission. If the issuing unit is a regional public transportation authority, the application must be accompanied by resolutions of the special tax board of that authority and of each of the boards of county commissioners of the counties organizing the authority approving of the application. The application shall state such facts and have attached to it such documents concerning the proposed bonds and the financial condition of the issuing unit as the secretary may require. The Commission may prescribe the form of the application.

Before he accepts the application, the secretary may require the governing board or its representatives to attend a preliminary conference to consider the proposed bond issue. If the issuing unit is a merged school administrative unit described in G.S. 115C-513, each county in which the merged unit is located may attend the preliminary conference.

After an application in proper form has been filed, and after a preliminary conference if one is required, the secretary shall notify the unit in writing that the application has been filed and accepted for submission to the Commission. The secretary's statement shall be conclusive evidence that the unit has complied with this section. (1953, c. 1121; 1971, c. 780, s. 2; 1989, c. 740, s. 5; 1991, c. 325, s. 6, c. 666, s. 6.)

§ 159-52. Approval of application by Commission.

(a)   In determining whether a proposed bond issue shall be approved, the Commission may consider:

(1)   Whether the project to be financed from the proceeds of the bond issue is necessary or expedient.

(2)   The nature and amount of the outstanding debt of the issuing unit.

(3)   The unit's debt management procedures and policies.

(4)   The unit's tax and special assessments collection record.

(5)   The unit's compliance with the Local Government Budget and Fiscal Control Act.

(6)   Whether the unit is in default in any of its debt service obligations.

(7)   The unit's present tax rates, and the increase in tax rate, if any, necessary to service the proposed debt.

(8)   The unit's appraised and assessed value of property subject to taxation.

(9)   The ability of the unit to sustain the additional taxes necessary to service the debt.

(10)   The ability of the Commission to market the proposed bonds at reasonable interest rates.

(11)   If the proposed issue is for a utility or public service enterprise, the probable net revenues of the project to be financed and the extent to which the revenues of the utility or enterprise, after addition of the revenues of the project to be financed, will be sufficient to service the proposed debt.

(12)   Whether the amount of the proposed debt will be adequate to accomplish the purpose for which it is to be incurred.

(13)   If the proposed bond issue is for a water system as described in G.S. 159-48(b)(21), whether a unit has prepared a local water supply plan in compliance with G.S. 143-355.

The Commission may inquire into and give consideration to any other matters which it may believe to have a bearing on whether the issue should be approved.

(b) The Commission shall approve the application if, upon the information and evidence it receives, it finds and determines:

(1) That the proposed bond issue is necessary or expedient.

(2) That the amount proposed is adequate and not excessive for the proposed purpose of the issue.

(3) That the unit's debt management procedures and policies are good, or that reasonable assurances have been given that its debt will henceforth be managed in strict compliance with law.

(4) That the increase in taxes, if any, necessary to service the proposed debt will not be excessive.

(5) That the proposed bonds can be marketed at reasonable rates of interest.

If the Commission tentatively decides to deny the application because it is of the opinion that any one or more of these conclusions cannot be supported from the information presented to it, it shall so notify the unit filing the application. If the unit so requests, the Commission shall hold a public hearing on the application at which time any interested persons shall be heard. The Commission may appoint a hearing officer to conduct the hearing, and to present a summary of the testimony and his recommendations for the Commission's consideration. (1931, c. 60, ss. 12, 13; 1971, c. 780, s. 1; 2011-374, s. 3.3.)

§ 159-53. Order approving or disapproving an application.

(a) After considering an application, and conducting a public hearing thereon if one is requested under G.S. 159-52(b), the Commission shall enter its order either approving or denying the application. An order approving an issue shall not be regarded as an approval of the legality of the bonds in any respect.

(b)   If the Commission shall enter an order denying an application, the proceedings under this Subchapter shall be at an end. (1931, c. 60, s. 14; 1971, c. 780, s. 1.)

§ 159-54. The bond order.

After or at the same time the application is filed with the Commission, a bond order shall be introduced before the governing board of the issuing unit. The bond order shall state:

(1)   Briefly and generally and without specification of location or material of construction, the purpose for which the bonds are to be issued, but not more than one purpose may be stated. For funding or refunding bonds a brief description of the debt, judgment, or obligation to be funded or refunded shall be sufficient.

(2)   The maximum aggregate principal amount of the bonds.

(3)   That taxes will be levied in an amount sufficient to pay the principal and interest of the bonds.

(4)   The extent, if any, to which utility or enterprise revenues are, or may be, pledged to payment of interest on and principal of the bonds pursuant to G.S. 159-47.

(5)   That a sworn statement of debt has been filed with the clerk and is open to public inspection.

(6)   If the bonds are to be approved by the voters, that the bond order will take effect when approved by the voters.

(7)   If the bonds are issued pursuant to G.S. 159-48(a)(1), (2), (3), or (5), that the bond order will take effect upon its adoption. If the bonds are to be issued pursuant to G.S. 159-48(a)(4), (6), or (7) or G.S. 159-48(b), (c), or (d) and are not to be submitted to the voters, that the bond order will take effect 30 days after its publication following adoption, unless it is petitioned to a vote of the people as provided in G.S. 159-60, and that in that event the order will take effect when approved by the voters.

When the bond order is introduced, the board shall fix the time and place for a public hearing thereon. (1917, c. 138, s. 17; 1919, c. 178, s. 3(17); c. 285, s. 2; C.S., s. 2938; 1921, c. 8, s. 1; Ex. Sess. 1921, c. 106, s. 1; 1927, c. 81, s. 9; 1931, c. 60, ss. 49, 55; 1933, c. 259, ss. 1, 2; 1935, c. 302, ss. 1, 2; 1949, c. 497, ss. 1, 3; 1957, c. 856, s. 2; 1971, c. 780, s. 1; 1973, c. 494, s. 6; 2012-156, s. 2.)

§ 159-55. Sworn statement of debt; debt limitation; statement of estimated interest on the bonds.

(a) After the bond order has been introduced and before the public hearing thereon, the finance officer (or some other officer designated by the governing board for this purpose) shall file with the clerk a statement showing the following:

(1) The gross debt of the unit, excluding therefrom debt incurred or to be incurred in anticipation of the collection of taxes or other revenues or in anticipation of the sale of bonds other than funding and refunding bonds. The gross debt (after exclusions) is the sum of (i) outstanding debt evidenced by bonds, (ii) bonds authorized by orders introduced but not yet adopted, (iii) unissued bonds authorized by adopted orders, and (iv) outstanding debt not evidenced by bonds. However, for purposes of the sworn statement of debt and the debt limitation, revenue bonds and project development financing debt instruments (unless additionally secured by a pledge of the issuing unit's faith and credit) shall not be considered debt and shall not be included in gross debt nor deducted from gross debt.

(2) The deductions to be made from gross debt in computing net debt. The following deductions are allowed:

a. Funding and refunding bonds authorized by orders introduced but not yet adopted.

b. Funding and refunding bonds authorized but not yet issued.

c. The amount of money held in sinking funds or otherwise for the payment of any part of the principal of gross debt other than debt incurred for water, gas, electric light or power purposes, or sanitary sewer purposes (to the extent that the bonds are deductible under subsection (b) of this section), or two or more of these purposes.

d. The amount of bonded debt included in gross debt and incurred, or to be incurred, for water, gas, or electric light or power purposes, or any two or more of these purposes.

e. The amount of bonded debt included in the gross debt and incurred, or to be incurred, for sanitary sewer system purposes to the extent that the debt is made deductible by subsection (b) of this section.

f. The amount of uncollected special assessments theretofore levied for local improvements for which any part of the gross debt (that is not otherwise deducted) was or is to be incurred, to the extent that the assessments will be applied, when collected, to the payment of any part of the gross debt.

g. The amount, as estimated by the governing board of the issuing unit or an officer designated by the board for this purpose, of special assessments to be levied for local improvements for which any part of the gross debt (that is not otherwise deducted) was or is to be incurred, to the extent that the special assessments, when collected, will be applied to the payment of any part of the gross debt.

(3) The net debt of the issuing unit, being the difference between the gross debt and deductions.

(4) The assessed value of property subject to taxation by the issuing unit, as revealed by the tax records and certified to the issuing unit by the assessor. In calculating the assessed value, the incremental valuation of any development financing district located in the unit, as determined pursuant to G.S. 159-107, shall not be included.

(5) The percentage that the net debt bears to the assessed value of property subject to taxation by the issuing unit.

(b) Debt incurred or to be incurred for sanitary sewer system purposes is deductible from gross debt when the combined revenues of the water system and the sanitary sewer system (whether or not the water and sewer system are operated separately or as a consolidated system) were sufficient to pay all operating, capital outlay, and debt service expenditures attributable to both systems in each of the three complete fiscal years immediately preceding the date on which the sworn statement of debt is filed. For the purposes of this subsection, the "revenues" of a water system and a sanitary sewer system include:

(1) Rates, fees, rentals, charges, and other receipts and income derived from or in connection with the system.

(2) Fees, rents, or other charges collected from other offices, agencies, institutions, and departments of the issuing unit at rates not in excess of those charged to other consumers, customers, or users.

(3) Appropriations from the fund balance of the prior fiscal year from the fund or funds established to account for the revenues and expenditures of the water system or sewer system pursuant to G.S. 159-13(a) of the Local Government Budget and Fiscal Control Act.

Before the sworn statement of debt is filed, the secretary shall determine to what extent debt incurred or to be incurred for sanitary sewer system purposes qualifies for deduction from gross debt pursuant to this subsection, and shall give his certificate to that effect. The secretary's certificate shall be filed with and deemed a part of the sworn statement of debt. The secretary's certificate shall be conclusive in the absence of fraud.

(c) No bond order shall be adopted unless it appears from the sworn statement of debt filed in connection therewith that the net debt of the unit does not exceed eight percent (8%) of the assessed value of property subject to taxation by the issuing unit. This limitation shall not apply to:

(1) Funding and refunding bonds.

(2) Bonds issued for water, gas, or electric power purposes, or two or more of these purposes.

(3) Bonds issued for sanitary sewer system purposes when the bonds are deductible pursuant to subsection (b) of this section.

(4) Bonds issued for sanitary sewers, sewage disposal, or sewage purification plants when the construction of these facilities has been ordered by the Environmental Management Commission, which Commission is hereby authorized to make such an order, or by a court of competent jurisdiction.

(5) Bonds or notes issued for erosion control purposes.

(6) Bonds or notes issued for the purpose of erecting jetties or other protective works to prevent encroachment by the ocean, sounds, or other bodies of water.

(d) At the time the bond order is introduced, the finance officer (or some other officer designated by the governing board for this purpose) shall file with the clerk a statement of the finance officer estimating the total amount of interest that will be paid on the bonds over the expected term of the bonds, if issued, and a summary of the assumptions upon which the estimate is based. The statement shall include a statement to the effect that the amount estimated is preliminary and is for general informational purposes only, that there is no assurance that the assumptions upon which the estimate is based will occur, that the occurrence of certain of the assumptions is beyond the control of the unit, and that differences between the actual circumstances at the time the bonds are issued from the assumptions included in the estimate could result in significant differences between the estimated interest and the actual interest on the bonds. The statement may include other qualifications as the finance officer deems appropriate. The validity of the bonds authorized by the order is not subject to challenge on the grounds that the actual interest cost of the bonds when issued is different than the amount set forth in the statement. The statement shall be filed with the Local Government Commission and maintained by the Clerk. (1917, c. 138, s. 19; 1919, c. 178, s. 3(19); c. 285, s. 4; C.S., s. 2943; 1921, c. 8, s. 1; Ex. Sess. 1921, c. 106, s. 1; 1927, c. 81, ss. 13, 14; c. 102, s. 1; 1931, c. 60, s. 51; 1933, c. 259, s. 1; c. 321; Ex. Sess. 1938, c. 3; 1955, c. 1045; 1959, c. 779, s. 10; 1967, c. 892, s. 4; 1969, c. 1092; 1971, c. 780, s. 1; 1973, c. 494, s. 7; c. 1262, s. 231; 1991, c. 11, ss. 2, 3; 1991 (Reg. Sess., 1992), c. 1007, s. 41; 2003-403, s. 4; 2013-200, s. 1.)

§ 159-56. Publication of bond order as introduced.

After the introduction of the bond order, the clerk shall publish it once with the following statement appended:

"The foregoing order has been introduced and a sworn statement of debt has been filed under the Local Government Bond Act showing the appraised value of the [issuing unit] to be $ _____ and the net debt thereof, including the proposed bonds, to be $ _____. The finance officer of the [issuing unit] has filed a statement estimating that the total amount of interest that will be paid on the bonds over the expected term of the bonds, if issued, is $ _____. The estimate is preliminary, is for general informational purposes only, and may differ from the actual interest paid on the bonds. A tax will [may] be levied to pay the principal of and interest on the bonds if they are issued. Anyone who wishes to be heard on the questions of the validity of the bond order and the advisability of issuing the bonds may appear at a public hearing or an adjournment thereof to be held at _____.

_____

Clerk"

The publication may include a summary of the assumptions upon which the estimate of the total amount of interest that will be paid on the bonds over the expected term of the bonds, if issued, is based, and may further state that there is no assurance that the circumstances included in the assumptions will occur, that the occurrence of certain of the assumptions is beyond the control of the issuing unit, and that differences between the actual circumstances at the time the bonds are issued from the assumptions included in the estimate could result in significant differences between the estimated interest and the actual interest on the bonds. The statement may include additional qualifications as the unit deems appropriate. The validity of bonds authorized to be issued pursuant to this act is not subject to challenge on the grounds that the actual interest cost of the bonds when issued is different than the amount set forth in the estimate referenced in the publication of the bond order as introduced. (1927, c. 81, s. 16; 1971, c. 780, s. 1; 2013-200, s. 2.)

§ 159-56.1. Certain proceedings ratified notwithstanding provisions of § 159-56.

All proceedings heretofore taken by the governing boards of units of local government in connection with the authorization of bonds are hereby ratified, approved, confirmed and in all respects validated, notwithstanding the provisions of G.S. 159-56; provided that the issuance of said bonds, the indebtedness to be incurred by the issuance thereof and the levy of a tax for the payment thereof shall have been approved at an election by a majority of the qualified voters of the unit voting thereon. (1973, c. 1172.)

§ 159-57. Hearing; passage of bond order.

On the date fixed for the public hearing, which shall be not earlier than six days after the date of publication of the bond order as introduced, the board shall hear anyone who may wish to be heard on the question of the validity of the order or the advisability of issuing the bonds. The hearing may be adjourned from time to time.

After the hearing, (and on the same day as the hearing, if the board so desires) the board may pass the order as introduced, or as amended. No amendment may increase the amount of bonds to be issued, nor substantially change the purpose of the issue. If the board wishes to increase the amount of bonds to be issued, or to substantially change the purpose of the issue, a new proceeding under this Article is required.

The provisions of any city charter, general law, or local act to the contrary notwithstanding, a bond order may be introduced at any regular or special meeting of the governing board and adopted at any such meeting by a simple majority of those present and voting, a quorum being present, and need not be published or subjected to any procedural requirements governing the adoption of ordinances or resolutions by the governing board other than the procedures set out in this Subchapter. Bond orders shall not be subject to the provisions of any city charter or local act concerning initiative and referendum. (1927, c. 81, s. 17; 1953, c. 1065, s. 1; 1971, c. 780, s. 1.)

§ 159-58. Publication of bond order as adopted.

After adoption, the clerk shall publish the bond order once, with the following statement appended:

"The foregoing order was adopted on the _____ day of _____, ____, and is hereby published this _____ day of _____, ____. Any action or proceeding questioning the validity of the order must be begun within 30 days after the date of publication of this notice. The finance officer of the [issuing unit] has filed a statement estimating that the total amount of interest that will be paid on the bonds over the expected term of the bonds, if issued, is $ _____. The estimate is preliminary, is for general informational purposes only, and may differ from the actual interest paid on the bonds.

Clerk"

The publication may include a summary of the assumptions upon which the estimate of the total amount of interest that will be paid on the bonds over the expected term of the bonds, if issued, is based, and may further state that there is no assurance that the circumstances included in the assumptions will occur, that the occurrence of certain of the assumptions is beyond the control of the issuing unit, and that differences between the actual circumstances at the time the bonds are issued from the assumptions included in the estimate could result in significant differences between the estimated interest and the actual interest on the bonds. The statement may include such additional qualifications as the unit deems appropriate. The validity of bonds authorized to be issued pursuant to this act is not subject to challenge on the grounds that the actual interest cost of the bonds when issued is different than the amount set forth in the estimate referenced in the publication of the bond order as adopted. (1917, c. 138, s. 20; 1919, c. 49, s. 1; c. 178, s. 3(20); C.S., s. 2944; 1921, c. 8, s. 1; Ex. Sess. 1921, c. 106, s. 1; 1927, c. 81, s. 19; 1971, c. 780, s. 1; 1999-456, s. 59; 2013-200, s. 3.)

§ 159-59. Limitation of action to set aside order.

Any action or proceeding in any court to set aside a bond order, or to obtain any other relief, upon the ground that the order is invalid, must be begun within 30 days after the date of publication of the bond order as adopted. After the expiration of this period of limitation, no right of action or defense based upon the invalidity of the order shall be asserted, nor shall the validity of the order be open to question in any court upon any ground whatever, except in an action or proceeding begun within the period of limitation prescribed in this section. (1917, c. 138, s. 20; 1919, c. 49, s. 1; c. 178, s. 3(20); C.S., s. 2945; 1921, c. 8, s. 1; Ex. Sess. 1921, c. 106, s. 1; 1927, c. 81, s. 20; 1971, c. 780, s. 1.)

§ 159-60. Petition for referendum on bond issue.

A petition demanding that a bond order be submitted to the voters may be filed with the clerk within 30 days after the date of publication of the bond order as introduced. The petition shall be in writing, and shall be signed by a number of voters of the issuing unit equal to not less than ten percent (10%) of the total number of voters registered to vote in elections of the issuing unit according to the most recent figures certified by the State Board of Elections. The residence address of each signer shall be written after his signature. The petition need not contain the text of the order to which it refers, and need not be all on one sheet.

The clerk shall investigate the sufficiency of the petition and present it to the governing board, with a certificate stating the results of his investigation. The governing board, after hearing any taxpayer who may request to be heard, shall thereupon determine the sufficiency of the petition, and its determination shall be conclusive.

This section does not apply to bonds issued pursuant to G.S. 159-48(a)(1), (2), (3), or (5). (1917, c. 138, s. 21; 1919, c. 49, ss. 1, 2; c. 178, s. 3(21); C.S., s. 2947; 1921, c. 8, s. 1; Ex. Sess. 1921, c. 106, s. 1; 1927, c. 81, s. 20; c. 102, s. 2; 1971, c. 780, s. 1; 1973, c. 494, s. 8.)

§ 159-61. Bond referenda; majority required; notice of referendum; form of ballot; canvass.

(a) If a bond order is to take effect upon approval of the voters, the affirmative vote or a majority of those who vote thereon shall be required.

(b) The date of a bond referendum shall be fixed by the governing board, but shall not be more than one year after adoption of the bond order, only on a date permitted by G.S. 163-287. The clerk shall mail or deliver a certified copy of the resolution calling a special bond referendum to the board of elections that is to conduct it within three days after the resolution is adopted, but failure to observe this requirement shall not in any manner affect the validity of the referendum or bonds issued pursuant thereto. Bond referenda shall be conducted by the board of elections conducting regular elections of the county, city, or special district. Several bond orders or other matters may be voted upon at the same referendum.

(c) The clerk shall publish a notice of the referendum at least twice. The first publication shall be not less than 14 days and the second publication not less than seven days before the last day on which voters may register for the referendum. The notice shall state the date of the referendum, the maximum amount of the proposed bonds, the purpose of the bonds, a statement that taxes will or may be levied for the payment thereof, and a statement as to the last day for registration for the referendum under the election laws then in effect.

(d)   The form of the question as stated on the ballot shall be in substantially the following words:

"Shall the order authorizing $ _____ bonds plus interest for (briefly stating the purpose) and providing that additional taxes may be levied in an amount sufficient to pay the principal of and interest on the bonds be approved?

[ ] YES

[ ] NO"

(e)   The board of elections shall canvass the referendum and certify the results to the governing board. The governing board shall then certify and declare the result of the referendum and shall publish a statement of the result once, with the following statement appended:

"Any action or proceeding challenging the regularity or validity of this bond referendum must be begun within 30 days after

_____

(date of publication)

_____

(title of governing board)"

The statement of results shall be filed in the clerk's office and inserted in the minutes of the board. (1917, c. 138, s. 22; 1919, c. 178, s. 3(22); c. 291; C.S., s. 2948; 1921, c. 8, s. 1; Ex. Sess. 1921, c. 106, s. 1; 1927, c. 81, ss. 22, 23, 25-27, 29; 1949, c. 497, ss. 2, 4; 1953, c. 1065, ss. 1, 2; 1971, c. 780, s. 1; 1973, c. 494, s. 9; 2013-200, s. 4; 2013-381, s. 10.26.)

§ 159-62. Limitation on actions contesting validity of bond referenda.

Any action or proceeding in any court to set aside a bond referendum, or to obtain any other relief, upon the ground that the referendum is invalid or was irregularly conducted, must be begun within 30 days after the publication of the statement of the results of the referendum. After the expiration of this period of limitation, no right of action or defense based upon the invalidity of or any irregularity in the referendum shall be asserted, nor shall the validity of the referendum be open to question in any court upon any ground whatever, except in an action or proceeding begun within the period of limitation prescribed in this section. (1917, c. 138, s. 22; 1919, c. 178, s. 3(22); c. 291; C.S., s. 2948; 1921, c. 8, s. 1; Ex. Sess. 1921, c. 106, s. 1; 1927, c. 81, s. 30; 1949, c. 497, s. 4; 1953, c. 1065, s. 2; 1971, c. 780, s. 1.)

§ 159-63. Repeal of bond orders.

A bond order may be repealed at any time before bonds or bond anticipation notes are issued thereunder. No referendum is required on the repeal of any bond order, nor is a petition for any such referendum permitted. (1971, c. 780, s. 1.)

§ 159-64. Within what time bonds may be issued.

Bonds may be issued under a bond order at any time within seven years after the bond order takes effect. Such period may be extended prior to the expiration of such period from seven years to 10 years as hereinafter provided. The board of the issuing unit shall file an application for Commission approval of such extension with the secretary of the Commission. The application shall state such facts and have attached to it such documents concerning such extension as the secretary may require. The Commission may prescribe the form of such application. In determining whether to approve such extension, the Commission may inquire into and give consideration to any matters which it believes may relate to such extension.

The Commission may enter an order approving a proposed extension of the maximum time period for issuing bonds under a bond order from seven to 10 years if, upon the basis of the information and evidence it receives, it finds and determines that governmental approvals relative to the purpose to be financed in whole or in part with the proceeds of the bonds cannot be obtained within seven years after the bond order has taken effect, that funds to be applied together with the proceeds of the bonds to finance the purpose for which the bonds are to be issued will not be available within seven years after the bond order has taken effect or that the proposed extension is necessary for other reasons that are not within the direct control of the issuing unit other than any order of any court. If the Commission enters an order denying such extension, then the proceedings under this section shall be at an end.

If the Commission enters an order approving a proposed extension of the maximum time period for issuing bonds under a bond order as provided in this section, then the board shall fix the time and place for a public hearing on such extension and the clerk shall publish such bond order once with the following statement appended:

"The foregoing order took effect on_____,_____. Anyone who wishes to be heard on the question of whether the maximum time period for issuing bonds under such order should be extended from seven years to 10 years after such date may appear at a public hearing or an adjournment thereof to be held at _____ on _____ at _____

(time)   (date)   (place)

_____

Clerk"

On the date fixed for such hearing, which shall be not earlier than six days after the date of publication of the bond order with appended statement as provided in this section, the board shall hear anyone who might wish to be heard on the question of whether the maximum time period for issuing bonds under the bond order should be extended from seven years to 10 years. The hearing may be adjourned from time to time.

After such hearing, the board may adopt an order providing that the maximum time period for issuing bonds under the bond order has been extended from seven to 10 years after the bond order has taken effect. Such order shall provide that it will take effect 30 days after its publication following adoption.

After adoption, the clerk shall publish once an order extending the maximum time period for issuing bonds under a bond order with the following statement appended:

"The foregoing order was adopted on the ____ day of_____,_____, and is hereby published this ____ day of_____, _____. Any action or proceeding questioning the validity of such order must be begun within 30 days after the date of publication of this notice.

_____

Clerk"

Any action or proceeding in any court to set aside an order extending the maximum time period for issuing bonds under a bond order, or to obtain any other relief, upon the ground that such order is invalid, must be begun within 30 days after the date of publication of such order as adopted. After the expiration of this period of limitation, no right of action or defense based upon the invalidity of such order shall be asserted nor shall the validity of such order be open to question in any court upon any ground whatever, except in an action or proceeding begun within the period of limitation prescribed in this section.

When the issuance of bonds under any bond order is prevented or prohibited by any order of any court, the period of time within which bonds may be issued under the bond order in litigation shall be extended by the length of time elapsing between the date of institution of the action or proceeding and the date of its final disposition.

When the issuance of bonds under any bond order, to finance public improvements in an area to be annexed, is prevented or prohibited by reason of litigation respecting the annexation and the Local Government Commission shall certify to such effect, the period of time within which bonds may be issued under the bond order shall be extended by the length of time elapsing between the date of institution of the litigation and the date of its final disposition.

The General Assembly may at any time prior to the expiration of the maximum time period herein provided extend the time for issuing bonds under bond orders.

When any such extension is effected or granted pursuant to this section, no further approval of the voters shall be required. (1917, c. 138, s. 24; 1919, c. 178, s. 3(24); C.S., s. 2950; 1921, c. 8, s. 1; Ex. Sess. 1921, c. 106, s. 1; 1927, c. 81; s. 32; 1939, c. 231, ss. 1, 2(d); 1947, c. 510, ss. 1, 2; 1949, c. 190, ss. 1, 2; 1951, c. 439, ss. 1, 2; 1953, c. 693, ss. 1, 3; 1955, c. 704, ss. 1, 2; 1969, c. 99; 1971, c. 780, s. 1; 1975, c. 545, s. 1; 1977, 2nd Sess., c. 1219, s. 36; 1979, c. 444, s. 1.)

§ 159-65. Resolution fixing the details of the bonds.

(a) After the bond order has been adopted, the board shall adopt a resolution fixing the details of the bonds. In fixing details of the bonds, the board is subject to these restrictions and directions:

(1) The dates for payment of installments of principal shall not exceed the maximum periods of usefulness prescribed by the Commission pursuant to G.S. 159-122.

(2) Bonds authorized by two or more bond orders may be consolidated into a single issue.

(3) Bonds of each issue shall have principal paid in annual installments, the first of which shall be payable not more than three years after the date of the bonds, and the last within the maximum maturity period prescribed by regulation of the Commission under G.S. 159-122.

(4) No installment of principal for any issue may be more than four times as great in amount as the smallest prior installment of principal for the same issue.

(5) Bonds of each issue may be issued from time to time in series with different provisions for each series. Each series shall be deemed a separate issue for the purposes of this section, except that two or more series may be considered to be a single issue under subdivisions (3) and (4) of this subsection if issued on the same day or two consecutive days.

(6) Any bond may be made payable on demand or tender for purchase as provided in G.S. 159-79, and any bond may be made subject to redemption prior to maturity, with or without premium, on such notice and at such time or times and with such redemption provisions as may be stated therein. When any such bond has been validly called for redemption and provision has been made for the payment of the principal thereof, any redemption premium, and the interest thereon accrued to the date of redemption, interest thereon shall cease.

(7) The bonds may bear interest at such rate or rates, payable semiannually or otherwise, may be in such denominations, and may be made payable in such kind of money and in such place or places within or without the State of North Carolina, as the board may determine.

(b) Subdivisions (a)(3) and (4) of this section do not apply to refunding bonds or to bonds purchased by a State or federal agency. Subdivisions (a)(3) and (4) also do not apply to bonds the interest on which is or may be includable in gross income for purposes of federal income tax, as long as the dates for payment of principal on these bonds have been approved by the Commission. For the purposes of subdivisions (a)(3) and (4) of this section and for bonds the interest on which is or may be includable in gross income for purposes of federal income tax, payment of an installment of principal may be provided for by the maturity of a bond, mandatory redemption of principal prior to maturity, a sinking fund, a credit facility as defined in G.S. 159-79, or any other means satisfactory to the Commission. (1917, c. 138, s. 25; 1919, c. 178, s. 3(25); C.S., s. 2951; 1921, c. 8, s. 1; Ex. Sess. 1921, c. 106, s. 1; 1933, c. 259, s. 1; 1951, c. 440, s. 1; 1953, c. 1206, s. 3; 1969, c. 686; 1971, c. 780, s. 1; 1973, c. 494, s. 10; cc. 883, 995; 1987, c. 585, s. 2; c. 586; 2003-388, s. 2.)

§ 159-66. Validation of former proceedings and actions.

(a) All proceedings and actions heretofore taken by the governing boards of units of local government and by the Local Government Commission to fix the details of bonds and to provide for the advertisement and sale thereof are hereby ratified, approved, confirmed and in all respects validated, notwithstanding the provisions of G.S. 159-65(4).

(b) This section shall apply to all bonds sold by the Local Government Commission between July 1, 1973, and February 18, 1974. (1973, c. 872, ss. 1, 2.)

§ 159-67. Procedures if a county votes to relocate the county seat.

Whenever the citizens of a county, by referendum, decide that the county's county seat, along with the courthouse and other county buildings and agencies, should be relocated, the board of county commissioners of that county shall forthwith begin discussions with the Local Government Commission concerning financing of the relocation. If bonds are to be issued for the relocation, or a financing agreement entered into, the board of commissioners shall apply to the Local Government Commission no later than 10 months after the day of the referendum. If a bond election is necessary, it shall be held no later than 22 months after the day of the referendum. (1975, c. 324, s. 5.)

§ 159-68. Certain provisions not applicable to refunding bonds.

The provisions of G.S. 159-56 and the provisions of this Article related to the holding of a public hearing prior to the adoption of the bond order do not apply to refunding bonds issued by a unit of local government so long as the refunding bonds do not extend the final maturity of the debt or obligation to be refunded and so long as the aggregate debt service over the life of the refunding bonds is less than the aggregate debt service on the debt or obligation to be refunded. When the conditions of this section are satisfied, a unit of local government may introduce a bond order, adopt a bond order, and adopt a sale resolution with respect to refunding bonds in one or more meetings of the unit's governing body. (2005-238, s. 3.)

§ 159-69. Reserved for future codification purposes.

§ 159-70. Reserved for future codification purposes.

§ 159-71. Reserved for future codification purposes.

Part 3. Funding and Refunding Bonds.

§ 159-72. Purposes for which funding and refunding bonds may be issued; when such bonds may be issued.

A unit of local government may issue funding and refunding bonds under this Article for the purposes listed in G.S. 159-48(a)(4), (5), (6), or (7). Funding bonds may be issued if the debt, judgment, or other obligation to be paid is payable at the time of the passage of the bond order or within one year thereafter. Refunding bonds may be issued at any time prior to the final maturity of the debt or obligation to be refunded. The proceeds from the sale of any refunding bonds shall be applied only as follows: either (i) to the immediate payment and retirement of the obligations being refunded or (ii) if not required for the immediate payment of the obligations being refunded such proceeds shall be deposited in trust to provide for the payment and retirement of the obligations being refunded, and to pay any expenses incurred in connection with such refunding, but provision may be made for the pledging and disposition of any amounts in excess of the amounts required for such purposes, including, without limitation, provision for the pledging of any such excess to the payment of the principal of and interest on any issue or series of refunding bonds issued pursuant to G.S. 159-78. Money in any such trust fund may be invested in (i) direct obligations of the United States government, or (ii) obligations the principal of and interest on which are guaranteed by the United States government, or (iii) to the extent then permitted by law in obligations of any agency or instrumentality of the United States government, or (iv) in certificates of deposit issued by a bank or trust company located in the State of North Carolina if such certificates shall be secured by a pledge of any of said obligations described in (i), (ii), or (iii) above having an aggregate market value, exclusive of accrued interest, equal at least to the principal amount of the certificates so secured. Nothing herein shall be construed as a limitation on the duration of any deposit in trust for the retirement of obligations being refunded but which shall not have matured and which shall not be presently redeemable or, if presently redeemable, shall not have been called for redemption.

The principal amount of refunding bonds issued pursuant to this section, together with the principal amount of refunding bonds, if any, issued under G.S. 159-78 in conjunction with refunding bonds issued pursuant to this section, shall not exceed the amount set forth in G.S. 159-78.

Except as expressly modified in this Part, funding and refunding bonds issued under the provisions of this Part shall be subject to the limitations and procedures set out in Parts 1 and 2 of this Article. (1917, c. 138, s. 16; 1919, c. 178, s. 3(16); C.S., s. 2937; 1921, c. 8, s. 1; Ex. Sess. 1921, c. 106, s. 1; 1927, c. 81, s. 8; 1929, c. 171, s. 1; 1931, c. 60, ss. 48, 54; 1933, c. 257, ss. 2-4; c. 259, ss. 1, 2; 1935, c. 302, ss. 1, 2; c. 484; 1939, c. 231, ss. 1, 2(c), 4(b); 1941, c. 147; 1943, c. 13; 1945, c. 403; 1947, cc. 520, 931; 1949, c. 354; c. 766, s. 3; c. 1270; 1953, c. 1065, s. 1; 1957, c. 266, s. 1; c. 856, s. 1; c. 1098, s. 16; 1959,

c. 525; c. 1250, s. 2; 1961, c. 293; c. 1001, s. 2; 1965, c. 307, s. 2; 1967, c. 987, s. 2; c. 1001, s. 1; 1971, c. 780, s. 1; 1973, c. 494, s. 11; 1977, c. 201, s. 1.)

§ 159-73. Financing or refinancing agreements.

Each unit of local government is authorized to enter into agreements with the holders of its outstanding debts for the settlement, adjustment, funding, refunding, financing, or refinancing of the debt. Such an agreement may contain any provisions not inconsistent with law and before the unit may enter into it, it must be approved by the Commission. (1971, c. 780, s. 1.)

§ 159-74. Test cases testing validity of funding or refunding bonds.

At any time after the procedure for authorizing the issuance of funding or refunding bonds has been completed, but before the issuance of the bonds, the issuing unit may institute an action in the Superior Court Division of the General Court of Justice in the county in which all or any part of the unit lies, to determine the validity of the bonds and the validity of the means of payment provided therefor. The action shall be in rem, and shall be against all of the owners of taxable property within the unit and all citizens residing in the unit, but it shall not be necessary to name each such owner or citizen in the summons or complaint. Jurisdiction of all parties defendant shall be acquired by publication of a summons once a week for three successive weeks, and jurisdiction shall be complete within 20 days after the date of the last publication. Any interested party may intervene in the action. Except as otherwise provided by this section, the action shall be governed by the Rules of Civil Procedure. (1931, c. 186, ss. 4, 5; 1935, c. 290, ss. 1, 2; 1937, c. 80; 1971, c. 780, s. 1.)

§ 159-75. Judgment validating issue; costs of the action.

A final decree of the General Court of Justice validating funding or refunding bonds or the financing or refinancing agreement shall be conclusive as to the validity of the bonds or the agreement.

The costs of any action brought under G.S. 159-74 shall be borne by the issuing unit, including a reasonable attorney's fee for the attorney assigned by the court to defend the interests of the citizens and taxpayers in general. (1931, c. 186, ss. 6, 7; 1935, c. 290, s. 3; 1971, c. 780, s. 1; 1973, c. 494, s. 12.)

§ 159-76. Validation of bonds and notes issued before March 26, 1931.

All bonds and notes issued before March 26, 1931, for which the issuing unit received an amount of money not less than the face amount of the bonds or notes and the proceeds of which have been spent for public purposes, and all bonds and notes subsequently issued to refund all or any portion of those bonds or notes, are hereby validated notwithstanding any lack of statutory authority or failure to observe any statutory provisions concerning the issuance of the bonds or notes. This section shall not validate any bonds or notes, the proceeds of which have been lost because of the failure of a bank. (1931, c. 186, s. 2; 1971, c. 780, s. 1; 1973, c. 494, s. 13.)

§ 159-77. Validation of all proceedings in connection with the authorization of bonds taken before April 28, 1975.

All proceedings heretofore taken by the governing boards of units of local government in connection with the authorization of bonds are hereby ratified, approved, confirmed and in all respects validated, notwithstanding the provisions of G.S. 159-61(c); provided that the issuance of said bonds shall have been approved at an election by a majority of the qualified voters of the unit voting thereon and that notice of said referendum shall have been published. (1975, c. 178.)

§ 159-78. Special obligation refunding bonds.

In conjunction with the issuance of refunding bonds pursuant to G.S. 159-72 or G.S. 159-84 a unit of local government may issue a series of refunding bonds which shall be payable from the excess of the amount required by a trust fund established pursuant to G.S. 159-72 or G.S. 159-84 to provide for the payment and retirement of the obligations being retired and the amount required to pay any expenses incurred in connection with such refunding to the extent such expenses are payable from said trust fund.

Such refunding bonds shall be special obligations of the municipality issuing them. The principal of and interest on such refunding bonds shall not be payable from the general funds of the municipality, nor shall they constitute a legal or equitable pledge, charge, lien, or encumbrance upon any of its property or upon any of its income, receipts, or revenues, except the trust fund established pursuant to G.S. 159-72 or G.S. 159-84 from which such refunding bonds are payable. Neither the credit nor the taxing power of the municipality is pledged for the payment of the principal or interest of such refunding bonds, and no holder of such refunding bonds has the right to compel the exercise of the taxing power of the municipality or the forfeiture of any of its property in connection with any default thereon. Every such refunding bond shall recite in substance that the principal of and interest on the bond is payable solely from the trust fund established for its payment and that the municipality is not obligated to pay the principal or interest except from such trust fund.

Any refunding bonds issued under this section shall be issued in compliance with the procedure set forth in Article 5 of this Chapter.

The principal amount of any issue of refunding bonds issued pursuant to G.S. 159-72 or G.S. 159-84, together with the principal amount of refunding bonds, if any, issued pursuant to this section in conjunction with a series of bonds issued under G.S. 159-72 or G.S. 159-84, shall not exceed the sum of the following: (i) the principal amount of the obligations being refinanced, (ii) applicable redemption premiums thereon, (iii) unpaid interest on such obligations to the date of delivery or exchange of the refunding bonds, (iv) in the event the proceeds from the sale of the refunding bonds are to be deposited in trust as provided by G.S. 159-72 or G.S. 159-84, interest to accrue on such obligations being refinanced from the date of delivery of the refunding bonds to the first or any subsequent available redemption date or dates selected, in its discretion, by the governing body of the unit of local government, or to the date or dates of maturity, whichever shall be determined by the governing body of the unit of local government to be most advantageous or necessary and (v) expenses, including bond discount, deemed by the governing body to be necessary for the issuance of the refunding bonds. (1977, c. 201, s. 2.)

§ 159-79. Variable rate demand bonds and notes.

(a)   (See note) Notwithstanding any provisions of this Chapter to the contrary, including particularly, but without limitation, the provisions of G.S. 159-65, G.S. 159-123 to G.S. 159-127, inclusive, G.S. 159-130, G.S. 159-138, G.S. 159-162, G.S. 159-164 and G.S. 159-172, a unit of local government, in fixing the details of general obligation bonds to be issued pursuant to this Article or general obligation notes to be issued pursuant to Article 9 of this Chapter, may provide that such bonds or notes

(1)   May be made payable from time to time on demand or tender for purchase by the owner provided a Credit Facility supports such bonds or notes, unless the Commission specifically determines that a Credit Facility is not required upon a finding and determination by the Commission that the proposed bonds or notes will satisfy the conditions set forth in G.S. 159-52;

(2)   May be additionally supported by a Credit Facility;

(3)   May be made subject to redemption prior to maturity, with or without premium, on such notice, at such time or times, at such price or prices and with such other redemption provisions as may be stated in the resolution fixing the details of such bonds or notes or with such variations as may be permitted in connection with a Par Formula provided in such resolution;

(4)   May bear interest at a rate or rates that may vary as permitted pursuant to a Par Formula and for such period or periods of time, all as may be provided in such resolution; and

(5)   May be made the subject of a remarketing agreement whereby an attempt is made to remarket the bonds to new purchases prior to their presentment for payment to the provider of the Credit Facility or to the issuing unit.

(a)   (For effective date, see note) Notwithstanding any provisions of this Chapter to the contrary, including particularly, but without limitation, the provisions of G.S. 159-65, G.S. 159-112, G.S. 159-123 to G.S. 159-127, inclusive, G.S. 159-130, G.S. 159-138, G.S. 159-162, G.S. 159-164 and G.S. 159-172, a unit of local government, in fixing the details of general obligation bonds to be issued pursuant to this Article, general obligation notes to be issued pursuant to Article 9 of this Chapter, or project development financing debt instruments or notes to be issued pursuant to Article 6 of this Chapter, may provide that the instruments or notes:

(1) May be made payable from time to time on demand or tender for purchase by the owner provided a Credit Facility supports such bonds or notes, unless the Commission specifically determines that a Credit Facility is not required upon a finding and determination by the Commission that the proposed bonds or notes will satisfy the conditions set forth in G.S. 159-52;

(2) May be additionally supported by a Credit Facility;

(3) May be made subject to redemption prior to maturity, with or without premium, on such notice, at such time or times, at such price or prices and with such other redemption provisions as may be stated in the resolution fixing the details of such bonds or notes or with such variations as may be permitted in connection with a Par Formula provided in such resolution;

(4) May bear interest at a rate or rates that may vary as permitted pursuant to a Par Formula and for such period or periods of time, all as may be provided in such resolution; and

(5) May be made the subject of a remarketing agreement whereby an attempt is made to remarket the bonds to new purchases prior to their presentment for payment to the provider of the Credit Facility or to the issuing unit.

(b) No Credit Facility, repayment agreement, Par Formula or remarketing agreement shall become effective without the approval of the Commission.

(c) As used in this section the following terms shall have the following meanings:

(1) "Credit Facility" means an agreement entered into by an issuing unit with a bank, savings and loan association or other banking institution, an insurance company, reinsurance company, surety company or other insurance institution, a corporation, investment banking firm or other investment institution, or any financial institution providing for prompt payment of all or any part of the principal (whether at maturity, presentment or tender for purchase, redemption or acceleration), redemption premium, if any, and interest on any bonds or notes payable on demand or tender by the owner issued in accordance with this section, in consideration of the issuing unit agreeing to repay the provider of such Credit Facility in accordance with the terms and provisions of a repayment agreement. A bank may include a foreign bank or branch or agency thereof the obligations of which bear the highest rating of at least one nationally-recognized

rating service and do not bear a rating below the highest rating of any nationally-recognized rating service which rates such particular obligations.

(2) "Par Formula" shall mean any provision or formula adopted by the issuing unit to provide for the adjustment, from time to time, of the interest rate or rates borne by any such bonds or notes so that the purchase price of such bonds or notes in the open market would be as close to par as possible.

(d) If the aggregate principal amount repayable by the issuing unit under a repayment agreement is in excess of the aggregate principal amount of bonds or notes secured by the related Credit Facility, whether as a result of the inclusion in the Credit Facility of a provision for the payment of interest for a limited period of time or the payment of a redemption premium or for any other reason, then the amount of unissued bonds or notes during the term of such repayment agreement shall not be less than the amount of such excess, unless the payment of such excess is otherwise provided for by agreement of the issuing unit subject to the approval of the Commission. In determining whether or not to grant such approval, the Commission shall consider, in addition to such other factors it may deem relevant, the ability of the issuing unit to pay such excess from other sources without incurring additional indebtedness secured by a pledge of the faith and credit of the issuing unit or levying additional taxes and the adequacy of such other sources to accomplish such purpose.

(e) Any bonds or notes issued pursuant to this section may be sold by the Commission at public or private sale according to such procedures as the Commission may prescribe and at such prices as the Commission determines to be in the best interest of the issuing unit, subject to the approval of the governing board of the issuing unit or one or more persons designated by resolution of the governing board of the issuing unit to approve such prices. (1987, c. 585, s. 1; 2003-403, s. 5.)

Article 5.

Revenue Bonds.

§ 159-80. Short title; repeal of local acts.

(a) This Article may be cited as "The State and Local Government Revenue Bond Act."

(b) It is the intent of the General Assembly by enactment of this Article to prescribe a uniform system of limitations upon and procedures for the exercise by all municipalities in North Carolina of the power to finance revenue bond projects through the issuance of revenue bonds and notes. To this end, all provisions of special, local, or private acts in effect as of July 1, 1973, authorizing the issuance of bonds or notes secured solely by the revenues of the projects for which the bonds or notes are issued or prescribing procedures therefor are repealed. No special, local or private act enacted or taking effect after July 1, 1973, may be construed to modify, amend, or repeal any portion of this Article unless it expressly so provides by specific reference to the appropriate section of this Article. It is further the intent of the General Assembly by enactment of this Article to provide an alternative and supplemental procedure for the exercise by the State of North Carolina of the power to finance revenue bond projects through the issuance of revenue bonds and notes. (1971, c. 780, s. 1; 1973, c. 494, s. 14; 1983, c. 554, ss. 1, 1.1.)

§ 159-81. Definitions.

The words and phrases defined in this section shall have the meanings indicated when used in this Article:

(1) "Municipality" means a county, city, town, incorporated village, sanitary district, metropolitan sewerage district, metropolitan water district, metropolitan water and sewerage district, county water and sewer district, water and sewer authority, hospital authority, hospital district, parking authority, special airport district, special district created under Article 43 of Chapter 105 of the General Statutes, regional public transportation authority, regional transportation authority, regional natural gas district, regional sports authority, airport authority, joint agency created pursuant to Part 1 of Article 20 of Chapter 160A of the General Statutes, a joint agency authorized by agreement between two cities to operate an airport pursuant to G.S. 63-56, and the North Carolina Turnpike Authority described in Article 6H of Chapter 136 of the General Statutes and transferred to the Department of Transportation pursuant to G.S. 136-89.182(b), but not any other forms of State or local government.

(2) "Revenue bond" means a bond issued by the State of North Carolina or a municipality pursuant to this Article.

(3) "Revenue bond project" means any undertaking for the acquisition, construction, reconstruction, improvement, enlargement, betterment, or extension of any one or combination of the revenue-producing utility or public

service enterprise facilities or systems listed in this subdivision, to be financed through the issuance of revenue bonds, thereby providing funds to pay the costs of the undertaking or to reimburse funds loaned or advanced by or on the behalf of either the State or a municipality to pay the costs of the undertaking.

A revenue bond project shall be (i) owned or leased as lessee by the issuing unit or (ii) owned by one or more of the municipalities participating in an undertaking established pursuant to Part 1 of Article 20 of Chapter 160A of the General Statutes. If the revenue bond project is owned by one or more municipalities as provided in (ii) of this subdivision, any one or more of the participating municipalities may each be an issuing unit consistent with their agreement to establish a joint undertaking. In addition, any joint agency established by participating municipalities pursuant to Part 1 of Article 20 of Chapter 160A of the General Statutes may be an issuing unit without owning the revenue bond project or leasing it as lessee.

The cost of an undertaking may include all property, both real and personal and improved and unimproved, plants, works, appurtenances, machinery, equipment, easements, water rights, air rights, franchises, and licenses used or useful in connection with the undertaking; the cost of demolishing or moving structures from land acquired and the cost of acquiring any lands to which the structures are to be moved; financing charges; the cost of plans, specifications, surveys, and estimates of cost and revenues; administrative and legal expenses; and any other expense necessary or incident to the project.

The following facilities or systems may be revenue bond projects under this subdivision:

a.   Water systems or facilities, including all plants, works, instrumentalities and properties used or useful in obtaining, conserving, treating, and distributing water for domestic or industrial use, irrigation, sanitation, fire protection, or any other public or private use.

b.   Sewage disposal systems or facilities, including all plants, works, instrumentalities, and properties used or useful in the collection, treatment, purification, or disposal of sewage.

c.   Systems or facilities for the generation, production, transmission, or distribution of gas (natural, artificial, or mixed) or electric energy for lighting, heating, or power for public and private uses, where gas systems shall include the purchase and/or lease of natural gas fields and natural gas reserves and the purchase of natural gas supplies, and where any parts of such gas systems may be located either within the State or without.

d. Systems, facilities and equipment for the collection, treatment, or disposal of solid waste.

e. Public transportation systems, facilities, or equipment, including but not limited to bus, truck, ferry, and railroad terminals, depots, trackages, vehicles, and ferries, and mass transit systems.

f. Public parking lots, areas, garages, and other vehicular parking structures and facilities.

g. Aeronautical facilities, including but not limited to airports, terminals, and hangars.

h. Marine facilities, including but not limited to marinas, basins, docks, dry docks, piers, marine railways, wharves, harbors, warehouses, and terminals.

i. Hospitals and other health-related facilities.

j. Public auditoriums, gymnasiums, stadiums, and convention centers.

k. Recreational facilities.

l. Repealed by Session Laws 2001-474, s. 36, effective November 29, 2001.

m. Economic development projects, including the acquisition and development of industrial parks, the acquisition and resale of land suitable for industrial or commercial purposes, and the construction and lease or sale of shell buildings in order to provide employment opportunities for citizens of the municipality.

n. Facilities for the use of any agency or agencies of the government of the United States of America.

o. Structural and natural stormwater and drainage systems of all types.

p. In the case of the North Carolina Turnpike Authority, a Turnpike Project, as defined in G.S. 136-89.181, including the planning and design of a Turnpike Project, that is designated by the Authority to be a revenue bond project.

q. Cable television systems.

(4) "Revenues" include all moneys received by the State or a municipality from, in connection with, or as a result of its ownership or operation of a revenue bond project or a utility or public service enterprise facility or system of which a revenue bond project is a part, including (to the extent deemed advisable by the State or a municipality) moneys received from the United States of America, the State of North Carolina, or any agency of either, pursuant to an agreement with the State or a municipality, as the case may be, pertaining to the project. (Ex. Sess. 1938, c. 2, s. 2; 1939, c. 295; 1941, c. 207, s. 2; 1951, c. 703, s. 1; 1953, c. 901, ss. 4, 5; c. 922, s. 1; 1965, c. 997; 1969, c. 1118, s. 1; 1971, c. 780, s. 1; 1973, c. 494, s. 15; 1975, c. 821, s. 2; 1977, c. 466, s. 3; 1979, c. 727, s. 4; c. 791; 1983, c. 554, ss. 2-2.2; 1985, c. 639, s. 3; 1987 (Reg. Sess., 1988), c. 976, s. 1; 1989, c. 168, ss. 37, 38; c. 643, s. 4; c. 740, s. 2; c. 780, s. 2; 1991, c. 508, s. 1; 1995 (Reg. Sess., 1996), c. 644, s. 3; 1997-393, s. 3; 1997-426, s. 6; 2001-414, s. 48; 2001-474, ss. 36, 37; 2002-133, ss. 6, 7; 2009-527, s. 2(e); 2010-165, s. 14; 2011-84, s. 4; 2013-50, s. 5.)

§ 159-82. Purpose.

The purpose of this Article is to establish a standard, uniform procedure for the financing by a municipality of revenue bond projects through the issuance of revenue bonds. Its provisions are intended to vest authority in and enable municipalities to secure and pay revenue bonds and the interest thereon solely out of revenues without pledging the faith and credit of the municipality. (1971, c. 780, s. 1; 1973, c. 494, s. 16.)

§ 159-83. Powers.

(a) In addition to the powers they may now or hereafter have, the State and each municipality shall have the following powers, subject to the provisions of this Article and of any revenue bond order or trust agreement securing revenue bonds:

(1) To acquire by gift, purchase, or exercise of the power of eminent domain or to construct, reconstruct, improve, maintain, better, extend, and operate, one or more revenue bond projects or any portion thereof without regard to location within or without its boundaries, upon determination (i) in the case of the State, by the Council of State and (ii) in the case of a municipality, by resolution of the governing board that a location wholly or partially outside its boundaries is necessary and in the public interest. The authority to exercise the power of eminent domain granted in this subdivision shall not apply to economic development projects described in G.S. 159-81(3)m., unless revenue bonds for the economic development project were approved by the Local Government Commission pursuant to G.S. 159-87 prior to August 15, 2006.

(2) To sell, exchange, transfer, assign or otherwise dispose of any revenue bond project or portion thereof or interest therein determined (i) in the case of the State, by the Council of State and (ii) in the case of a municipality, by resolution of the governing board not to be required for any public purpose.

(3) To sell, furnish, and distribute the services, facilities, or commodities of revenue bond projects.

(4) To enter into contracts with any person, firm, or corporation, public or private, on such terms (i) in the case of the State, as the Council of State and (ii) in the case of a municipality, as the governing board may determine, with respect to the acquisition, construction, reconstruction, extension, betterment, improvement, maintenance, or operation of revenue bond projects, or the sale, furnishing, or distribution of the services, facilities or commodities thereof.

(5) To borrow money for the purpose of acquiring, constructing, reconstructing, extending, bettering, improving, or otherwise paying the cost of revenue bond projects, to issue its revenue bonds or bond anticipation notes therefor, in the name of the State or a municipality, as the case may be, and to pledge, mortgage, or grant a security interest in all or a portion of the real and personal property, whether owned or leased, comprising any revenue-producing utility or public service enterprise facilities or systems acquired, constructed, reconstructed, extended, bettered, or improved with the proceeds of the borrowing. Property subject to a mortgage, deed of trust, security interest, or similar lien pursuant to this subdivision may be sold at foreclosure in any manner permitted by the instrument creating the encumbrance, without compliance with any other provision of law regarding the disposition of publicly owned property. The granting of a lien on, or security interest in, hospital or health-related real or tangible personal property and the conveyance of this

property pursuant to the provisions of the lien or security interest are not subject to the provisions of G.S. 131E-8, 131E-13, or 131E-14.

(6) To establish, maintain, revise, charge, and collect such rates, fees, rentals, tolls, or other charges, free of any control or regulation by the North Carolina Utilities Commission or any other regulatory body except as provided in G.S. 159-95 for the use, services, facilities, and commodities of or furnished by any revenue bond project, and to provide methods of collection of and penalties for nonpayment of such rates, fees, rentals, tolls, or other charges. The rates, fees, rentals, tolls and charges so fixed and charged shall be such as will produce revenues at least sufficient with any other available funds to meet the expense and maintenance and operation of and renewals and replacements to the revenue bond project, including reserves therefor, to pay when due the principal, interest, and redemption premiums (if any) on all revenue bonds or bond anticipation notes secured thereby, and to fulfill the terms of any agreements made by the State or the issuing municipality with the holders of revenue bonds issued to finance all or any portion of the cost of the project.

(7) To pledge all or part of any proceeds derived from the use of on-street parking meters to the payment of the cost of operating, maintaining, and improving parking facilities whether on-street or off-street, and the principal of and the interest on revenue bonds or bond anticipation notes issued for on-street or off-street parking facilities.

(8) To pledge to the payment of its revenue bonds or bond anticipation notes and interest thereon revenues from one or more revenue bond projects and any leases or agreements to secure such payment, including revenues from improvements, betterments, or extensions to such projects thereafter constructed or acquired as well as the revenues from existing systems, plants, works, instrumentalities, and properties of the projects to be improved, bettered, or extended.

(8a) In the case of any county, city, town, or incorporated village, to make loans or advances to a municipality to provide funds to the municipality to pay any costs of any revenue bond project. Funds received by a municipality in reimbursement of a loan or advance shall be distributed and restricted as provided in G.S. 159-27.1.

(9) To appropriate, apply, or expend for the following purposes the proceeds of its revenue bonds, notes issued in anticipation thereof, and revenues pledged under any resolution or order authorizing or securing the

bonds: (i) to pay interest on the bonds or notes and the principal or redemption price thereof when due; (ii) to meet reserves and other requirements set forth in the bond order or trust agreement; (iii) to pay the costs of the revenue bond projects authorized in the bond order, reimburse funds loaned or advanced for the costs of these revenue bond projects in accordance with the bond order, and provide working capital for initial maintenance and operation until funds are available from revenues; (iv) to pay and discharge revenue bonds and notes issued in anticipation thereof; (v) to pay and discharge general obligation bonds issued under Article 4 of this Chapter or under any act of the General Assembly, when the revenues of the project financed in whole or in part by the general obligation bonds will be pledged to the payment of the revenue bonds or notes.

(10) To make and enforce rules and regulations governing the use, maintenance, and operation of revenue bond projects.

(11) To accept gifts or grants of real or personal property, money, material, labor, or supplies for the acquisition, construction, reconstruction, extension, improvement, betterment, maintenance, or operation of any revenue bond project and to make and perform such agreements or contracts as may be necessary or convenient in connection with the procuring or acceptance of such gifts or grants.

(12) To accept loans, grants, or contributions from, and to enter into contracts and cooperate with the United States of America, the State of North Carolina, or any agency thereof, with respect to any revenue bond project.

(13) To enter on any lands, waters, and premises for the purpose of making surveys, borings, soundings, examinations, and other preliminary studies for constructing and operating any revenue bond project.

(14) To retain and employ consultants and other persons on a contract basis for rendering professional, financial, or technical assistance and advice and to select and retain subject to approval of the Local Government Commission the financial consultants, underwriters and bond attorneys to be associated with the issuance of any bonds and to pay for services rendered by underwriters, financial consultants or bond attorneys out of the proceeds of any such issue with regard to which the services were performed.

(15) Subject to any provisions of law requiring voter approval for the sale or lease of utility or enterprise systems, to lease to or from any person, firm, or corporation, public or private, all or part of any revenue bond project, upon such

terms and conditions as and for such term of years, not in excess of 40 years, (i) in the case of the State, as the Council of State and (ii) in the case of a municipality, as the governing board may deem advisable to carry out the provisions of this Article, and to provide in such lease for the extension or renewal thereof and, if deemed advisable, for an option to purchase or otherwise lawfully acquire the project upon terms and conditions therein specified.

(16)   To execute such instruments and agreements and to do all things necessary or therein in the exercise of the powers herein granted, or in the performance of the covenants or duties of the State or a municipality, as the case may be, or to secure the payment of its revenue bonds.

(b)   Any contract, agreement, lease, deed, covenant, or other instrument or document evidencing an agreement or covenant between bondholders or any public agency and the State or a municipality issuing revenue bonds with respect to any of the powers conferred in this section shall be approved by the commission.

(c)   In addition to the powers they may now or hereafter have, the State and each municipality shall have the following powers, notwithstanding any provisions of this Article to the contrary, in connection with the development of new and existing seaports and airports:

(1)   To acquire, construct, own, own jointly with public and private parties, lease as lessee, mortgage, sell, lease as lessor, or otherwise dispose of lands and facilities and improvements, including undivided interests therein;

(2)   To finance and refinance for public and private parties seaport and airport facilities and improvements that relate to, develop, or further waterborne or airborne commerce and cargo and passenger traffic, including commercial, industrial, manufacturing, processing, mining, transportation, distribution, storage, marine, aviation, and environmental facilities and improvements;

(3)   To secure any such financing or refinancing by all or any portion of its revenues, income or assets or other available moneys associated with any of its seaport or airport facilities and with the facilities and improvements to be financed or refinanced, and by foreclosable liens on all or any part of its properties associated with any of its seaport or airport facilities and with the facilities and improvements to be financed or refinanced, but in no event to create a debt secured by a pledge of its faith and credit.

(d)   In addition to the powers they may now or hereafter have, the State and each municipality shall have the following powers, notwithstanding any provisions of this Article or any other statute to the contrary, in connection with the development of facilities for the use of any agency or agencies of the government of the United States of America:

(1)   To acquire, construct, own jointly with public and private parties, lease as leasor or leasee, mortgage, sell, or otherwise dispose of lands, facilities and improvements, including undivided interests therein and to do so, regardless of the provisions of any other statute, on such terms (i) in the case of the State, as the Council of State and (ii) in the case of a municipality, as the governing board may deem advisable to carry out the provisions of this subsection;

(2)   To finance and refinance facilities and related improvements for the use of any agency of the government of the United States of America;

(3)   To secure any such financing or refinancing by all or any portion of the revenue, income or assets or other available monies associated with such facilities and improvements to be financed or refinanced, and by foreclosable liens on all or any part of the facilities and improvements to be financed or refinanced, but in no event to create a debt secured by a pledge of its faith and credit.

(e)   Repealed by Session Laws 2001-174, s. 39, effective November 29, 2001.

(f)   In addition to the powers they may now or hereafter have, each municipality has the power to finance and refinance the cost of water treatment facilities and related transmission mains, and their expansion and improvement, all or some portion of which may be located on land leased from an authority created under the provisions of G.S. 162A-3.1, for a term not less than the term of the obligations issued or otherwise incurred for the purpose. The authority may own or operate (or both) such facilities and mains and may contract with one or more of the political subdivisions that are members of the authority for operation of all or portions thereof. For this purpose, each municipality has, in addition to the powers it has under applicable law, all the powers under G.S. 162A-6(b) of an authority created under G.S. 162A-3.1, and the political subdivisions that are members of the authority and that contract with such municipality for a supply of water and a portion of the capacity of the water treatment facilities and mains shall have all the powers of political subdivisions under G.S. 162A-6(b) and G.S. 162A-16 contracting with an authority created under G.S. 162A-3.1. This provision is supplemental to the other provisions of this Article. (Ex. Sess., 1938, c. 2, s. 3; 1951, c. 703, ss. 2, 3; 1953, c. 922, s. 2; 1969, c. 1118, s. 2; 1971, c. 780, s. 1; 1973, c. 494, s. 17; 1983, c. 554, ss. 3-4; 1985, c. 723, s. 2; 1985 (Reg. Sess., 1986), c. 795, s. 1; c. 933, s. 4; 1987 (Reg. Sess., 1988), c. 976, s. 2; 1989, c. 168, ss. 39, 40; 1991, c. 508, s. 2; 2001-474, ss. 38, 39; 2005-238, s. 4; 2005-249, s. 1; 2006-224, s. 3; 2006-259, s. 47.)

§ 159-84. Authorization of revenue bonds.

The State and each municipality is hereby authorized to issue its revenue bonds in such principal amount as may be necessary to provide sufficient moneys for the acquisition, construction, reconstruction, extension, betterment, improvement, or payment of the cost of one or more revenue bond projects, including engineering, inspection, legal and financial fees and costs, working capital, interest on the bonds or notes issued in anticipation thereof during construction and, if deemed advisable by the State or a municipality, as the case may be, for a period not exceeding two years after the estimated date of completion of construction, establishment of debt service reserves, and all other expenditures of the State or the municipality, as the case may be, incidental and necessary or convenient thereto.

Subject to agreements with the holders of its revenue bonds, the State or each municipality, as the case may be, may issue further revenue bonds and refund outstanding revenue bonds whether or not they have matured. Revenue bonds may be issued partly for the purpose of refunding outstanding revenue bonds and partly for any other purpose under this Article. Revenue bonds issued to refund outstanding revenue bonds shall be issued under this Article and not Article 4 of this Chapter or any other law.

Refunding bonds may be issued at any time prior to the final maturity of the debt or obligation to be refunded. The proceeds from the sale of any refunding bonds shall be applied only as follows: either, (i) to the immediate payment and retirement of the obligations being refunded or (ii) if not required for the immediate payment of the obligations being refunded such proceeds shall be deposited in trust to provide for the payment and retirement of the obligations being refunded, and to pay any expenses incurred in connection with such refunding, but provision may be made for the pledging and disposition of any amounts in excess of the amounts required for such purposes, including, without limitation, provision for the pledging of any such excess to the payment of the principal of and interest on any issue or series or [of] refunding bonds issued pursuant to G.S. 159-78. Money in any such trust fund may be invested in (i) direct obligations of the United States government, or (ii) obligations the principal of and interest on which are guaranteed by the United States government, or (iii) to the extent then permitted by law in obligations of any agency or instrumentality of the United States government, (iv) certificates of deposit issued by a bank or trust company located in the State of North Carolina if such certificates shall be secured by a pledge of any of said obligations described in (i), (ii), or (iii) above having any aggregate market value, exclusive of accrued interest, equal at least to the principal amount of the certificates so secured. Nothing herein shall be construed as a limitation on the duration of any deposit in trust for the retirement of obligations being refunded but which shall not have matured and which shall not be presently redeemable or, if presently redeemable, shall not have been called for redemption.

The principal amount of refunding bonds issued pursuant to this section, together with the principal amount of refunding bonds, if any, issued under G.S. 159-78 in conjunction with refunding bonds issued pursuant to this section, shall not exceed the amount set forth in G.S. 159-78. (1953, c. 692; 1969, c. 1118, s. 4; 1971, c. 780, s. 1; 1977, c. 201, s. 3; 1983, c. 554, s. 5.)

§ 159-85. Application to Commission for approval of revenue bond issue; preliminary conference; acceptance of application.

(a) Neither the State nor a municipality may issue revenue bonds under this Article unless the issue is approved by the Commission. The State Treasurer or the governing board of the issuing municipality or its duly authorized agent, as the case may be, shall file an application for Commission approval of the issue with the secretary of the Commission. If the issuing municipality is a regional public transportation authority, the application must be accompanied by a resolution of the special tax board of that authority approving of the application. The application shall state such facts and have attached to it such documents concerning the proposed revenue bonds and the financial condition of the State or the issuing municipality, as the case may be, and its utilities and enterprises as the secretary may require. The Commission may prescribe the form of the application.

(b) Before he accepts the application, the secretary may require (i) in the case of the State, the State Treasurer or (ii) in the case of a municipality, the governing board or its representatives to attend a preliminary conference at which time the secretary and his deputies may informally discuss the proposed issue and the timing of the steps taken in issuing the bonds.

(c)　　After an application in proper form and order has been filed, and after a preliminary conference if one is required, the secretary shall notify the State Treasurer or the municipality, as the case may be, in writing that the application has been filed and accepted for submission to the Commission. The secretary's statement shall be conclusive evidence that the State or the municipality, as the case may be, has complied with this section.

(d)　　Repealed by Session Laws 2001-474, s. 39. (Ex. Sess. 1938, c. 2, s. 9; 1949, c. 1081; 1967, c. 555; 1969, c. 688, s. 2; 1971, c. 780, s. 1; 1973, c. 494, s. 18; 1983, c. 554, s. 6; 1989, c. 168, s. 41; c. 740, s. 6; 2001-474, s. 39.)

§ 159-86. Approval of application by Commission.

(a)　　In determining whether a proposed revenue bond issue shall be approved, the Commission may consider:

(1)　　Whether the project to be financed from the proceeds of the revenue bond issue is necessary or expedient.

(2)　　Whether the proposed project is feasible.

(3)　　The State's or the municipality's, as the case may be, debt management procedures and policies.

(4)　　Whether the State or the municipality, as the case may be, is in default in any of its debt service obligations.

(5)　　Whether the probable net revenues of the project to be financed will be sufficient to service the proposed revenue bonds.

(6)　　The ability of the Commission to market the proposed revenue bonds at reasonable rates of interest.

The Commission may inquire into and give consideration to any other matters that it may believe to have a bearing on whether the issue should be approved.

(b) The Commission shall approve the application if, upon the information and evidence it receives, it finds and determines:

(1) That the proposed revenue bond issue is necessary or expedient.

(2) That the amount proposed is adequate and not excessive for the proposed purpose of the issue.

(3) That the proposed project is feasible.

(4) That the State's or the municipality's, as the case may be, debt management procedures and policies are good, or that reasonable assurances have been given that its debt will henceforth be managed in strict compliance with law.

(5) That the proposed revenue bonds can be marketed at reasonable interest cost to the State or the municipality, as the case may be. (1971, c. 780, s. 1; 1983, c. 554, ss. 7, 8.)

§ 159-87. Order approving or denying the application.

(a) After considering an application the Commission shall enter its order either approving or denying the application. An order approving an issue shall not be regarded as an approval of the legality of the bonds in any respect.

(b) If the Commission enters an order denying the application, the proceedings under this Article shall be at an end. (1971, c. 780, s. 1.)

§ 159-88. Adoption of revenue bond order.

(a) At any time after an application is filed with the Commission for the issuance of revenue bonds, (i) in the case of the State, the Council of State and (ii) in the case of a municipality, the governing board of the municipality may adopt a revenue bond order pursuant to this Article.

(b) Notwithstanding the provisions of any city charter, general law, or local act, a revenue bond order may be introduced at any regular or special meeting of the governing board of a municipality and adopted at such a meeting by a simple majority of those present and voting, a quorum being present, and need not be published or subjected to any procedural requirements governing the adoption of ordinances or resolutions by the governing board other than the procedures set out in this Article. Revenue bond orders are not subject to the provisions of any city charter or legal act concerning initiative or referendum.

(c) Notwithstanding any other provision of this Article, no bond order authorizing the issuance of revenue bonds of the State shall be adopted by the Council of State until such time as the General Assembly shall have enacted legislation authorizing the undertaking of the revenue bond project to be financed and fixing the maximum aggregate principal amount of revenue bonds that shall be issued for such purpose, and such legislation shall have taken effect.

(d) Repealed by Session Laws 2001-474, s. 39, effective November 29, 2001. (1971, c. 780, s. 1; 1973, c. 494, s. 19; 1983, c. 554, s. 9; 1989, c. 168, s. 42; 2001-474, s. 39; 2012-156, s. 3.)

§ 159-89. Special covenants.

A revenue bond order or a trust agreement securing revenue bonds may be between the State or the issuing municipality and a bank or trust company located within or without the State of North Carolina, and may contain covenants as to any of the following:

(1) The pledge of all or any part of revenues received or to be received from the undertaking to be financed by the bonds, or the utility or enterprise of which the undertaking is to become a part.

(2) Rates, fees, rentals, tolls or other charges to be established, maintained, and collected, and the use and disposal of revenues, gifts, grants, and funds received or to be received.

(3) The setting aside of debt service reserves and the regulation and disposition thereof.

(4) The custody, collection, securing, investment, and payment of any moneys held for the payment of revenue bonds.

(5)	Limitations or restrictions on the purposes to which the proceeds of sale of revenue bonds then or thereafter to be issued may be applied.

(6)	Limitations or restrictions on the issuance of additional revenue bonds or notes; the terms upon which additional revenue bonds or notes may be issued and secured; or the refunding of outstanding or other revenue bonds.

(7)	The procedure, if any, by which the terms of any contract with bondholders may be amended or abrogated, the percentage of revenue bonds the bondholders of which must consent thereto, and the manner in which such consent may be given.

(8)	Events of default and the rights and liabilities arising thereupon, the terms and conditions upon which revenue bonds issued under this Article shall become or may be declared due before maturity, and the terms and conditions upon which such declaration and its consequences may be waived.

(9)	The preparation and maintenance of a budget with respect to the expenses of the State or a municipality, as the case may be, for the operation and maintenance of revenue bond projects.

(10)	The retention or employment of consulting engineers, independent auditors, and other technical consultants in connection with revenue bond projects.

(11)	Limitations on or the prohibition of free service by revenue bond projects to any person, firm, or corporation, public or private.

(12)	The acquisition and disposal of property for revenue bond projects.

(13)	Provisions for insurance and for accounting reports and the inspection and audit thereof.

(14)	The continuing operation and maintenance of the revenue bond project or the utility or enterprise of which it is to become a part. (Ex. Sess. 1938, c. 2, s. 6; 1971, c. 780, s. 1; 1983, c. 554, s. 10; 2003-388, s. 1.)

§ 159-90. Limitations on details of bonds; additional provisions.

(a) In fixing the details of revenue bonds, the State or the issuing municipality, as the case may be, shall be subject to the following restrictions and directions:

(1) The maturity dates may not exceed the maximum maturity periods prescribed by the Commission for general obligation bonds pursuant to G.S. 159-122. For bonds issued in reimbursement of a loan or advance, the maximum maturity period to be used in determining the maturity dates of the bonds shall be the maximum permissible period prescribed by the Commission for the original project for which the loan or advance was expended, calculated from the date the original project is completed.

(2) Any bond may be made subject to redemption prior to maturity, including redemption on demand of the holder, with or without premium, on such notice and at such time or times and with such redemption provisions as may be stated. When any such bond shall have been validly called for redemption and provision shall have been made for the payment of the principal thereof, any redemption premium, and the interest thereon accrued to the date of redemption, interest thereon shall cease.

(3) The bonds may bear interest at such rate or rates, payable semiannually or otherwise, may be in such denominations, and may be payable in such kind of money and in such place or places within or without the State of North Carolina, as the State Treasurer or the issuing municipality, as the case may be, may determine.

(b) In addition to the foregoing provisions of this section, in fixing the details of revenue bonds the State or the issuing municipality, as the case may be, may provide that bonds

(1) May be made payable from time to time on demand or tender for purchase by the owner provided a Credit Facility supports such bonds, unless the Commission specifically determines that a Credit Facility is not required upon a finding and determination by the Commission that the proposed bonds will satisfy the conditions set forth in G.S. 159-86(b);

(2) May be additionally supported by a Credit Facility;

(3) May be made subject to redemption prior to maturity, with or without premium, on such notice and at such time or times and with such redemption provisions as may be stated in the bond order or trust agreement or with such

variations as may be permitted in connection with a Par Formula provided in such bond order or trust agreement;

(4) May bear interest, notwithstanding the provisions of G.S. 159-125(a), at a rate or rates that may vary as permitted pursuant to a Par Formula and for such period or periods of time, all as may be provided in the bond order or trust agreement; and

(5) May be made the subject of a remarketing agreement whereby an attempt is made to remarket the bonds to new purchasers prior to their presentment for payment to the provider of the Credit Facility or to the issuing municipality or the State.

No Credit Facility, repayment agreement, Par Formula or remarketing agreement shall become effective without the approval of the Commission.

As used in this subsection, the following terms shall have the following meanings:

"Credit Facility" means an agreement entered into by an issuing municipality or by the State Treasurer on behalf of the State with a bank, savings and loan association or other banking institution, an insurance company, reinsurance company, surety company or other insurance institution, a corporation, investment banker or other investment institution, or any financial institution providing for prompt payment of all or any part of the principal (whether at maturity, presentment for purchase, redemption or acceleration), redemption premium, if any, and interest on any bonds payable on demand or tender by the owner issued in accordance with this section, in consideration of the issuing municipality or the State agreeing to repay the provider of such Credit Facility in accordance with the terms and provisions of such repayment agreement, provided, that any such repayment agreement shall provide that the obligation of the issuing municipality or the State thereunder shall have only such sources of payment as are permitted for the payment of bonds issued under this Article.

"Par Formula" shall mean any provision or formula adopted by the issuing municipality or the State to provide for the adjustment, from time to time, of the interest rate or rates borne by any such bonds so that the purchase price of such bonds in the open market would be as close to par as possible. (Ex. Sess. 1938, c. 2, s. 5; 1949, c. 1081; 1967, c. 100, s. 1; c. 711, s. 2; 1969, c. 688, s. 1; 1971, c. 780, s. 1; 1983, c. 554, s. 11; 1985, c. 265, s. 1; 1991, c. 508, s. 4.)

§ 159-91. Lien of revenue bonds.

(a) All revenue bonds issued under this Article shall be equally and ratably secured by a pledge, charge, and lien upon revenues provided for in the bond order, without priority by reason of number, or of dates of bonds, execution or delivery, in accordance with the provisions of this Article and of the bond order; except that the State or a municipality may provide in a revenue bond order that revenue bonds issued pursuant thereto shall to the extent and in the manner prescribed in the order or agreement be subordinated and junior in standing, with respect to the payment of principal and interest and the security thereof, to any other revenue bonds.

(b) Any pledge made by the State or a municipality pursuant to this Article shall be valid and binding from the date of final passage of the bond order upon the issuance of any bonds or bond anticipation notes thereunder. The revenues, securities, and other moneys so pledged and then held or thereafter received by the State or a municipality, as the case may be, or any fiduciary shall immediately be subject to the lien of the pledge without any physical delivery thereof or further act, and the lien of the pledge shall be valid and binding as against all parties having claims of any kind in tort, contract, or otherwise against the State or a municipality, as the case may be, without regard to whether such parties have notice thereof. The bond order by which a pledge is created need not be filed or recorded in any manner other than as provided in this Chapter. (1971, c. 780, s. 1; 1983, c. 554, s. 12.)

§ 159-92. Status of revenue bonds under Uniform Commercial Code.

Whether or not the revenue bonds and interest coupons appertaining thereto are of such form and character as to be investment securities under Article 8 of the Uniform Commercial Code as enacted in this State, all revenue bonds represented by instruments and interest coupons appertaining thereto issued under this Article are hereby made investment securities within the meaning of and for all the purposes of Article 8 of the Uniform Commercial Code as enacted in this State, subject only to the provisions of the bonds pertaining to registration. (1971, c. 780, s. 1; 1983, c. 322, s. 3.)

§ 159-93. Agreement of the State.

The State of North Carolina does pledge to and agree with the holders of any revenue bonds or revenue bond anticipation notes heretofore or hereafter issued by the State or any municipality in this State that so long as any such bonds or notes are outstanding and unpaid the State will not limit or alter the rights vested in the State or the municipality at the time of issuance of the bonds or notes to establish, maintain, revise, charge, and collect such rates, fees, rentals, tolls, and other charges for the use, services, facilities, and commodities of or furnished by the revenue bond project in connection with which the bonds or notes, or bonds or notes refunded by the bonds or notes, were issued as shall produce revenues at least sufficient with other available funds to meet the expense of maintenance and operation of and renewal and replacements to such project, including reserves therefor, to pay when due the principal, interest, and redemption premiums (if any) of the bonds or notes, and to fulfill the terms of any agreements made with the bondholders or noteholders, nor will the State in any way impair the rights and remedies of the bondholders or noteholders until the bonds or notes and all costs and expenses in connection with any action or proceedings by or on behalf of the bondholders or noteholders, are fully paid, met, and discharged. (1971, c. 780, s. 1; 1973, c. 494, s. 20; 1983, c. 554, s. 13.)

§ 159-94. Limited liability.

(a) Revenue bonds shall be special obligations of the State or the municipality issuing them. The principal of and interest on revenue bonds shall not be payable from the general funds of the State or the municipality, as the case may be, nor shall they constitute a legal or equitable pledge, charge, lien, or encumbrance upon any of its property or upon any of its income, receipts, or revenues, except the funds which are pledged under the bond order authorizing the bonds. Neither the credit nor the taxing power of the State or the municipality, as the case may be, are pledged for the payment of the principal or interest of revenue bonds, and no holder of revenue bonds has the right to compel the exercise of the taxing power by the State or the municipality, as the case may be, or the forfeiture of any of its property in connection with any default thereon. Every revenue bond shall recite in substance that the principal of and interest on the bond is payable solely from the revenues pledged to its payment and that the State or the municipality, as the case may be, is not obligated to pay the principal or interest except from such revenues.

(b) Repealed by Session Laws 2001-474, s. 39. (Ex. Sess. 1938, c. 2, s. 7; 1953, c. 922, s. 3; 1971, c. 780, s. 1; 1983, c. 554, s. 14; 1989, c. 168, s. 43; 2001-474, s. 39.)

§ 159-95. Approval of State agencies.

The general design and plan of any revenue bond project undertaken for water systems or facilities or sewage disposal systems or facilities shall be subject to the approval of the Commission for Public Health or the State Environmental Management Commission to the same extent that such projects would be if they were not financed by revenue bonds, and the provisions of the revenue bond order shall be consistent with any requirements imposed on the project by the Commission for Public Health or the State Environmental Management Commission. No revenue bond project for the acquisition or construction of systems or facilities for the generation, production, or transmission of gas or electric power may be undertaken by the State or a municipality unless the State or municipality, as the case may be, shall first obtain a certificate of convenience and necessity from the North Carolina Utilities Commission. (Ex. Sess. 1938, c. 2, s. 9; 1949, c. 1081; 1967, c. 555; 1969, c. 688, s. 2; 1971, c. 780, s. 1; 1973, c. 476, s. 128; c. 494, s. 21; c. 1262, s. 23; 1983, c. 554, s. 15; 2007-182, s. 2.)

§ 159-96. Limitation on extraterritorial operation of enterprises financed by revenue bonds.

(a) Each utility or public service enterprise listed in G.S. 159-81(3), if financed wholly or partially by revenue bonds issued under this Article, shall be owned or operated by the municipality for its own use and for the use of public and private consumers residing within its corporate limits or, in the case of a joint agency or undertaking established pursuant to Part 1 of Article 20 of Chapter 160A of the General Statutes, for the use of the municipalities that established the joint agency or undertaking and for the use of the public and private consumers residing within their corporate limits. A utility or public service enterprise financed wholly or partially by revenue bonds, when operated primarily for the municipality's own use and for users within its corporate limits or, in the case of two or more municipalities participating in a joint agency or undertaking, when operated primarily for the use of the municipalities that established the joint agency or undertaking, may be operated incidentally for users outside the corporate limits of either the issuing unit or a participating municipality. Provided, however, that revenue bonds may be issued for the purpose of financing in whole or in part mass transit systems, aeronautical facilities, marine facilities and systems, systems or facilities for the generation, production, transmission, or distribution of gas (natural, artificial, or mixed), facilities and equipment for the collection, treatment or disposal of solid waste, notwithstanding that such systems, facilities or equipment may be operated for users outside the corporate limits of a municipality that is an issuing unit where the municipality finds that the systems, facilities, or equipment so financed would benefit the municipality or, in the case of two or more municipalities participating in a joint agency or undertaking, where the municipalities that are the issuing units find that the systems, facilities, or equipment so financed would benefit the municipalities that established the joint agency or undertaking.

Revenue bonds may not be issued for the purpose of financing in whole or in part systems or facilities for the transmission or distribution of gas (natural, artificial, or mixed) to users outside the corporate limits of a municipality to whom service is available or will be available within a reasonable time from a local distribution natural gas utility pursuant to a certificate of public convenience and necessity issued by the North Carolina Utilities Commission. A finding by the governing body of a municipality that is an issuing unit that the systems or facilities to be provided by the financing will not provide service to users to whom such service is available or will be available within a reasonable time from a local distribution natural gas utility shall be conclusive upon (i) the expiration of a 45 day period following the making of such finding, (ii) the mailing by the municipality of a copy of such notice within five days after the making of such finding to any local distribution company certificated to provide service to the area in which the facilities are to be located, and (iii) the absence of a written objection to such finding being mailed by any such certificated local distribution company to the municipality by not later than five days prior to the end of such 45 day period, all such mailings to be properly given or made if sent by United States registered mail, return receipt requested, postage prepaid. Time shall be computed pursuant to G.S. 1A-1, Rule 6(a).

(b)   A revenue bond project financed wholly or partially by revenue bonds of the State may be located either within or without the State and, when operated primarily for the State's own use and for users within the State, may be operated incidentally for users outside the State.

(c) Repealed by Session Laws 2001-474, s. 39, effective November 29, 2001.

(d) Notwithstanding the provisions of subsections (a) and (b) of this section and G.S. 160A-312, municipalities may acquire sewage collection and disposal systems and water supply and distribution systems located within and without the corporate limits of such municipalities and finance such acquisition with revenue bonds. Further, municipalities may own, maintain and operate such acquired systems, enlarge and improve such acquired systems and finance the enlargement and improvement of such acquired systems with revenue bonds. This subsection applies only to acquisitions by municipalities financed by revenue bonds during the calendar year ending December 31, 1989.

(e) In the case of a Turnpike Project of the North Carolina Turnpike Authority, the Turnpike Project may be located anywhere in the State the Authority is authorized to maintain a Turnpike Project. (1971, c. 780, s. 1; 1973, c. 1325; 1983, c. 554, s. 16; c. 795, s. 5; 1989, c. 168, s. 44; c. 263; 1991, c. 511, s. 1; 2001-414, s. 50; 2001-474, s. 39; 2002-133, s. 8.)

§ 159-97. Taxes for supplementing revenue bond projects.

(a) For the purpose of supplementing the revenues of a revenue bond project, as defined in this section, any county or city may covenant with, or may enter into an agreement with a municipality for the benefit of the holders of revenue bonds of the issuing municipality issued pursuant to this Article, whereby such county or city agrees to:

(1) Levy for the life of all revenue bonds issued in connection with the revenue bond project an annual property tax not in excess of the rate set forth in the question submitted to voters as hereinafter provided, such levy to be based upon the operating supplement requirement, as defined in this section, or

(2) Levy for the life of the revenue bonds in respect of which such tax is being levied an annual property tax not in excess of the rate required to pay the principal of and the interest on the aggregate principal amount of revenue bonds set forth in the question submitted to the voters as hereinafter provided, such levy to be based upon the debt service reserve supplement requirement, as defined in this section.

When any such covenant has been made or any such agreement has been entered into, the issuing municipality shall determine, and, in those instances in which the issuing municipality is not also the taxing county or city, the issuing municipality shall certify to the governing board of the taxing county or city, by not later than June 1 of each fiscal year the amount required, determined as hereinafter provided, to be raised by taxation by such county or city in the next fiscal year. The county or city is obligated to levy such tax only to the extent that an operating supplement requirement or a debt service reserve supplement requirement shall occur during the fiscal year preceding the fiscal year in which the tax is to be levied. In no event shall the county or city be required to levy a tax in excess of the rate required to be levied in accordance with the approval of the voters as provided in subsection (c). When any such tax is to be levied, the county or city shall include in its budget ordinance an appropriation to the issuing municipality or the appropriate fund, as the case may be, equal to the estimated yield of the tax levy, and shall pay such appropriation to the issuing municipality or transfer moneys to the appropriate fund in equal monthly installments unless another mutually satisfactory schedule of payments is agreed upon.

(b) A covenant made, or the pledge of an agreement entered into, by a county or city pursuant to this section shall be effected by the provisions of the revenue bond order or the trust agreement securing revenue bonds of the issuing municipality and where the issuing municipality is not also the taxing county or city a resolution of the county or city approving the appropriate provisions of the bond order or trust agreement relating to the pledge of the tax. If the taxing county or city is not the issuing municipality, it shall file an application for approval of the resolution with the secretary of the Commission in the manner provided in G.S. 159-149, and the Commission shall determine whether to approve the application as provided by G.S. 159-151 and 159-152; provided, however, that G.S. 159-148 and 159-150 shall have no application to this section.

(c) A covenant made, or agreement entered into, by a county or city pursuant to this section shall take effect only if approved by the affirmative vote of a majority of those who vote thereon in a referendum held in the taxing county or city. The referendum shall be called and held as provided in G.S. 159-61, except that

(1) The ballot proposition shall be in substantially one of the following forms:

Operating Supplement Requirement:

"Shall the (order or agreement) binding the (taxing county or city) to levy annually a tax on property not in excess of _____ cents on the one hundred dollars ($100.00) value of property subject to taxation for the purpose of supplementing the revenues of (revenue bond project) in instances where the gross revenues of the project are estimated to be less than the estimated total costs of the (i) current operating expenses of the project, (ii) amount required to maintain the debt service reserve by repaying any withdrawals therefrom in respect of all outstanding bonds issued in connection with the project and (iii) debt service on all outstanding bonds issued in connection with the project, all as defined in such (order or agreement), the proceeds of such tax to be used for the payment of the current operating expenses of the project so long as any revenue bonds issued therefor remain outstanding and unpaid, be approved?

[ ] Yes

[ ] No"

Debt Service Reserve Supplement Requirement:

"Shall the (order or agreement) binding the (taxing county or city) to levy annually, without limitation as to rate or amount, a tax on property subject to taxation for the purpose of supplementing the revenues of (revenue bond project) for maintaining the debt service reserve required by said (order or agreement) in connection with the issuance of not in excess of $ _____ revenue bonds of (the issuing municipality), so long as any of such revenue bonds remain outstanding and unpaid, be approved?

[ ] Yes

[ ] No"

and

(2)   The published statement of result shall have the following statement appended:

"Any action or proceeding challenging the regularity or validity of this supplemental tax referendum must be begun within 30 days after (date of publication).

(title of governing board)."

(d) Any action or proceeding in any court to set aside a supplemental tax referendum held under this section, or to obtain any other relief, upon the ground that the referendum is invalid or was irregularly conducted, must be begun within 30 days after the publication of the statement of the result of the referendum. After the expiration of this period of limitation, no right of action or defense based upon the invalidity of or any irregularity in the referendum shall be asserted, nor shall the validity of the referendum be open to question in any court upon any ground whatever, except in an action or proceeding begun within the period of limitation prescribed in this subsection.

(e) An order or agreement submitted to and approved by the voters pursuant to this section may be repealed at any time before bonds are issued pursuant thereto.

(f) In instances where the taxing county or city is not the issuing municipality, such county or city may levy taxes as provided for in this section in respect of a revenue bond project located outside its corporate limits provided that such county or city is entitled by law to appoint one or more members of the governing body of such municipality.

(g) For the purposes of this section,

(1) A "revenue bond project" is limited, notwithstanding the provisions of G.S. 159-81, to (i) aeronautical facilities, including but not limited to airports, terminals and hangars, (ii) hospitals and other health-related facilities, and (iii) systems, facilities and equipment for the collection, treatment or disposal of solid waste within the meaning of said G.S. 159-81;

(2) An "operating supplement requirement" occurs when, as set forth in the budget prepared by the issuing municipality in respect of the revenue bond project, the estimated cost in the next succeeding fiscal year of the (i) current operating expenses of the revenue bond project, (ii) amount required to maintain the debt service reserve by repaying any withdrawals therefrom in respect of all outstanding bonds issued in connection with the revenue bond project, and (iii) debt service on all outstanding bonds issued in connection with the revenue bond project, are in excess of the pledged revenues of the revenue

bond project for such fiscal year as estimated by the issuing municipality, excluding taxes levied pursuant to this section; provided, however, that the amount of the operating supplement requirement shall not exceed the total amount of the current operating expenses of the revenue bond project mentioned in clause (i) above, and

(3)   A "debt service reserve supplement requirement" occurs when there have been withdrawn from the debt service reserve any moneys for the purpose of paying debt service on the bonds in respect of which the supplemental tax has been authorized by the voters; provided, however, that the amount of the debt service reserve supplement requirement shall not exceed the amount so withdrawn.

(h)   Any covenant or agreement of a county or city made pursuant to this section, and the obligations assumed thereby, shall be excludable from the gross debt of the county or city for purposes of the statement of debt mentioned in G.S. 159-55.

(i)   For the purposes of this section the terms county or city shall include a special airport district with respect to financing of aeronautical facilities. (1973, c. 786, s. 1; 1979, c. 727, s. 5; 1983, c. 795, s. 6.)

§ 159-98. Reserved for future codification purposes.

Article 5A.

Capital Appreciation Bonds.

§ 159-99. Definition; terms and conditions.

(a)   Capital Appreciation Bond Defined. - For purposes of this Article, the term "capital appreciation bond" means a bond that meets all of the following conditions:

(1)   It is sold, at public or private sale, at a price substantially less, as conclusively determined by the issuer of the bond, than the principal amount of the bond.

(2)   Compounded interest on the bond is payable at maturity.

(3) The bond is designated as a capital appreciation bond within the meaning of this Article by the proceedings of the issuer of the bond providing for its issuance.

(b) Calculating Principal Amount. - For purposes of calculating the aggregate principal amount of bonds within the meaning of any constitutional or statutory limitation on the incurrence of debt, the aggregate principal amount of any capital appreciation bonds is the aggregate of the initial offering prices at which the bonds are offered for sale to the public, including private or negotiated sales, or sold to the initial purchaser of the bonds in a private placement, in either case without reduction to reflect underwriters' discount or placement agents' or other intermediaries' fees.

(c) Terms and Conditions. - The proceedings providing for the issuance of any capital appreciation bonds may provide for the issuance of terms bonds or serial bonds, or both, the establishment of sinking funds for or the redemption of term bonds, the issuance of capital appreciation bonds at the same time and as part of the same issue of any other type of bonds, the method of calculating the principal amount of any such capital appreciation bonds outstanding for the purpose of determining, within the meaning of the proceedings and otherwise, application of debt service provisions, funds into which debt service payments are to be deposited, application of redemption provisions, bondowners' voting rights and consents, pro rata application of available funds, and any other matters the issuer considers appropriate. (1987, c. 650; 2004-170, ss. 40(a), 40(c).)

§ 159-100. Authorization.

(a) Revenue Bond Act. - The State and local governmental units are authorized to issue capital appreciation bonds pursuant to the provisions of The State and Local Government Revenue Bond Act.

(b) Local Government Bond Act. - Local governmental units are authorized to issue capital appreciation bonds pursuant to the provisions of The Local Government Bond Act. In connection with the issuance of a series of bonds containing capital appreciation bonds issued by local governmental units pursuant to The Local Government Bond Act, the Local Government Commission may require that annual debt service on the series of bonds be as nearly level or equal as possible taking into consideration prevailing financial techniques, including, without limitation, the postponement of principal maturities in early years of the issue and the use of capitalized interest. The Local Government Commission may also limit the amount of a series of bonds that may be issued as capital appreciation bonds and to make the issuance of any capital appreciation bonds subject to a finding by the Commission or the issuer that the issuance of the bonds will not increase the aggregate amount of debt service payable on the series of bonds of which the capital appreciation bonds constitute a part.

(c) Future Acts. - Local governmental units are authorized to issue capital appreciation bonds pursuant to the provisions of any law enacted in the future. (1987, c. 650; 2004-170, ss. 40(b), 40(c).)

Article 6.

Project Development Financing Act.

§ 159-101. Short title.

This Article may be cited as the "North Carolina Project Development Financing Act." (2003-403, s. 2.)

§ 159-102. Unit of local government defined.

For the purposes of this Article, the term "unit of local government" means a county or a municipal corporation. (2003-403, s. 2.)

§ 159-103. Authorization of project development financing debt instruments; purposes.

(a) Each unit of local government may issue project development financing debt instruments pursuant to this Article and use the proceeds for one or more of the purposes for which any unit may issue general obligation bonds pursuant to the following subdivisions of G.S. 159-48: (b)(1), (3), (7), (11), (12), (16), (17), (19), (21), (23), (24), or (25), (c)(1), (4), (4a), or (6), or (d)(3), (4), (5), (6) or (7), or (b)(13) excluding stadiums, arenas, golf courses, swimming pools, wading pools, or marinas. In addition, the proceeds may be used for any service or facility authorized by G.S. 160A-536 to be provided in a municipal service district, but no such district need be created.

For the purpose of this Article, the term "capital costs" as defined in G.S. 159-48(h) also includes (i) interest on the debt instruments being issued or on notes issued in anticipation of the instruments during construction and for a period not exceeding seven years after the estimated date of completion of construction and (ii) the establishment of debt service reserves and any other reserves reasonably required by the financing documents. The proceeds of the debt instruments may be used either in a development financing district established pursuant to G.S. 160A-515.1 or G.S. 158-7.3 or, if the use directly benefits private development forecast by the development financing plan for the district, outside the development financing district. The proceeds may be used only for projects that enable, facilitate, or benefit private development within the development financing district, the revenue increment of which is pledged as security for the debt instruments. This subsection does not prohibit the use of proceeds to defray the cost of providing water and sewer utilities to a private development in a project development financing district.

(b)   Subject to agreement with the holders of its project development financing debt instruments and the limitation on duration of development financing districts set out in this Article, each unit of local government may issue additional project development financing debt instruments and may issue debt instruments to refund any outstanding project development financing debt instruments at any time before the final maturity of the instruments to be refunded. General obligation bonds issued to refund outstanding project development financing debt instruments shall be issued under the Local Government Bond Act, Article 4 of this Chapter. Revenue bonds issued to refund outstanding project development financing debt instruments shall be issued under the State and Local Government Revenue Bond Act, Article 5 of this Chapter.

Project development financing debt instruments may be issued partly for the purpose of refunding outstanding project development financing debt instruments and partly for any other purpose under this Article. Project development financing debt instruments issued to refund outstanding project development financing debt instruments shall be issued under this Article and not under Article 4 of this Chapter.

(c) If the private development project to be benefited by proposed project development financing debt instruments affects tax revenues in more than one unit of local government and more than one affected unit of local government wishes to provide assistance to the private development project by issuing project development financing debt instruments, then those units may enter into an interlocal agreement pursuant to Article 20 of Chapter 160A of the General Statutes for the purpose of issuing the instruments. The agreement may include a provision that a unit may pledge all or any part of the taxes received or to be received on the incremental valuation accruing to the development financing district to the repayment of instruments issued by another unit that is a party to the interlocal agreement. (2003-403, s. 2; 2007-395, s. 1.)

§ 159-104. Application to Commission for approval of project development financing debt instrument issue; preliminary conference; acceptance of application.

A unit of local government may not issue project development financing debt instruments under this Article unless the issue is approved by the Local Government Commission. The governing body of the issuing unit shall file with the secretary of the Commission an application for Commission approval of the issue. At the time of application, the governing body shall publish a public notice of the application in a newspaper of general circulation in the unit of local government. The application shall include any statements of facts and documents concerning the proposed debt instruments, development financing district, and development financing plan, and the financial condition of the unit, required by the secretary. The Commission may prescribe the form of the application.

Before accepting the application, the secretary may require the governing body or its representatives to attend a preliminary conference in order to discuss informally the proposed issue, district, and plan and the timing of the steps to be taken in issuing the debt instruments. The development financing plan need not be adopted by the governing body at the time it files the application with the secretary. However, before the Commission may enter its order approving the debt instruments, the governing body must adopt the plan and make the findings described in G.S. 159-105(b)(1) and (5).

After an application in proper form and order has been filed, and after a preliminary conference if one is required, the secretary shall notify the unit in writing that the application has been filed and accepted for submission to the Commission. The secretary's statement is conclusive evidence that the unit has complied with this section. (2003-403, s. 2.)

§ 159-105. Approval of application by Commission.

(a) In determining whether to approve a proposed project development financing debt instrument issue, the Commission may inquire into and consider any matters that it considers relevant to whether the issue should be approved, including:

(1) Whether the projects to be financed from the proceeds of the project development financing debt instrument issue are necessary to secure significant new project development for a development financing district.

(2) Whether the proposed projects are feasible. In making this determination, the Commission may consider any additional security such as credit enhancement, insurance, or guaranties.

(3) The unit of local government's debt management procedures and policies.

(4) Whether the unit is in default in any of its debt service obligations.

(5) Whether the private development forecast in the development financing plan would likely occur without the public project or projects to be financed by the project development financing debt instruments.

(6) Whether taxes on the incremental valuation accruing to the development financing district, together with any other revenues available under G.S. 159-110, will be sufficient to service the proposed project development financing debt instruments.

(7) The ability of the Commission to market the proposed project development financing debt instruments at reasonable rates of interest.

(b) The Commission shall approve the application if, upon the information and evidence it receives, it finds all of the following:

(1) The proposed project development financing debt instrument issue is necessary to secure significant new economic development for a development financing district.

(2) The amount of the proposed project development financing debt is adequate and not excessive for the proposed purpose of the issue.

(3) The proposed projects are feasible. In making this determination, the Commission may consider any additional security such as credit enhancement, insurance, or guaranties.

(4) The unit of local government's debt management procedures and policies are good, or that reasonable assurances have been given that its debt will henceforth be managed in strict compliance with law.

(5) The private development forecast in the development financing plan would not be likely to occur without the public projects to be financed by the project development financing debt instruments.

(6) The proposed project development financing debt instruments can be marketed at reasonable interest cost to the issuing unit.

(7) The issuing unit has, pursuant to G.S. 160A-515.1 or G.S. 158-7.3, adopted a development financing plan for the development financing district for which the instruments are to be issued. (2003-403, s. 2.)

§ 159-106. Order approving or denying the application.

(a) After considering an application, the Commission shall enter its order either approving or denying the application. An order approving an issue is not an approval of the legality of the debt instruments in any respect.

(b) Unless the debt instruments are to be issued for a development financing district for which a project development financing debt instrument issue has already been approved, the day the Commission enters its order approving an application for project development financing debt instruments is also the effective date of the development financing district for which the instruments are to be issued.

(c) If the Commission enters an order denying the application, the proceedings under this Article are at an end. (2003-403, s. 2.)

§ 159-107. Determination of incremental valuation; use of taxes levied on incremental valuation; duration of the district.

(a) Base Valuation in the Development Financing District. - After the Local Government Commission has entered its order approving a unit of local government's application for project development financing debt instruments, the unit shall immediately notify the tax assessor of the county in which the development financing district is located of the existence of the development financing district. Upon receiving this notice, the tax assessor shall determine the base valuation of the district, which is the assessed value of all taxable property located in the district on the January 1 immediately preceding the effective date of the district. If the unit or an agency of the unit acquired property within the district within one year before the effective date of the district, the tax assessor shall presume, subject to rebuttal, that the property was acquired in contemplation of the district, and the tax assessor shall include the value of the property so acquired in determining the base valuation of the district. The unit may rebut this presumption by showing that the property was acquired primarily for a purpose other than to reduce the incremental tax base. After determining the base valuation of the development financing district, the tax assessor shall certify the valuation to: (i) the issuing unit; (ii) the county in which the district is located if the issuing unit is not the county; and (iii) any special district, as defined in G.S. 159-7, within which the development financing district is located.

(b) Adjustments to the Base Valuation. - During the lifetime of the development financing district, the base valuation shall be adjusted as follows:

(1) If the unit amends its development financing plan, pursuant to G.S. 160A-515.1 or G.S. 158-7.3, to remove property from the development financing district, on the succeeding January 1, that property shall be removed from the district and the base valuation reduced accordingly.

(2) If the unit amends its development financing plan, pursuant to G.S. 160A-515.1 or G.S. 158-7.3, to expand the district, the new property shall be added to the district immediately. The base valuation of the district shall be increased by the assessed value of the taxable property situated in the added territory on the January 1 immediately preceding the effective date of the district.

(3) Repealed by Session Laws 2007-395, s. 2, effective August 20, 2007.

Each time the base valuation is adjusted, the tax assessor shall immediately certify the new base valuation to: (i) the issuing unit; (ii) the county if the issuing unit is not the county; and (iii) any special district, as defined in G.S. 159-7, within which the development financing district is located.

(c) Revenue Increment Fund. - When a unit of local government has established a development financing district, and the project development financing debt instruments for that district have been approved by the Commission, the unit shall establish a separate fund to account for the proceeds paid to the unit from taxes levied on the incremental valuation of the district. The unit shall also place in this fund any moneys received pursuant to an agreement entered into under G.S. 159-108.

(d) Levy of Property Taxes Within the District. - Each year the development financing district is in existence, the tax assessor shall determine the current assessed value of taxable property located in the district. The assessor shall also compute the difference between this current value and the base valuation of the district. If the current value exceeds the base value, the difference is the incremental valuation of the district. In each year the district is in existence, the county, and if the district is within a city or a special district as defined by G.S. 159-7, the city or the special district shall levy taxes against property in the district in the same manner as taxes are levied against other property in the county, city, or special district. The proceeds from ad valorem taxes levied on property in the development financing district shall be distributed as follows:

(1) In any year in which there is no incremental valuation of the district, all the proceeds of the taxes shall be retained by the county, city, or special district, as if there were no development financing district in existence.

(2) In any year in which there is an incremental valuation of the district, the amount of tax due from each taxpayer on property in the district shall be distributed as provided in this subdivision. The net proceeds of the following taxes shall be paid to the government levying the tax: (i) taxes separately stated and levied solely to service and repay debt secured by a pledge of the faith and credit of the unit; (ii) nonschool taxes levied pursuant to a vote of the people; (iii) taxes levied for a municipal or county service district; and (iv) taxes levied by a taxing unit in a development financing district established by a different taxing unit and for which there is no increment agreement between the two units. All remaining taxes on property in the district shall be multiplied by a fraction, the

numerator of which is the base valuation for the district and the denominator of which is the current valuation for the district. The amount shown as the product of this multiplication shall, when paid by the taxpayer, be retained by the county, city, or special district, as if there were no development financing district in existence. The net proceeds of the remaining amount shall, when paid by the taxpayer, be turned over to the finance officer of each issuing unit, who shall place this amount in the special revenue increment fund required by subsection (c) of this section. As used in this section, "net proceeds" means gross proceeds less refunds, releases, and any collection fee paid by the levying government to the collecting government.

(e) Effect of Annexation or District Established by a County. - If a city annexes land in a development financing district established by a county pursuant to G.S. 158-7.3, the proceeds of all taxes levied by the city on property within the district shall be paid to the city unless the city enters into an agreement with the county pursuant to this subsection, and the annexed land in the county's district that subsequently becomes a part of the city does not count against the city's five-percent (5%) limit under G.S. 158-7.3 or G.S. 160A-515.1 unless the city and the county enter into an agreement pursuant to this section. The city and the county may enter into an increment agreement under which the city agrees that city taxes on part or all of the incremental valuation in the district shall be paid into the revenue increment fund for the district. An increment agreement may be entered into when the district is established or at any time after the district is established. The increment agreement may extend for the duration of the district or for a shorter time agreed to by the parties.

(f) Use of Moneys in the Revenue Increment Fund. - If the development financing district includes property conveyed or leased by the unit of local government to a private party in consideration of increased tax revenue expected to be generated by improvements constructed on the property pursuant to G.S. 158-7.1, an amount equal to the tax revenue taken into account in arriving at the consideration, less the increased tax revenue realized since the construction of the improvement, shall be transferred from the Revenue Increment Fund to the county, city, or special district as if there were no development financing district in existence. Any money in excess of this amount in the Fund may be used for any of the following purposes, without priority other than priorities imposed by the order authorizing the project development financing debt instruments:

(1) To finance capital expenditures (including the funding of capital reserves) by the issuing unit in the development financing district pursuant to the development financing plan.

(2) To meet principal and interest requirements on project development financing debt instruments and debt instrument anticipation notes issued for the district.

(3) To repay the appropriate fund of the issuing unit for any moneys actually expended on debt service on project development financing debt instruments pursuant to a pledge made pursuant to G.S. 159-111(b).

(4) To establish and maintain debt service reserves for future principal and interest requirements on project development financing debt instruments and debt instrument anticipation notes issued for the district.

(5) To meet any other requirements imposed by the order authorizing the project development financing debt instruments.

If in any year there is any money remaining in the Revenue Increment Fund after these purposes have been satisfied, it shall be paid to the general fund of the county and, if applicable, of the city and any special district as defined by G.S. 159-7, in proportion to their rates of ad valorem tax on taxable property located in the development financing district.

(g) Duration of District. - A development financing district shall terminate at the earlier of (i) the end of the thirtieth year after the effective date of the district or (ii) the date all project development financing debt instruments issued for the district have been fully retired or sufficient funds have been set aside, pursuant to the order authorizing the debt instruments, to meet all future principal and interest requirements on the instruments. (2003-403, s. 2; 2005-238, s. 5; 2007-395, s. 2; 2010-95, s. 39.)

Vision Books Order Form

Fax Orders: 1-980-299-5965

Phone Orders: 1-704-898-0770

E-mail Orders: www.visionbooks.org

Mail Orders: Vision Books, LLC
P.O. Box 42406
Charlotte, NC 28215

Shipp To:
Name_____
Address_____
City_____State_____Zip_____
Phone_____Fax_____
Email_____@_____

Bill To: We can bill a third party on your behalf.
Name_____
Address_____
City_____State_____Zip_____
Phone___(_____)_____Fax_____
Email_____@_____

Pamphlet Number ($15.00 Each)	Qty	Total Cost
_____	_____	_____
_____	_____	_____
_____	_____	_____
_____	_____	_____
_____	_____	_____
_____	_____	_____
_____	_____	_____
<u>Full Volume Set 1-92</u>	<u>92 Pamphlets</u>	<u>1,380.00</u>

Free Shipping & Handling on Full Volume Orders
Add $1.00 Shipping & Handling Per Pamphlet $_____

Total Cost $_____

Thank you for your support. Management!

DID YOU ENJOY THIS BOOK?

Vision Books, LLC would like to hear from you! If you or someone you know has been fasely imprisoned, we would like to hear your story. If the 'North Carolina Criminal Law and Procedure' has had an effect in your life or if you have suggestions, we would like to hear from you. Send your letters to:

Vision Books, LLC
Attn: Staff Writers
P.O. Box 42406
Charlotte, NC 28215
Email: staff@visionbooks.org

Order Additional Copies:

Fax Orders: 1-980-299-5965

Phone Orders: 1-704-898-0770

E-mail Orders: www.visionbooks.org

Mail Orders: Vision Books, LLC
                       P.O. Box 42406
                       Charlotte, NC 28215

www.ingramcontent.com/pod-product-compliance
Lightning Source LLC
Chambersburg PA
CBHW051629170526
45167CB00001B/112